Christmas Memories
with Recipes

Christmas Memories with Recipes

WINGS BOOKS
NEW YORK

This 1999 edition is published by Wings Books®, an imprint of Random House Value Publishing, Inc. 201 East 50th Street, New York, N.Y. 10022. Published by arrangement with W. H. Freeman and Company, New York.

Wings Books® and colophon are registered trademarks of Random House Value Publishing, Inc.

Random House
New York • Toronto • London • Sydney • Auckland
http://www.randomhouse.com/

Printed and bound in the United States of America

Library of Congress Cataloging–in–Publication Data
Christmas memories with recipes.
p. cm.
Originally published: 1st ed. New York : Farrar, Straus & Giroux, 1988, in series: Kitchen arts & letters.
Includes index.
ISBN 0-517-10190-4
1. Christmas cookery. 2. Christmas.
TX739.2.C45C464 1994
641.5'68—dc20   94-10843
CIP

9 8 7 6 5

Contents

A Note to the Reader

ALL OF OUR HOLIDAY CELEBRATIONS are laced with a web of memories, often stretching back to our childhoods, and Christmas is surely the most memory-laden. As we unpack the ornaments for the tree or chop the candied orange peel for the fruitcake, we think of all the times we've done this before. These recollected experiences become a vital part of our celebrations.

The well-polished traditions of Christmas bring us back to memories of our families and friends, sometimes to one sparkling and unforgettable holiday, sometimes to a Christmas that turned hardship into celebration, sometimes to a blur of Christmases that are difficult to untangle from one another but remain tied together with the common thread of happy familiarity. The sounds, the smells, the tastes of our past Christmases are with us as we gather every year and enrich each new celebration. We find ourselves again in kitchens steaming with good cooking, breathing in spicy fragrances and wrapping endless parcels of cookies. Often we find ourselves preparing the dishes our mothers and fathers made years before, so our children can share in our past.

Christmas Memories with Recipes is a mosaic of holiday recollections by twenty-five cooks and writers from all parts of the Americas and Europe. They share with us memories of their varied holidays, some with sleigh bells, snow-fringed pines, and Christmas puddings, some with more exotic flavor and setting. For those, like Evan Jones, who are accustomed to a New England version of Christmas, the sunny glow of California and the whole-food cooking of Laurel's Kitchen or the whole baby goat, tamales, and firecrackers of Felipe Rojas-Lombardi's Lima may seem improbable, but the elaborate preparations and the drawn-out excitement are immediately familiar. In the preparations, in the time we take and the care we

A Note to the Reader

spend as we work with our friends and families, rests much of the joy of the holiday.

We hope you will read and use this book with pleasure, sharing these rich moments and marvelous foods with the writers who have taken us into their memories and their celebrations.

Recipes by Category

Appetizers

Soups

Breads and Coffeecakes

Cakes, Puddings, and Pies

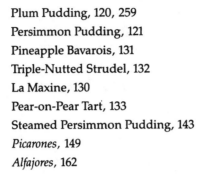

Recipes by Category

Cookies and Confections

Beverages

Sauces, Condiments, and Relishes

Recipes by Category

Christmas Memories
with Recipes

Evan Jones

A NORTHEAST KINGDOM IDYLL

If ever a holiday was destined for postcard immortality, it is Christmas in snow-blanketed New England. Evan Jones, the writer and historian of American food, here goes behind that scene, showing that it is backed by true pleasure in the outdoors coupled with the warmth of a lovingly prepared meal based on native ingredients.

MAYBE THE WAY TO SAY IT is that Christmases make a mosaic of nostalgia. My memories begin with the year the first ice skates were the parental gifts for my siblings and me, and there is an odd bit of sentiment for the friend whose handmade cradle, much later, was his celebration of my own first child's inaugural Christmas.

Yuletides in the Middle West were at least as white as those I have experienced in New England and no less festive than others I've spent in Europe, or on a tropical island. Snow seems to be, as I look back, the thing that matters. Once, at L'Auberge Maillane, outside Cannes, a sparkler twinkled on a minuscule Christmas tree that adorned our small table when the feast was brought, and sure enough, within hours the whole Mediterranean coast was buried in snow by Europe's most awesome winter storm in decades.

Snowfall certifies the childhood celebrations of my wife Judith's Vermont recollections at least as much as it does my own, and so we drive north habitually to Bryn Teg, eager for the sight of our summer pastures smoothed out in white blankets and the spruces and Scotch pines and cedars creaking when a cold wind stirs them. Our country haven is in the Northeast Kingdom, a domain that might have been designed for Christmas.

3

Perched on our slope of Stannard Mountain, with a long view of Mansfield's peak to the west, Bryn Teg can be reached only by climbing one gently winding hill road after another. Snowplows burrow along, piling white banks with new layers to make way for the school bus, but the roller-coaster lane that leads up to our house gets no public service. A neighbor whose truck has been converted for the season into a road scraper must be prevailed upon, and only providence knows how many passes his plow must make to clear the last quarter-mile of our Christmas journey.

Chances are more than good that in any given year there will be snow for the holiday, but still we weren't prepared in 1984 for what the days before Christmas managed to accumulate. No sooner had one ration of snow settled down in a quiet winter wonderland than another foot of white stuff fell upon the Northeast Kingdom. In an effort to ease our coming, our neighboring plowman had already pushed his way up to the house five times. Still we were forced to make another pleading telephone call, and then as we stopped in the village we persuaded a garage to rent us a four-wheel-drive Jimmy-X with axles elevated enough to traverse snowed-in terrain.

At Christmas as well as at other times, country people can be ambivalent about winter storms. The writer Edward Hoagland, who has a place a few miles up the road, observed with sorrow that "barns go broken-backed under the weight of snow." And earlier in this century Wilson Bentley, from another nearby community, was so enchanted by the winter's mantle that he spent a lifetime photographing snowflakes. He printed almost six thousand microphotos of individual flakes and sold two hundred of them to Tiffany's to be used as intricate models for hexagonal designs in cut diamonds. However, along with almost everybody else, *I* want snow that knows its place, disintegrating on the roof from heat within the building and lingering on window ledges just long enough to please the eye with its mysterious multiplicity of frozen crystals.

I also like the idea of snow being practical, which in 1984 was what it turned out to be for the skiers in the family. As our high-wheeled vehicle grunted into fourth gear to negotiate the hilly driveway, I looked out at the white vastness of the frozen pond we had carved out of a swampy spot the year before; its snowy counterpane was far too thick to be easily removed for skating, but the land that shoulders this small lake was ideal for cross-country gliding up to the high ground of summer meadows. The snow shimmered crisply in failing light, and cries went up from the back seat to affirm the skiers' possibility of at least an informal slalom race down that unblemished whiteness.

We piled out, toting baggage and cartons of provisions into the warmth of the house. The furnace was doing its job all right, but the teenagers, Alexandra and Matthew, made it plain that their need was for logs to be ignited immediately in the Rumford fireplace while Bronwyn, their mother, and Judith, my wife, put into the fridge the things that might spoil in the kitchen's rising temperature (a fire had already been started in the cast-iron stove by our thoughtful neighbor).

In any season, the kitchen is the marrow, the essence of the house. Beams, eight by ten inches, support the low ceiling, and a wrought-iron lamp hangs near the Welsh cupboard, whose shelves are laden with local pottery. Two large windows look toward the sunset, two more over the sink toward the split-leaf maple we planted in the yard and on to the woods creeping threateningly toward rolling pastures. In December it's a temptation to eye the scattered evergreens there and think of Christmas decorations festooning one of them indoors.

The big black six-burner stove, wedged between an auxiliary corner sink and the refrigerator, which we painted black, is the reason, we sometimes tell each other, that we bought the house. There were many, many reasons, of course, but the compelling appeal of this generously proportioned stove, fueled by outdoor tanks of propane, is clearly evident as it sits stolidly, comfortably, on the terra-cotta tile floor. It seems to have been invented to turn out feasts for a gathered family.

We planned that year to fill the oven with a plump goose we would bring back from Ralph Persons's place on the edge of the village. And well before the main event of Christmas Day, there were holiday cookies to be baked in lamb-shaped pottery forms and hung on the tree, and there would be sweet-potato ginger rolls, and a Yankee parsnip pie, among other pastries. We had plenty of time to get ready for Christmas Eve, which was to be shared in part with the LeCours family in the village. Most important, more urgent than all else was the shopping trip that had to be made, no matter what weather might turn up.

In the morning the sky had begun to clear. High, feathery cirrus clouds drifted above us, and a bevy of bluejays started upward off the squeaking snow crust as we came out the back door. Although haze obscured Mount Mansfield on the far horizon, our high-wheeled red and white vehicle, with its heater oozing warmth, seemed full of assurances as we headed toward Hardwick. The threat of more snow had diminished, and we made it without incident to the village shopping mall.

About a half hour later we turned into the Mackville road to get to the Persons poultry farm. Ralph is a loitering sort of man, cheerful when he's not wary of strangers, and he takes pleasure in exhibiting his various birds to friends. He plucked from her roost a gold-flecked Bantam hen that clutched his arm, then a Rembrandt-colored mallard duck, the morning light catching its burnished purples, greens, and blues; and he showed off a white Leghorn, telling us with a grin of mischief that this was the one that laid suntanned eggs. Ralph is a hero to his fine feathered friends, yet it doesn't seem to pain him when he sentences one to the roasting pan. He was still smiling when we took the road toward home with our denuded goose.

Judith was out of the car just in time to point a camera at the tree expedition coming out of the woods. Matt and Alexandra had felled a well-girthed pine in the fledgling woods on the north side of the house. Rising palely from the chimney into the white-blue sky was a ribbon of wood smoke. Young Matt, cold enough from his search for the most acceptable evergreen, pushed energetically across the snow, dragging his needly burden indoors to a place near the living-room fire.

We set up the frosty, sharp-quilled tree on the metal base, and soon it was decorated with all-white lights, shimmering slivers of foil, opalescent balls, and the two ornate birds that had been part of so many other Christmases. When, as evening came, the strings of bulbs were set alight and their mild heat warmed the green boughs, there was a faint aroma, more woodsy than flowerlike, that is characteristic of white pines at yuletide in the Northeast Kingdom.

When Judith and I went outdoors to stand in deep snow under remote starlight, the sky had turned so mysteriously deep and dark that we lingered to look at the shadowed trees, every thin branch outlined and motionless. The stalks of autumn marigolds rose, as if petrified, out of the bright snow. Downslope from us, our small deep lake appeared cupped and white, tall blue spruces on its shoulders as stalwart as sentinels, guarding the frozen surface.

The next day we had the *réveillon* party to look forward to. We joined the LeCours family on Church Street, where we found tiny Violette LeCours, her face flushed and dewy, surrounded by children and grandchildren who had gathered from as far away as Virginia. All of them were gifted singers, and Mrs. LeCours was a gifted cook as well. She had wanted us to know how a French family from the Gaspé Peninsula observed its traditional Noel, and she drew us into her dining room–kitchen (the carpeted parlor was too formal).

On the well-used table was the tourtière, the classic meat pie served on Christmas Eve, after Mass. "In my grandmother's time it was sure to be on every Christmas table, but it's not so common now," she said. "They say it was originally a pigeon pie." Hers, like most of the tourtières served by the local French, was dependent on good pork shoulder and was seasoned with onion, cinnamon, and cloves. It is rich fare that fuels the body—a rewarding thing to have on coming inside from a freezing winter day. There was also a *bûche de Noël*, not surprisingly, and lots of other sweets for the big family to share, but the high point of *réveillon* for the LeCourses was the singing, the *chansons* rendered in solos and in harmonies. The music of Violette LeCours and her lively, cheerful progeny echoed in our minds as we returned to Bryn Teg in a light snowfall.

On our own, the habitual high point of Christmas Eve is the midnight service at the Church of St. John the Baptist—no bells pealing in cadence, no *réveillon* as a prospect. The little village church is attached to a house, its interior garlanded with greenery and bright red rosettes of poinsettias. The simple wooden pews

Evan Jones

are packed shoulder to shoulder with parishioners in from the cold, wearing their heavy outdoor garments throughout the service, leaning together as they stand for the hymns. It is a moment of joy for Judith, who enfolds us all in her own sure radiance.

When the last good night had been said on the church steps and we were once more crowded into our drift-defying multi-geared jeep, a carol, "It Came upon a Midnight Clear," was a failed prophecy. Wilson Bentley's delicate flakes began floating down to cover the day-old snow. With the heavy wipers squeegeeing on the windshield, we had news of what Christmas Day was to be.

"Like being at sea on a transatlantic liner," Judith said when we woke up in the early light. Bryn Teg was a floating vessel becalmed within sight of a mountain horizon. Only the dark splotches of trees interrupted the wide, downy valley that stretched outward just below us. All the month's other snowfalls were as nothing compared to the inches of white powder that now covered everything. In the living room, the children had already turned on the lights of the tree they had chosen in the woods, and it was beautiful, with boxed presents bracing its trunk at the bottom and the color of its ornaments glinting against the outdoor backdrop framed by the windows. Opening the bounty of gifts continued as we demolished a New England country breakfast of waffles, maple syrup, and homemade link sausages, plus the *boudin blanc* we'd transported from New York.

By now, sunlight lay on the stretching fields of snow like the thinnest film of gold. For Matt and Alex, it was pure challenge. With his own patented mixture of bravado and teenage charm that invariably melted any resistance that might come from his mother, Matt borrowed the jeep to take his sister to the Burke Mountain ski slopes. They would be back before the hour set for the Christmas feast, they promised jauntily; then they were suddenly gone, leaving behind the reassuring tracks of snow tires.

Seeing the children disappear so adventurously was all that Judith and Bronwyn needed. There was time before the goose would have to slide into the big black stove and no better way to use the interval than to clamp on their skis for an hour of cross-country sport. The high ground above the pond was clear enough now to have become almost blue in reflecting the light-filled sky. Up across the bulging pasture the skis took them, their snowy wake trailing behind them like double ribbons, until they vanished from sight. Later, when I looked out, I saw Judith headed home, doing a downward snowplow, and Bronwyn frolicking in a zigzag Christie turn. "We saw pawprints!" they both cried when they burst into the kitchen. "Was it a fox?" Judith asked rhetorically. "There wasn't a sound except the skis and the boughs creaking." And Bronwyn added in quick maternal concern, "No sign of the kids?"

It turned out Matt had lost his way after leaving Highway 5. On whatever roads they turned into, Alex said, there was a plow wedging up ridges of snow to frustrate them. Glad as he was to have found the road home, Matt clumped down the cellar steps to bring up wood, complaining that the living-room hearth had been reduced to a bed of red coals instead of licking flames. At least he could fix *that*.

What we all fixed was Christmas dinner. In anticipation, I had telephoned an Indian entrepreneur in Minnesota, with the result that we were stocked with plenty of wild rice; as a sentimental nod toward my youth I wanted some of it to be used in stuffing the goose. I'd also been delegated to produce the Bryn Teg soup from the fiddlehead ferns that a friend had gathered in early May and which we froze for use throughout the year. But defter hands were needed to turn out the pumpkin timbales Judith had first made as a child with a Vermont aunt, and she was now making a batch for dinner in our islanded house. Meantime, on the white marble slab Bronwyn was shaping the dough for sweet-potato rolls the size of Ping-Pong balls, and their generous ginger seasoning was perfuming the air.

"Snow!" We chorused the word as in the same instant we saw the wet stuff hitting the kitchen windowpanes and clinging to the branches of the young maple tree in the yard. The new "flaky torrent" (in a poet's nimble phrase) called for special celebration, and at a word from me Matthew found the cold bottle of champagne and eased off its caged cork. As Alex checked the flame under the small white onions in their creamy sauce, we

Evan Jones

9

lifted our glasses. The youngsters, not needing alcohol, found their own chilled drinks.

By the time the goose had wafted its aromatic signals from the oven and the feast in all its Vermont splendor drew us to our places at the table, there was no knowing how long we might be snowed in—nor did any of us think we cared. As plates were filled in the candlelight with food we had all had a hand in preparing, there were looks of smug success on all the faces at the table. Outside, the snow came tumbling down, undeterred in the dark. Inside, Matthew's fire would keep us warm of heart; his sister's smile needed no refueling. We felt blessed, and ready for the duration.

Roast Goose
with Wild Rice, Hazelnut, and Apple Stuffing

1 goose (9 to 12 pounds)
Salt
3 to 4 cups cooked wild rice
⅔ cup coarse-chopped hazelnuts
2 large green apples, peeled, cored, and cubed
½ cup fine-chopped onion
2 teaspoons dried savory
3 tablespoons chopped parsley
Freshly ground pepper
Flour
SERVES 6 TO 8

Remove the neck, heart, and gizzard from the goose and put them in a saucepan with 4 cups water. Let simmer gently, partially covered, for several hours, until reduced to slightly less than 2 cups. Season the broth to taste with salt.

For the stuffing, mix together the wild rice, nuts, apples,

onion, and herbs, seasoning to taste with salt and pepper. Fill the cavity of the goose with the stuffing, skewer closed, and lace string around the skewers, then truss the bird. Roast in a preheated 325-degree oven, breast side down, for 1½ hours, drawing off the fat as it accumulates, then turn and roast another 1½ hours, or slightly more for an 11–12-pound bird. When done, the juices should run clear when the bird is pricked where the thigh attaches to the body.

Pour off all but 1 tablespoon of the fat, then sprinkle a little flour over the bottom of the roasting pan—1 to 2 tablespoons, depending on how thick you like your gravy. Set the pan over low heat and stir for 2 minutes, scraping up all the browned bits. Add the reserved goose broth and whisk until smooth. Taste and season with salt and pepper and serve in a gravy boat alongside the bird. Remove trussing strings and skewers before carving.

Sweet-Potato Ginger Rolls

1 tablespoon active dry yeast
2 tablespoons sugar
2 tablespoons nonfat dry milk
1 tablespoon grated fresh gingerroot
1 teaspoon grated orange rind
1 teaspoon coarse salt or ½ teaspoon table salt
⅛ teaspoon freshly grated nutmeg
2 tablespoons soft butter
¾ cup mashed sweet potatoes
3½ cups all-purpose flour, preferably unbleached
1 egg beaten with 1 teaspoon water
Sesame seeds
MAKES 36 ROLLS

In a medium-size bowl dissolve the yeast in ¼ cup of luke-warm water. Combine the sugar and dry milk with 1 cup of warm water and add to the yeast along with the grated ginger, orange rind, salt, and nutmeg. Whip the butter into the mashed potatoes and combine with yeast mixture. Stir the flour in and then beat

11

the mixture for 1 minute. Cover the bowl with plastic wrap and place over a pan of warm water to rise until double in volume—about 45 minutes.

Turn out onto a floured work surface, punch down, and knead very lightly a few turns. Pull off pieces of dough slightly smaller than a Ping-Pong ball and, since they will be very sticky, just roll lightly with floured hands to form a ball. Arrange on one or two greased baking sheets large enough to hold the three dozen rolls side by side without crowding. Cover with a kitchen towel and let rise in a warm place for 30 minutes. Paint with the beaten egg and sprinkle sesame seeds on top.

Bake in a preheated 350-degree oven for 25 minutes. Serve warm.

Pumpkin Timbales

2 cups mashed baked pumpkin
1½ teaspoons finely minced fresh gingerroot
1 tablespoon maple syrup
¼ teaspoon freshly grated nutmeg
3 eggs, lightly beaten
¼ cup half-and-half
Salt and freshly ground pepper
SERVES 8

Mix all the ingredients together, seasoning to taste with salt and pepper. Pour the mixture into 8 lightly buttered muffin tins or custard cups, filling them two-thirds full, and place them in a pan of simmering water. Bake for 5 minutes in a preheated 350-degree oven, then lower the heat to 325 degrees and bake another 30 minutes, or until set (a skewer inserted in the center should come out clean). Let rest 5 minutes before unmolding.

Julia Child

THE LOG OF
A BÛCHE

Julia Child has never watched her extremely popular Show Number 251, for reasons she explains here. With Simone Beck and Louise Bertholle, Child brought the techniques and joys of French cooking to the United States in the two volumes of MASTERING THE ART OF FRENCH COOKING. *The beginnings of that classic work can be glimpsed here.*

I THINK WITH WONDER not only of my gastronomic innocence but also of my worldly innocence when, some forty years ago, we landed at Le Havre and I saw my first native Frenchmen. Hearty blue-bloused porters they were, tough and jolly; I had expected all Frenchmen to be formal, distant, delicate, small, and equipped with thin waxed mustaches. To find ruddy, well-muscled, normal-looking men was reassuring. They packed us into our not very new blue Buick, and off we drove to Paris via Rouen. I was ecstatic over the very French look of the French countryside, I swooned over the romantically half-timbered houses, I was utterly awed by the great cathedral, and quite delirious over our lunch at La Couronne. We started with oysters, followed with one of their famous duck dishes. While husband Paul commandeered a fat ripe Comice pear for dessert and an equally fat wedge of Camembert, I went for the pastries.

Such an array was utterly intoxicating and quite new to me. Where had I been all those years? I didn't know what most of the beautifully decorated items were, and my four words of French were not adequate for an explanation. But I did recognize a tart when I saw one, and cream puffs, and rum babas. However, this was my first encounter with the lush elaboration of the French petit four, especially those that were cunningly walled in leaves

13

of chocolate and decorated with buttery swirls. I was particularly entranced, too, with a chocolate cake fairly hidden under a forest of mushrooms. Of course, they were not actual mushrooms, as I found upon sampling them, but perfect meringue facsimiles.

How we made our way to Paris along the Seine after our glorious lunch I don't remember, but it was 1948, shortly after World War II, and automobiles, especially big American models, were few. In fact our blue Buick brought forth such wondering remarks as *"Oo-là! Quelle baignolle!"*—quite a bathtub you've got there, as Paul interpreted for me. He had spent years in France before World War II and spoke the language beautifully, one reason he had been posted to the American embassy in Paris.

We were fortunate indeed to find almost at once a wonderfully old-fashioned apartment, the whole third floor of a large private house, on the Rue de l'Université just across from the Place de la Concorde. It came with a playful little brown *poussiquette* (my first cat—many firsts here) who was an efficient mouser, a kitchen on the fourth floor that looked out onto the walled garden of one of the French ministries, and a fulsome set of Louis XVI furniture.

As soon as we were settled, I took steps to enlarge my French vocabulary, thanks to two-hour daily lessons at Berlitz plus frequent conversations with a lively French friend who took on my education, and at the Cordon Bleu cookery school, where all the teaching was in French.

By Christmas time I was getting a grip on the language, had mastered a number of such basics as handmade mayonnaise, and had even made, filled, and frosted several real, totally French cakes. Proud of my pastry prowess, I was knowingly inspecting a swish pastry shop on the Rue du Bac when I saw those meringue mushrooms again, this time scattered over the top of a log-shaped cake. *"Commandez votre Bûche de Noël,"* urged a pretty sign in elegant script by its side.

That's when I saw my first yule-log cake. Although they are common enough now, could they have *not* existed in America then? Perhaps they did in New York, but not where I came from. This *bûche* did look quite like a real log, its chocolate frosting cunningly made to resemble the bark of a tree. There was even a knot in the log, and a cut branch, its yellow woodlike inside showing. The mushrooms, dusted with cocoa powder and nestling along part of its top and sides, gave it a fittingly woodsy look, which was only enhanced by a casually draped veil of spun caramel. I've seen many a yule-log cake since, but most of them have been covered with sugar flowers and green bits; pastry chefs are not always known for their sophistication of design. None of the confections I've seen in recent years has had the elegance of this particular French *bûche*, a beautiful piece of work in its directness and simplicity.

Although I admired it extravagantly, I never attempted a *bûche de Noël* of my own until almost twenty years later, when we were in the midst of our black-and-white television series, *The French Chef*. It was Show Number 78, and would be aired in time for Christmas. In those days we did them "live on tape"; in other words, once the cameras started rolling, you didn't stop for anything short of dismemberment of the cook or an out-and-out fire in the kitchen. Most of our programs then were half-hours devoted to a single process or recipe. The *bûche* offered just the right elements—drama, fun, and a goodly number of basic techniques.

The *bûche* is really a jelly roll, starting with a sponge-cake batter, a fine basic that shows the proper beating together of egg yolks and sugar, the whipping of egg whites to stiff shining peaks of perfection, plus the technique of folding them together. It's baked in a flat jelly-roll pan about 12 by 18 inches, giving you that special technique, plus the little trick of how in the world to get the cake out of the pan. Further challenges are the filling, the frosting, and the mushrooms; in this case a meringue base with various additions serves to make all three—egg whites again, but with a difference.

The black-and-white *bûche*, Show Number 78, went off without incident, as I remember. The only trouble I had was the next day, when I took the standby *bûche* to a winter weekend in New Hampshire. Except for its final spun-caramel veil, the log was splendidly frosted, I had the mushrooms in an airtight container, and everything survived the automobile trip nicely. I made the caramel just before dinner, finished the decorations, and set the log out in the woodshed to stay cold.

15

After our host's marvelous wild pheasant and a sprightly salad and cheese course, I went out to bring in my masterpiece. Unaware that it was not only cold out there in the woodshed but damp as well, I found my caramel had collapsed in wispy droplets upon my decor. Woe indeed. There was nothing for me to do but bring it in, attempting to wear a smile over my stiff upper lip—one must never, ever apologize! I didn't mention the caramel collapse as I rapidly displayed the *bûche* and served it forth. Probably it was not even noticed. Anyway it was suitably admired, and they ate up every crumb.

The real drama came some years later, when we did another *bûche de Noël.* It was Show Number 251 in the midst of our color series. I always say "we" speaking of the shows because a team of loyal public-television volunteer cooks worked with me from the beginning of the *French Chef* series, through many experiences, both harrowing and hilarious.

Our first disaster was on the very early morning of taping day. We had made a number of naked jelly-roll sheets the day before and had rolled them up for safekeeping. Unfortunately, someone had stored them in the freezer rather than in the refrigerator. Naturally when one of the cooks tried to unroll them they broke into big pieces. Quick! Make and bake at least two more.

I had wanted to show that a *bûche* is not only for Christmas but could be for other festivities such as the Fourth of July. Our thought was to display on the table at the end a finished *bûche* for the Glorious Fourth. Although we like to have everything wonderfully edible, since we eat our work when the show is over, time was fleeting, and so we faked that one cake by rolling up, icing, and very carefully decorating a copy of the Boston *Globe.*

Finally we were ready to shoot, and the relentless cameras began to roll. What I didn't realize was that, probably unnerved by our troubles, I had made the barklike chocolate frosting too thick, so that it oozed with difficulty from my pastry tube and did not adhere to the cake very well. I could see what I was doing on my side of the *bûche,* but the frosting on the back side—the camera side, which the audience saw but which I couldn't—kept peeling off.

After struggling with my side I looked up into the camera,

right into the viewer's eyes, presumably to offer a deathless observation; what I saw was an "idiot card," a scrawled message to me: "Turn it around!" What did that mean? I couldn't see the peeling side of the cake, so it didn't register. I kept fussing confusedly with my side, looked up again—into the audience's eyes—and a new idiot card: "Frosting peeling off." I finally got the message and turned the *bûche* around. Indeed, hardly a line of frosting had stuck on. But time was wasting, and I still had the spun caramel to make. I managed to spread on the frosting with a spatula (much easier than the pastry tube anyway), assuring my viewers with every stroke not to worry, that all would be perfectly loglike in the end, and it actually was. Then on to the caramel, the final decoration of mushrooms, a garland of holly, and off to the dining room, where the *bûche* display awaited us.

After a few jolly final words I pointed to the Fourth of July *bûche*. Intending to finish with a flourish, I held two sparklers over a decorative candle, and as soon as they were sending off the proper bursts, I lifted them high, to plunge them dramatically into the sides of our all-American *bûche*. Of course I had forgotten that *that* one was not a *bûche* at all but a dressed-up Boston *Globe*. And of course as I enthusiastically plunged the sparklers into that unyielding *bûche*, they bent almost double in my hands. Mustering some presence of mind, I quickly raised them high again, and signed off fast with my usual *"Bon appétit."*

I never did see that show and have no idea how it went over. In spite of my troubles we got plenty of requests for the recipe when it ran and still get numerous demands when it goes on repeats, which indicates the show mightn't have been all that bad.

Here is the recipe—in a slightly updated version. If you don't have to do it for television, it should go like a breeze and, I can assure you, will eat like a dream.

Julia Child

A Bûche de Noël

Although an ordinary sponge-cake recipe is fine for the jelly-roll cake, or sponge sheet as it is often called, the orange and almond formula suggested here will make it far more interesting. To simplify mechanics, the frosting and filling as well as the mushrooms are all from the same egg-white-and-sugar meringue mixture.

MAKES A 10-INCH LOG SERVING 8 TO 10

FOR THE ORANGE/ALMOND SPONGE SHEET
3 egg yolks
½ cup granulated sugar
Grated rind and strained juice of 1 medium orange
¾ cup blanched almonds ground with 3 tablespoons granulated
    sugar
¼ teaspoon almond extract
½ cup plain bleached cake flour in a sifter
3 "large" egg whites
3 additional tablespoons granulated sugar
Confectioner's sugar in a sieve or sifter

MERINGUE BASE FOR THE FILLING, FROSTING, AND
MUSHROOMS
3 "large" egg whites
Pinch of salt
Scant ¼ teaspoon cream of tartar
1⅓ cups granulated sugar

BASE FOR THE FILLING AND FROSTING
12 ounces semisweet baking chocolate melted with ⅓ cup strong
    coffee
1 tablespoon vanilla extract
2 to 3 tablespoons dark Jamaican rum
4 tablespoons (½ stick) unsalted butter, softened

FOR THE FILLING
½ stick additional softened butter

18

FOR DECORATION
2 to 3 tablespoons unsweetened cocoa in a tea strainer, and the sieve or sifter of confectioner's sugar

FOR THE SPUN CARAMEL VEIL
1 cup granulated sugar
3 tablespoons white corn syrup

SPECIAL EQUIPMENT SUGGESTED
A jelly-roll pan about 11 by 17 inches; butter, wax paper, and flour for the pan; an electric blender or food processor for the almonds; a table-model electric mixer for the meringue; a pastry bag with ⅜-inch tube opening and a separate tube with ⅛-inch opening, for the mushrooms; a buttered and floured no-stick pastry sheet for the mushrooms; a serving board to hold the log; plenty of wax paper; an oiled broom handle suspended between 2 chair backs and newspapers on the floor, for the caramel.

THE SPONGE SHEET
Preparing the pan. Preheat the oven to 375 degrees. Line the jelly-roll pan with buttered wax paper, leaving a 2-inch overhang at each end. Roll flour in the pan and shake out excess.

The cake batter. Using a wire whisk or hand-held electric mixer, beat the 3 egg yolks in a 3-quart bowl, gradually sprinkling in the ½ cup of sugar. When the mixture is thick and pale yellow, beat in the grated orange rind and juice, the almonds, and the almond extract. Slowly sift in the flour, while blending with the whisk. In a very clean separate bowl with clean beaters, beat the egg whites to soft peaks; sprinkle in the 3 tablespoons of sugar and continue beating to form stiff, shining peaks. Stir a quarter of the egg whites into the batter; delicately fold in the rest.

Baking the jelly roll. Immediately turn the batter into the prepared pan; bang it lightly but firmly on your work surface to settle it, and place it at once in the middle level of the preheated 375-degree oven. Bake about 10 minutes, until it has very lightly colored and the top is springy—do not overbake or the cake will crack when you roll it up.

1 9

Cooling and storing. Sprinkle the top of the cake with a 1/16-inch layer of confectioner's sugar; cover with a sheet of wax paper and a lightly dampened towel. Reverse onto a tray or baking sheet. Then while the cake is still warm, holding an end of the wax paper, lift off the jelly-roll pan. Carefully peel the wax paper off the cake. Sift another 1/16-inch layer of sugar over the cake and roll it up in the damp towel; place in a plastic bag to keep it from drying out, and refrigerate. (The cake must be cold before you fill and frost it.)

● *Ahead-of-time note:* The sponge sheet will keep nicely 2 or 3 days in the refrigerator or you may freeze it for several weeks—but to prevent its breaking, be sure to let it defrost completely before unrolling it.

THE MERINGUE BASE—ITALIAN MERINGUE

Beat the egg whites in the electric mixer until foaming throughout; add the salt and cream of tartar and continue beating until soft peaks are formed. Turn mixer speed to slow. In a small saucepan bring the sugar and ½ cup water to the simmer, remove from heat, and swirl the pan until the sugar has dissolved completely and the liquid is perfectly clear. Cover the pan tightly and boil to the soft-ball stage (238 degrees). Using moderately slow speed, gradually whip the hot syrup into the egg whites; increase speed to fast and continue at high speed for 5 minutes, until egg whites form stiff shining peaks and have completely cooled. Plan to use the meringue promptly.

MERINGUE MUSHROOMS

Preheat the oven to 200 degrees. Scoop a quarter of the meringue into the pastry bag and squeeze out 8 to 10 half-inch domes on the pastry sheet, to serve as mushroom caps. Hold the 1/8-inch tube over the end of the pastry bag and squeeze out 8 to 10 conical shapes ¾ inch high, for the stems. Bake about 1 hour in the middle level of the oven, until the meringues push easily off the pastry sheet—they should color no more than a darkish cream. Return unused meringue to the main mixture.

● *Ahead-of-time note:* Meringues may be made in advance and frozen.

THE FILLING AND FROSTING

Beat the smoothly melted chocolate into the meringue, along with the vanilla, rum, and soft butter. Remove two-thirds of the mixture to a bowl and refrigerate; this is the frosting. Beat the additional half stick of soft butter into the remaining meringue; this is the filling.

FILLING THE CAKE

Unroll the sponge sheet and slice a quarter inch off the long sides so that the cake will roll easily. Spread the filling over the top of the sheet. Roll it up from one of the small ends and you have made the log shape. Neatly slice a narrow slanting piece from each end of the log. With a small knife dig a hole in an upper side of the log and insert a piece of the scrap to simulate a bump or a branch. Place the log seam-side down on the serving board and slip double sheets of wax paper under the edge of each side and the two ends—to catch frosting spills.

FROSTING THE LOG

Beat 2 or more spoonfuls of sifted cocoa into the frosting mixture to make it a spreadable consistency. (Reserve 2 spoonfuls of frosting for the mushrooms.) Leaving the two ends free, frost the cake using a flexible metal spatula, then scumble it with the spatula and a fork to give it a rough barklike look.

● *Ahead-of-time note:* Refrigerate the log if you are not continuing; it will keep nicely for a day—if you can find a non-mashing cover for it.

FINAL DECORATIONS, JUST BEFORE SERVING

The mushrooms. With a small knife, pierce a hole in the bottom of each meringue mushroom cap, insert a bit of the frosting (or softened butter) into the hole and then the pointed end of a meringue stem. Arrange the mushrooms in tasteful clusters upon the log and sprinkle the log with a dusting of confectioner's sugar to give a snowy effect. Dust the tops of the mushrooms with cocoa powder tapped from the sieve.

The caramel veil. Bring the sugar to the simmer with the corn syrup and one-third cup water in a small saucepan; when the mixture is completely dissolved and clear, cover tightly and boil to the caramel stage. Let it cool two to three minutes, until it forms thick strands when lifted with a fork. Then dip the fork into the syrup and wave it over the broomstick, to form long hanging threads of caramel.

The finale. Lift the caramel strands off the broomstick; drape them over the yule log. Decorate the serving board with sprigs of holly if you wish, and the *bûche de Noël* is ready to serve.

Edna Lewis

CHRISTMAS
IN FREETOWN

In THE TASTE OF COUNTRY COOKING, *Edna Lewis recalls an almost forgotten countryside, where families grew or gathered everything they ate. Here she tells how preparation for the holidays began early, when the black walnuts ripened, and the actual celebration was a bright break in the hard routine of a small family farm.*

WHEN I WAS A GIRL growing up in the small farming community of Freetown, Virginia, preparations for Christmas started in early September, when we children went out to gather black walnuts, hickory nuts, and hazelnuts. Hazelnuts grew along the edge of the woods on low bushes, but hickories and black walnuts grew on tall trees, and we waited until they fell to the ground before racing the squirrels to collect them. The black walnuts and hickory nuts had to be gathered early in the fall to give them time to dry out in the sun to help in removing the outer shell. If they were not dry, it was almost impossible to crack their firm inner shells. When they were ready, we'd wedge an upturned flatiron between our knees, put a dried nut on the hard surface, and take a hammer to the nut. Using a nut pick or sometimes a hairpin, we'd pry the nutmeats from the shell—rich, flavorful nutmeats that, even on those warm, bright days, filled us with happy anticipation because we knew they would be baked into delicious Christmas cakes and cookies.

Whenever she saw a break of a day or two from the September harvest, Mother would set about making the fruitcake. It was a family affair that my older sister and I cheerfully participated in. Outside it might be rainy and blowing, but in the snug kitchen the sweet smells of dried fruit, grated fresh nutmeg, and spices

23

kept us warm and happy. Mother bought the dried fruit from the store, and the fragrant mix of citron, dried candied lemon and orange peel, and seedless raisins seemed to us wonderfully exotic. We took turns chopping quantities of sticky fruit, which we then put into a big bowl and marinated with wine and brandy. The batter for the cake was so heavy we spelled each other during stirring or laid an extra hand on the sturdy wooden spoon. Finally the cake was mixed, and Mother spooned the batter into two prepared pans, where it sat overnight to marinate and mellow. The next day, whether it was still raining or not, Mother baked the cakes. When they had cooled completely, she wrapped them, still encased in the brown paper that lined the pans, in cheesecloth and put them in a large crock or lard can to age during the months before Christmas. Since most everyone cooked with lard in those days, wide-mouthed ten-gallon lard cans were common in every household. One cake was set on the bottom of the can, and a partition made of several slats of wood was propped over it so that a second cake could fit in the can. Every few weeks or so, we lifted out the cakes and sprinkled them with a glassful of brandy, rum, or whiskey to keep them moist and flavorful. Come Christmas, we unwrapped the cakes, sliced one up to give away, and put the other on the sideboard to be enjoyed by family and guests during the coming week.

In early December, as Christmas approached, we began baking cookies, pies, and cakes and, to our delight, making candy. We never had candy at any other time of the year, and so the chocolate and caramel fudge and peanut brittle we made at Christmas time were treasured treats. All the candy was really sweet— just the way we liked it! Cookies were not as important at Christmas when I was young as they seem to be now or may have been in other communities; the ones we made were simple sugar cookies with no special decorations. At other times of the year, Mother baked thick chewy buttermilk cookies with sugary tops.

I always associate oysters with Christmas. The country store stocked barrels of shucked oysters, and we children were sent up to the store to fill our buckets with them. Mother made oyster stew for Christmas Eve supper, fried oysters with cornmeal coating for Christmas breakfast, and escalloped oysters for Christmas dinner. The fruitcake, cookies, pies, and candies came out on Christmas Eve—but only for show; we couldn't indulge until the next day. After Christmas Eve supper, we decorated the tree with strings of popcorn we had made a few days earlier. Sometimes we colored the popcorn with colored confectioner's sugar to add brightness to the tree. We also garlanded it with shiny twisted gold cord and often set little white candles nestled in puffs of cotton on the tree. I think I liked these candles best of all, even though they were never lit for fear of fire. Another of my favorite decorations was the red paper bells Mother hung about the house. They folded up flat for storage, but when opened, the bells were big and bold. Ropes of running cedar were strung all over the house until not a corner was left bare.

Christmas morning was heralded by fireworks. My father got us up before dawn and we huddled together in the cold, dark morning while he set off noisy Roman candles and lit our sparklers, which, as we became more awake and excited, we swung around and around, swooping up and down, making lovely trails of light. These fireworks were big excitement in Freetown for us children, and if our older neighbors did not completely share the excitement, well, that was all right. They knew they were set off by my father, the youngest parent in the community, and they had come to expect them every Christmas morning.

Mother always hung new long stockings by the fireplace for us after we had gone to bed on Christmas Eve, and after the fireworks we hurried inside to open them. There was always an orange in the toe of the stocking. By Christmas morning the gentle heat of the banked fire had warmed the oranges up so that their aroma trickled up the stairs to our rooms—our first Christmas greeting. There were also Brazil nuts and hazelnuts and little celluloid dolls. We did not get any other presents the way children do now.

After Christmas breakfast, Mother began preparing Christmas dinner, which was served at noon, early enough to give the men plenty of time at the table before twilight and chores. We invited some old people my grandfather's age and a friend or two, but mostly it was only our own family (eight or ten of us, depending on which of our cousins were staying with us) who gathered

Edna Lewis

25

around the table. Hog killing was just over, and there was fresh pork such as spareribs, liver pudding, and whatever else we had not put down to cure. In Freetown we grew, hunted, or foraged most of our food, so because it was hunting season, alongside the traditional escalloped oysters, the chicken, and the rabbit was a panful of quail or snipe. We had white and sweet potatoes, turnips, and a leafy green, which at that time of year usually was watercress. After the meal came dessert—mincemeat pie, caramel layer cake, coconut cake, fruitcake, and candy.

When we had finished eating, the visiting began. We ran out into the cold, darkening afternoon to our neighbors' houses, where we sampled some of their desserts or candies or whatever they offered. We had already exchanged some foods with the neighbors right after Christmas breakfast; now the back-and-forth visiting and eating would continue all week. The adults in Freetown worked hard the rest of the year, and they took full advantage of this week to relax and enjoy themselves. We also used this time to visit old friends who lived a distance from Freetown. It was bitter cold during December and January in Virginia, and after hitching the horse to the surrey, our parents bundled us children up under heavy blankets and off we went.

Christmas week always ended too soon for us. In a few days, though, it was New Year's Eve, when traditional black-eyed peas were made for good luck and we feasted on more meats and vegetables, as well as the leftover desserts from Christmas. We went to bed early as usual, but the adults stayed up and ate supper after midnight. On New Year's Day, Mother took down all the decorations, and when everything had been packed away in boxes for the next year, the house looked strangely bare. We were a little sad, but took comfort in the knowledge that the joyous week would repeat itself the next year and the one after that and after that. It had been a wonderful time of sharing and eating and visiting and good times.

Edna Lewis's Christmas Fruitcake

1 cup diced (about ½ inch) glazed candied orange peel
1 cup diced (about ½ inch) glazed candied lemon peel
2 cups diced (about ½ inch) citron
1 cup currants
2 cups seedless raisins, chopped
½ cup dry red wine
½ cup brandy
3½ cups all-purpose flour
1 teaspoon ground cinnamon
2 teaspoons freshly grated nutmeg
½ teaspoon ground cloves
1 teaspoon ground allspice
½ teaspoon ground mace
1 teaspoon baking powder
½ teaspoon salt
1 cup plus 6 tablespoons (2¾ sticks) butter, at room temperature
2 cups brown sugar, packed
5 eggs, separated
½ cup sorghum molasses

MAKES 1 TEN-INCH TUBE CAKE OR 2 NINE-INCH
LOAVES

Mix all the fruit in a large bowl and pour in the wine and brandy. Stir gently and set aside to marinate for a few hours.

Butter a 10-inch tube pan or two 9-by-5-by-3-inch loaf pans and line it (or them) with clean parchment paper. Butter the paper.

Sift the flour with the spices twice. Add the baking powder and salt and sift again.

Put the butter into a large mixing bowl and cream until satiny. Add sugar and, using an electric mixer, cream until light and fluffy. Beat the egg yolks slightly and then add them to the bowl. Mix the batter well before you start to add the flour-spice mixture. Stir the batter as you add the flour, a little at a time, stirring well after each addition. When the flour is thoroughly incorporated, add the molasses and stir. Finally, stir in the fruit and any soaking liquid in the bowl.

Put the egg whites in a grease-free bowl and beat with a clean beater until they hold stiff peaks. Fold them into the batter thoroughly and then spoon the batter into the prepared pan (or pans). Cover loosely with a clean cloth and let the batter sit overnight in a cool place to mellow.

On the next day, heat the oven to 250 degrees. Place the fruitcake on the middle rack of the oven and bake for 3½ to 4 hours. After 1½ hours, cover the pan with a piece of brown paper (do not use foil) or set the pan in a paper bag and return it to the oven.

When the cake has baked for 3½ hours, remove it from the oven and listen closely for any quiet, bubbling noises. If you "hear" the cake, it needs more baking. Or test the cake with a toothpick or cake tester. If the toothpick or tester comes out of the center of the cake clean, the cake is ready to take from the oven. Put it on a wire rack to cool, still in the pan.

When the cake is completely cool, turn it out of the pan (or pans), leaving the brown-paper lining on the cake. Wrap the cake with parchment, then aluminum foil, and pack the cake in a tin. Homemade fruitcakes need air, so punch a few holes in the lid of the tin or set the cover loosely on the tin.

Set the tin in a cool, undisturbed place, and every two or three weeks before Christmas, open the foil and sprinkle the cake with a liqueur glassful of brandy, wine, or whiskey. The liquor will keep the cake moist and flavorful and help preserve it as well.

Craig Claiborne

DISTANT
CHRISTMASES

In his newspaper columns and influential NEW YORK TIMES cookbooks, Craig Claiborne introduced the American public to the foods of almost all nations. Here he talks of his own introduction to what were then very exotic dishes. When Claiborne recalls his own strongest holiday memories, however, he returns to his roots in the South.

THE CHRISTMASES THAT PASS most often through my mind are from my early childhood, the most dramatic being when I was about four years old and, in a moment of innocence, set my family's home ablaze. However, most of my Christmases have been celebrated in distant places, places I didn't choose but found myself in come the holiday season.

When I was young, the thought of travel was beyond childhood fantasy. I was born in 1920 in a small Mississippi village called Sunflower. My father, who had been a fairly well-off plantation owner at the time of my birth, had lost almost everything—the homestead, landholdings, and a cotton gin among other things—and I assumed that the scope of my travels for the rest of my life would be bounded on the north by Memphis and on the south by New Orleans.

World War II drastically altered my orientation. And not the least of these alterations is a long list of vivid Christmas memories from all over the world and of the food on which I dined each December 25.

Take my first holiday as an enlisted man, a yeoman, which is to say a male secretary in uniform, aboard the heavy cruiser, the U.S.S. *Augusta*. It was November 1942, and we were involved in the invasion of North Africa. On November 8, when the smoke

29

had cleared, I went ashore at Casablanca. And it was there that I sampled, for the first time in my life, "foreign" food. The dish on which I dined was couscous, served in the private home of a Moroccan and his wife. The dining room and kitchen were perfumed with scents I had never before encountered, including cumin, coriander, saffron, cinnamon, and ginger. It was my first great, abandoned, wild love affair with food, and my enthusiasm was undoubtedly apparent, for I and another colleague from the battleship were invited back for an evening meal on Christmas Day. Our hosts were Muslim, and it was a tribute to our immediate friendship that they offered the second invitation. It was a far cry from roast turkey and stuffing. We dined seated, as is the Moroccan custom, on a floor covered with brightly colored pillows, and on both occasions we ate with our fingers—no knives or forks—while sipping a Moroccan red wine which was served, I feel quite certain, as a gesture to the American guests; the customary drink for couscous in a Moroccan home is a very sweet mint tea.

In recalling those ghosts of Christmases past, my brain follows a hopscotch pattern.

About thirty-five years ago, for instance, I was back in uniform, this time as a commissioned officer in the Korean conflict. I was stationed on a very small, little-known Pacific atoll named Kwajalein. On Christmas Eve, moved by old-fashioned sentiment, a group of us decided to act as herald angels and sing carols to all the families who lived in the quonset huts around and about those primitive palm- and coconut-tree–lined thoroughfares.

In preparation for the event we spent an hour or so each afternoon rehearsing *a capella* such traditional fare as "Silent Night," "It Came upon a Midnight Clear" and "O Come, All Ye Faithful." We were pretty much impressed with our barroom harmonies, but when the evening for serenading rolled around there were dark-gray storm clouds overhead, a rapidly falling barometer, and a temperature hovering around 125 degrees.

We let our sentiments dictate and duly clambered aboard a six-wheel flatbed truck, pulling our khaki-colored camouflage jackets around our bodies. Then the deluge arrived. It rained, and without respite. It appeared that the floodgates of heaven had opened, determined to drown out our voices. That, plus winds of hurricane-like intensity. But we were determined to finish what we had started and defiantly sang those songs of praise and greeting. And so on Christmas morning I awakened with a pounding headache, a shaking body, and a fever that seemed destined to foreshadow pneumonia. Happily that did not develop.

A few of my colleagues arrived at my bedside bearing a cafeteria tray and, among other restoratives, a bottle of gin, which in those days could be purchased at navy stores for 65 cents a fifth. The tray consisted of cold roast turkey with sage dressing, an overly thickened giblet gravy which resembled a rudely colored mucilage, and out-of-a-bottle cranberry sauce. And for dessert, a sliver of pumpkin pie whose cold, starchy crust was also gravy-gray.

On reflection I have wondered whether that meal might not have been a turning point in my life. In any event, it was about that time that I decided that my one great goal was to write about the good life and all that that entails, including the art and bliss of dining well. I applied for admission to a hotel school in Lausanne, and before my stay on that atoll was ended, my future had been charted irremediably.

Some years before, an episode not wholly unrelated to my military and culinary life had occurred, another Christmas moment. The year was 1946, and I had recently returned to my family after spending many months in uniform during World War II. I recall awakening on Christmas morning and going into the living room, where an enormous, billowing pyramid of a tree had been installed. It stood floor to ceiling and was bedecked with tinsel ropes of gold and silver and myriad lights, under which was arrayed an impressive assortment of gifts. Among them were three gifts that bore my name: a chafing dish, which, in that long-ago era, was considered fashionable; a card stating that a brace of freshly killed pheasant was waiting to be plucked from the refrigerator; and a copy of Irma Rombauer's *Joy of Cooking*, which I still treasure in my home library.

A short while earlier, I had shed my navy uniform and moved into a small apartment on Chicago's near North Side. When it was time for me to return there on the day after Christmas, I boarded a train in Memphis with my chafing dish, my brace of game birds, and my Rombauer solidly in hand. I arrived in Chicago in a ferocious snowstorm, a wind-chill factor in the sub-zeros, and not a taxi in sight. I walked blindly to the nearest subway and somehow I did make it home, gifts intact.

Somewhere, in one food publication or another, I had read that game should be properly hung before cooking. (I was amused a long while later at my hotel school to learn that the French word for hanging game or other meat is *mortifier*, which literally means to gangrene or necrotize!) In my innocence, I proceeded to hang my pheasants in my small, rather too-well-heated apartment. I tied a string around the neck of each bird and hooked the other ends around the faucets of the kitchen sink. As they hung, I telephoned friends to invite them to a special meal on the following weekend, and they accepted readily. As Friday approached, of course, the stench became unbearable, the air in those cramped heated quarters unbreathable.

I hastily cut the strings from the faucets and tossed the birds out the window and into the high-piled snow. I now have absolutely no recollection of what I served my guests at that post-Christmas feast so many innocent years ago.

I briefly mentioned a jarring moment in my life that preceded my naval career by what seems like eons, and that is the Christmas I set fire to my home. We were still living in my small town, Sunflower, in the heart of the Mississippi Delta, and my family had a faithful black servant named Albert—last name unknown—on whom my family and I relied to keep me out of harm's way.

On the day after Christmas, Albert had been charged with removing the Christmas tree from near the family hearth and shellacking the hardwood floors in the living room. I had found, among the toys in my Christmas stocking, a box of sparklers which enchanted my eyes as they burned. As they burned, I loved to whirl them around and around until they were spent. It was a brilliant winter morning with sunlight streaming through the double doors of the room, and in order to extinguish a sparkler I had recently lit, I plunged it into the liquid shellac being applied to the floor with a mop. The shellac exploded, sending the varnish sputtering in all directions. The room was aflame within seconds, and I fled screaming and yelling, crying and terrified at the magnitude of what I had done. Fortunately a fire crew arrived within minutes and the fire was extinguished.

When I think of the food of my childhood and early years, it is breakfast that I recall with the greatest pleasure. My family always sat down to an abundant meal for that first meal of the day—generally of bacon or sausage or ham plus buttered grits and buttered biscuits, homemade preserves (my favorite was fig), and piping hot coffee. No one gave a second thought to calories or cholesterol in those days—eating was too much fun.

But breakfast on Christmas morning was something special. The entire family would crawl or bounce out of bed at the first sign of the light of day, and the children in their flannel nighties would rush to the Christmas tree or stockings suspended from the mantelpiece to discover the hidden wonders from Santa Claus. The gifts would be unwrapped in something of a wild-eyed, pulse-racing frenzy and continue until the stockings had been totally emptied of toys and tangerines, dried raisins, pecans, and Brazil nuts. And then the morning feast would begin. The family members would arrange themselves around the table, the center of which would be well burdened with one platter of fried ham; a sauceboat of red-eye gravy; a basket of hot-from-the-oven biscuits; assorted jams and preserves; a platter of smothered quail (the word "smothered" refers to the fact that the birds were browned all over in butter, then covered closely with a plate or lid that fit directly on top of the birds and the plate covered with weights) cooked until the meat was almost falling off the bones. Freshly brewed coffee was always at hand.

On Christmas afternoon there was also, to my mind, a surprising annual ritual, surprising because both my parents were teetotalers, and alcohol, other than the pharmaceutical sort, was absolutely forbidden in my home. Each Christmas, however, my mother would ask a neighbor to buy her a pint of bootleg bourbon (it was during Prohibition and my home state was dry). She would then assemble her rich-as-Croesus eggnog, made with an abundance of eggs and heavy cream, and temper it with a bit of bourbon. She would also pour a generous quantity out of the bourbon bottle over the homemade fruitcakes, which would be sliced and served with the eggnog.

Smothered Quail

6 cleaned quail, about ¼ pound each
Salt to taste if desired
Freshly ground pepper to taste
5 tablespoons butter
3 tablespoons all-purpose flour
2½ cups boiling chicken broth
1 teaspoon Worcestershire sauce
Juice of half a lemon
SERVES 3 TO 6

Preheat the oven to 325 degrees.

Sprinkle each quail inside and out with salt and pepper.

Heat the butter in a skillet, preferably of black cast iron, and when it is quite hot, add the quail. Brown the birds on all sides, turning occasionally to brown evenly, about 5 minutes.

Transfer the quail to a platter. Sprinkle the fat in the skillet with flour. Cook, stirring, until the flour takes on a hazelnut color. Add the broth, stirring rapidly with a wire whisk until the sauce is thickened and smooth. Add the Worcestershire sauce and lemon juice. Return the quail to the skillet and turn them in the sauce. Cover with a tight-fitting lid. Place in the oven and bake 45 minutes or longer, or until the quail are thoroughly tender.

Fried Country Ham with Red-Eye Gravy

1 slice country ham, about 1 pound, preferably center-cut
¾ cup strong, freshly brewed coffee
SERVES 2 TO 4

Cut off a strip of fat from the outside rim of the ham, leaving a portion of the fat intact. Cut the strip of fat into small cubes. Using a sharp knife, cut the fat remaining on the ham at intervals down to the meat.

Put the cubed fat into a skillet, preferably of black cast iron, and cook, stirring, until the fat is rendered. Scoop out and discard the rendered pieces of fat. Add the ham slice to the skillet and fry until nicely browned on one side. Turn the slice and continue frying until brown and cooked through.

Remove the ham slice. Pour the coffee into the skillet and cook, stirring, about 1 minute. Cut the ham slice into 2 to 4 pieces and serve the gravy on the side, to be poured over grits and/or spooned over the ham pieces.

Grits

Grits are usually sold "regular" or "quick cooking." The finest grits are stone-ground. They are available from many mail-order shops including Early's Honey Stand, Post Office Box K, Spring Hill, Tennessee 37174. Cook them according to package directions. When cooked, the grits should be eaten piping hot. To serve, make a well or indentation in each serving and place butter and/ or red-eye gravy in the depression.

Craig Claiborne

Mississippi Delta Eggnog

8 large eggs, separated
¾ cup sugar
1 cup bourbon
½ cup heavy cream
Nutmeg
SERVES 8

Put the egg yolks and sugar into the bowl of an electric mixer and beat until light and lemon-colored.

Gradually add the bourbon, beating on low speed.

In a separate bowl whip the cream until stiff. Fold it into the egg-yolk mixture.

In a clean bowl whip the egg whites until stiff and fold them into the eggnog. Serve in goblets, preferably silver, with a generous grating of nutmeg on top.

Betty Fussell

A DEPRESSION

CHRISTMAS

In I HEAR AMERICA COOKING, *Betty Fussell told of her personal search through American regional cooking. Her childhood Christmases, set in the Depression, are a way station on that search.*

AS A CHILD, I could never understand why a chicken with its head cut off could run around like crazy but a person could not. I knew what chickens could do because wherever we lived in California, in the middle of an orange grove or on a busy street in the middle of Riverside, my grandparents always kept chickens in the backyard. My grandmother fed them corn and collected their eggs. I made pets of them and hauled them around our yard in my little red wagon, like a tumbrel in *A Tale of Two Cities*, until my grandfather gave them the ax.

I knew that a person with his head cut off could not run around because at the Fox Riverside Theater I had seen Ronald Colman get the ax. While I knew that every one of my pet chickens was destined, eventually, for the guillotine, I cried more over Colman than for any of my Minnies and Annabels. Why it was a far, far better thing that Colman lose his head than keep it, I was not altogether sure. And while unlike Madame Defarge, I did not anticipate the fall of the ax on man or chicken with any relish, I did learn early to accept decapitation as a fact of life. I see now that the hard facts of the Depression merely heightened the faith of my Calvinist family that holidays were holy days and that neither food nor any other good came without sacrifice.

My grandfather's task for Easter, the Fourth of July, my birth-

37

day, my brother's birthday, and most importantly Christ's birthday was to sacrifice a chicken. Grandfather, whom my father called Pater, was a true paterfamilias when we all moved, along with my father's new wife after the death of his old one, into a house so heavily mortgaged that my father finished paying for it the same year he retired from a lifetime of teaching biology and botany at Riverside Polytechnic High School. Pater was the one who said the blessing before every meal and who opened the Bible after every breakfast, while we knelt by our chairs, to lead us in morning worship. Pater wielded the Bible as he wielded the ax—with the authority of Abraham. What the divinely sent ram was to Abraham, the chicken was to my grandfather, who conveyed to my brother and me, on our knees beside the dining table that stood in for an altar, that we should thank a wise and beneficent Providence for having sent chickens to stand in for us.

Killing a chicken for Christ was an act of contrition and atonement. Pater would sharpen his ax on a grinding stone by the wooden board he set on a trestle well away from the sheets drying on lines in the yard. Next he would haul a large bucket of hot water from the basement sink. Only then would he look over the flock of Rhode Island Reds, clucking and scratching for worms, to find the fattest, choicest hen. The chosen one was not nearly as compliant as Isaac. As my grandfather lunged, the bird squawked and scrabbled for cover. My job was to shoo the bird back toward Grandfather. Once he had it cornered, he would grab the bird by the neck, swing it a couple of times in the air like a lasso, thunk it down on the board, and chop off its head. The head would lie still enough, but the body rose like a feathered Lazarus, blood spouting, wings flapping, clawed feet rushing to and fro, with my grandfather running after it to keep the laundry pure as Ivory Snow. When my grandmother, on one occasion or another, would tell me to stop running around like a chicken with its head cut off, I was fairly warned.

Pater made short work of the feathers, plunging the body into the bucket to bring forth a dripping corpse half its former size and to pluck its feathers as deftly as my grandmother tatted lace. He would then singe the pinfeathers over a gas burner next to the sink. I liked the smell of burnt skin, like the smell of snuffed candles, and I liked to watch the way he cleaned the bird by cutting out the crop from its neck, then slitting the vent and removing the entrails to disentangle gall bladder, liver, heart, and gizzard, as if he were some divinating prophet. I got to look for eggs. If we were lucky, I might find half a dozen embryonic eggs the size of my thumb, all yellow yolk, and if we were really lucky, a double-yolked one. That was an augury as propitious as a free Fudgsicle stick.

The chickens we raised were also propitious. They were as free-range as any *poularde de Bresse* and twice as big as a Perdue. These were chickens to put meat on your bones, and if they were old enough to be tough, we cooked them long enough to weaken their resistance. A Christmas chicken had to be big enough to serve six people one piece each, with wings, back, neck, and pope's nose available upon request. Nothing went to waste, including the wishbone. As the youngest, I claimed the wishbone as my birthright and let it dry on my butter plate during dinner so that it would be brittle enough for wishing on after dessert. I chose Grandfather for my wishmate because I knew that at the last moment he would slip his thumb down his side of the bone to break it first so that my wish would come true. My wishbone wish was the same as my bedtime prayer: "Make me a good girl and let me be happy." I was too young to know what an oxymoron was.

My grandmother's job was to make the stuffing. She favored one of stale breadcrumbs or corn bread, mixed with chopped olives and hard-boiled eggs to supplement the embyronic ones. I have a note in her hand for a turkey dressing of "1 cube of butter and two 12-cent loaves." Bread certainly was cheap, but so were home-raised eggs and canned black pitted jumbo olives, which California more or less invented in the early part of the century.

My father was chief cook and bottle washer, as he would say, and his job was to cook chicken the way his mother had taught him on the farm in Edgerton, Kansas. The farm way was to braise chicken more than roast it because the point was to get a flood of yellow gravy in which to drown both chicken and mashed potatoes. Father would make a flour-and-butter paste to cover breast and legs, then add water and cover the roasting pan until

3 9

the final stretch, when, in a concession to California suntans, he would uncover the pan to give the chicken a good brown skin.

To my father, a chicken was only a chicken, but mashed potatoes were divine. Their preparation was a liturgy. In peeling potatoes he reenacted his naval purgatory in the Great War when, a sailor boy from Kansas, he glimpsed paradise in San Francisco and decided Kansas was hell. In boiling potatoes he again thanked the Providence that had led his ancestors west from Ireland before the potato famine. And in mashing potatoes, with the wood-and-wire potato masher still popular in the 1930s, he celebrated the union of science and art in which a solid was transformed into an airy cloud, pure, white, and free of lumps.

At Christmas the companion vegetable he favored was canned peas and carrots. When I try to convince my children that in the Depression canned food was not a deprivation but a luxury, they have to imagine an America in which most people lived or had lived on farms and spent most of each summer putting up produce in blue Mason jars with screw lids. Once off the farm, my school-teacher father continued to put up each summer at least 100 quarts of tomatoes, 50 quarts of cherries, and another 50 of peaches. What my father considered a treat was canned Del Monte peaches or, even better, canned Del Monte pears. As for vegetables, not to have to shell peas or peel and dice carrots or sterilize jars or fear botulism was a blessing on the order of Christ's taking on flesh in a manger of hay.

My stepmother's job was to fuss at the rest of us. She was careful not to sully her professional life with domestic chores and, considering our crowded quarters, she had a point. A doctor of osteopathy, she had turned a small room between our living and dining rooms into a treating room for patients who were attracted by the sign on the front of our house, "Dr. Elizabeth Blake Harper, D.O." Our kitchen was an even smaller room at the rear of the dining room, but we extended it by the back screened porch, which housed a wooden icebox and shelf after shelf of my father's Mason jars. My stepmother was good at fussing, and the exacting rituals of Christmas—the extra-long morning prayers, the opening of the stockings hung with care over the gas heater, the opening of the presents under a skeletal tree of silver icicles and cotton blobs of snow above a carpet of pine needles—gave her talents full scope.

She met the challenge of Christmas bravely, beginning with Christmas Eve, when she commandeered the kitchen to execute her one culinary contribution to our household, scrambled eggs and brains. In our house this was not a sophisticated French dish cloaked with capers and *beurre noir*, but poverty food—cheap and, to most of my friends, disgusting. To me brains were lovely, not only for their creamy softness but because they redeemed the plain scrambled eggs that were our common everyday supper. Little did I dream that eggs fresh from the nest, annealed with nothing but sweet butter, would in my adult years be scarce as hen's teeth and precious as repentance.

Perhaps my stepmother regarded the cooking of brains as a medical duty, since there was a touch of the laboratory in her manner of prepping them. She soaked the convoluted mass for an hour or two before removing their membranes with fingers accustomed to anatomical dissection. She then blanched the brains with vinegar and pulled them in small pieces ever so carefully to add to the eggs. Maybe she took over the brains department in our kitchen to prove that she could cook if she wanted to, and maybe I later took up cooking to prove that cooking was as noble an occupation as osteopathy.

For Christmas dinner my brother's job was to make root-beer floats for dessert. Since stores were closed on Christmas Day, my father had to buy the quart of vanilla ice cream the night before. When we still had only an icebox, we hoped that Christmas would be sunny but not too hot. Once we had bought our first white enameled electric refrigerator, however, my father still bought ice cream at the last possible moment because he thought flavor leaked out in prolonged storage. My brother, who hated domestic chores in general and kitchen ones in particular, loved opening the iced bottles of root beer for the floats. Brother Bob was our official family rebel, and as soon as his wrist was strong enough, he took to opening real beer bottles with an avidity that only a teetotaling childhood can provoke.

Root beer, both in name and substance, was suspect in our family but not entirely proscribed. Coca-Cola, tea, and coffee *were*

41

prohibited. My grandparents drank hot water diluted with Postum, my parents drank Postum diluted with milk, and my brother and I drank milk fortified with Horlick's Malted or with Ovaltine. Root beer was a Christmas indulgence and as resonant of holiday cheer at our table as a flaming pudding at the table of Tiny Tim. First my brother would put a scoop of ice cream into each former jelly glass and then pour the root beer from a sufficient height to maximize the head of foam. If no one was looking, he'd blow the foam straight at my pigtails, a pleasure second only to making gross sucking noises with his straw.

My main job was to set the table. In some households this might have seemed routine, but in mine it was a challenge. When we got our new refrigerator, we kept it in one corner of the dining room for both convenience and display. It augmented considerably a décor of paper curtains at the window, green and yellow linoleum on the floor, and brown oilcloth on the table. In another corner we kept a tall varnished dresser that held a Zenith radio, a nearly always empty box of Kleenex, and a full variety of specimen jars—a few beetles, a dozen butterflies, a snake memorialized in formaldehyde. My father renewed the jars and wallpaper every few years, exchanging green flowers on a cream background for rose flowers on brown, but the curtains we changed several times a winter, or at least after every good smudge that saved the orange crop but ruined the curtains.

From the dresser I would remove an ecru cloth of machine-made lace and spread it carefully over the oilcloth, adjusting sides and ends. I stuck red candles in pottery candlesticks, even though sun would pour through the window for our noontime dinner. I would cut flowers in the yard to compose a centerpiece, ignoring common poinsettias that grew rampant as hollyhocks beside the house, and choosing instead a trio of gardenias from the bush behind the garage. I must have patterned my table from the pages of *Good Housekeeping*, for I arranged our Rogers silverplate and my grandmother's Kansas flower-rimmed china with a true appreciation of the finer things. I made place cards from my father's index cards and set out a relish bowl of carrot sticks, celery, and black olives, along with the jar of Hellmann's mayonnaise that my father was never without. If there was no iceberg lettuce or Jell-O salad to put it on, he spread mayonnaise instead of butter on his roll.

My secondary job was to help my grandmother make divinity fudge. Recently I stumbled on a recipe for it in my grandmother's favorite—actually her only—cookbook, *Our Women's Exchange*, published by the Women's General Missionary Society of Xenia, Ohio, in 1910. With straight pins from her pincushion, my grandmother pinned to its pages recipes cut from newspapers or written out on scraps of paper in her neat hand. Each page was headed by an appropriate Biblical quotation, and under the rubric "Hear, ye careless daughters," the women of Xenia confirmed my grandmother's belief in salvation through thrift. "Old shoes, bones and other objectionable sights in the ordinary alley, and even dead rats, do great service when planted at the base of grapevines or small trees," the women wrote. "One of the grandest grapevines in England is planted where a large number of horses which had died from some epidemic disease had been buried years and years before." The grapevine may have been suspect in my grandmother's eyes, but the regeneration of living plants from dead horses was to her as powerful an exemplum of God's eternal promise as a babe in a manger.

The very name divinity fudge recommended it to my grandmother and to other Midwestern women for whom a nut- and fruit-laden fudge stood in for fruitcake laden with demon rum. The silken texture of divinity fudge recommended it to me, and I loved to beat the egg whites and thickened syrup with a spoon until my arm nearly fell off and my grandmother's took over. Today's electric mixer can do this beating in a trice, but in the Depression an electric mixer was strictly for the rich, and we beat happily with a rotary beater or a cheap metal kitchen spoon.

Grandmother was a good beater. Despite the fact that at ninety-six pounds she was a mere wisp of a thing, all bone and wire, her arm was as steady as a motor and her humor considerably better. It amazed me the way she could metamorphose the sticky stuff into a smooth cream, angelically white. For California tots like myself who had never seen snow, divinity fudge was a vision of White Christmas long before Bing crooned against a backdrop of Hollywood soap flakes.

Betty Fussell

43

While she beat, my grandmother would sing what the twenty froggies sang who went to school down beside the wishing pool: "First you work and then you play." God's lessons were as eloquent in fudge as in decapitated chickens if the interpreter was acute. Because whether or not I kept my head, I wanted to tread the path of righteousness all the way to heaven, I beat that fudge as hard as I could. And after dinner I sang as hard as I could around the Baldwin upright piano, beside the stockings emptied of oranges and walnuts and potatoes, beside the tree denuded of needles and packages wrapped in Woolworth's paper, beneath the mistletoe above the treating-room door.

On Christmas Day we sang together of shepherds as poor as ourselves, or poorer, because they had no orange juice. We sang of shepherds in the field who had surely brought chickens as well as lambs to the manger and who had forever escaped Herod's sword as we had escaped the blizzards of Kansas. We sang of Orient kings and silent nights and angel voices heard on high across oceans and centuries to make our Christmas anything but depressing and to make our holiday chicken holy.

Chicken from Scratch, with Yellow Gravy and Olive & Egg Dressing

First raise your chicken to get 5 to 6 pounds dressed weight. Then sharpen an ax and cut off its head, scald the body in hot water, pluck the feathers, and remove obstinate pinfeathers with tweezers. Singe the bird on all sides over a gas flame. Cut the legs off below the joint and remove the oil bag above the tail. Cut a slit in the neck and remove the crop and windpipe. Cut off the neckbone close to the body but leave a good length of skin. Enlarge the vent horizontally, cut the entrails loose, and remove them, being careful not to burst the blue-green gall bag attached to the liver. Discard the gall bag, but save the liver, heart, gizzard, and any eggs. Split the gizzard and remove the insides and inner lining. Wash the chicken well inside and out with cold water and let it dry.

Stuff the crop lightly with Olive & Egg Dressing (see below) and close the neck skin along the back with skewers to hold the dressing in place. Stuff the body cavity lightly with the same dressing and tie the ends of the legs together around the tail. Put the bird on a rack in a roasting pan with a cover and rub the breast and legs with a mixture of 4 tablespoons flour, 4 tablespoons butter, and 1 teaspoon salt. Add a cup of boiling water to the bottom of the pan, cover the pan tightly, and roast at 350 degrees. Uncover halfway through and add more water if needed. If you want the meat to fall off the bone (which is the way we cooked our chickens), allow about 30 minutes a pound. A 5- to 6-pound chicken will take about 2½ hours. By current standards, however, 20 minutes a pound is sufficient to produce a bird that is moist as well as fork tender. In any case, remove the cover of the roasting pan for the final half hour of cooking, basting the bird well to brown its skin.

SERVES 8, WITH LEFTOVERS

Yellow Gravy

Simmer the giblets, along with a sliced onion, carrot, and 2 celery stalks, in water to cover while the chicken is roasting. Remove the liver after 5 minutes and cook the remaining giblets until the gizzard is tender. Chop all the giblets fine and add the strained broth and giblets to the liquid in the roasting pan once the chicken is done and removed to a serving platter. (The liquid should total 2½ to 3 cups.) Mix 2 tablespoons of flour with 2 tablespoons softened butter. Gradually beat in ½ cup milk or cream and stir the mixture into the roasting-pan liquid. Bring to the boil and simmer about 10 minutes, adding salt and pepper to taste. Pour into a sauceboat and serve separately.

MAKES 3–4 CUPS

Olive & Egg Dressing

1 small onion, chopped
2 tablespoons butter
1 cup coarse breadcrumbs or crumbled corn bread
2 hard-boiled eggs, chopped
½ cup pitted black olives, chopped
½ teaspoon powdered sage
Salt and pepper to taste
MAKES ABOUT 2 CUPS DRESSING

Sauté the onion in the butter until the onion softens. Add the crumbs, eggs, olives, seasonings, and any embryonic eggs found in the chicken. Spoon stuffing into the cavities of the breast and body.

Father's Mashed Potatoes

6 large baking potatoes
⅓ to ½ cup milk
Butter
Salt and pepper to taste
SERVES 6

Peel potatoes, cut them in quarters, and drop them into a pot of boiling salted water. Boil until potatoes are fork tender, drain them well, and mash them with a strong fork or potato masher, or put them through a potato ricer. In a separate pan, heat the milk with 4 tablespoons of butter until the butter melts. Add this liquid gradually to the potatoes, beating them with a large spoon. "The more they are beaten, the nicer they become." Season well with salt, put them in a dish, make a well in the center, and add an additional lump of butter. Sprinkle the top with pepper.

To keep mashed potatoes warm, put them in a baking dish, dip a knife in cream or milk, and smooth over the top, wetting every part of the exposed surface. Place the dish in a warm oven until ready to serve.

Scrambled Eggs with Brains

1 pound calves' brains
1 tablespoon vinegar or lemon juice
8 eggs
⅓ cup milk
Salt and pepper to taste
3 tablespoons butter
Parsley for garnish
SERVES 6

Soak brains in cold water for at least an hour. Remove as much of the membrane as you can without tearing the flesh. Put the brains in a saucepan, cover with boiling water, add the vinegar or lemon juice, and simmer very gently about 15 minutes. Drain, cool, and remove more membrane if possible. Delicately pull the brains into small pieces.

Beat the eggs with the milk, salt, and pepper. Add the brains to the eggs. Melt the butter in a large cast-iron skillet and add the egg mixture, stirring continuously with a spatula or spoon over low heat until the eggs begin to thicken and form soft curds. Remove from the heat immediately, sprinkle with parsley, and serve.

Grandmother's Divinity Fudge

2 cups sugar
½ cup light corn syrup
2 egg whites
1 teaspoon vanilla extract
1 tablespoon lemon juice
1 cup chopped nuts
MAKES ABOUT 4 DOZEN SQUARES

Cover the sugar with the syrup and ½ cup water in a small saucepan and bring to a boil. Cover the pan and boil without stirring for 3 minutes to dissolve all crystals. Continue boiling

Betty Fussell

rapidly until the mixture reaches the soft-ball stage (240 degrees on a candy thermometer). Off heat, add the vanilla extract and lemon juice.

While the sugar syrup is boiling, whip the egg whites in a large bowl until soft peaks form. As soon as the syrup is ready, pour it immediately in a thin stream into the egg whites, beating constantly until the mixture cools and stiffens. Fold in the nuts and spread the fudge on an oiled 14-by-16-inch baking sheet. When it is cold, cut into squares. (On a wet day, the candy may never stiffen much. If so, drop blobs of it onto an oiled sheet to make circles.)

Jane Grigson

IN DULCI JUBILO:

A TABLE FOR

CAROLERS

On Christmas Eve carolers brighten the holidays as they go from house to house, bringing their songs and stopping for a warming treat. Jane Grigson has written expertly on fruits and vegetables, sausages and fish, but here she tells of familiar homey food that sustains the comfort of the holiday season.

ONE OF MY EARLIEST MEMORIES is of my father singing at Christmas. *Adeste, fideles, Laeti triumphantes.* He had a lovely tenor voice, clear, unaffected, warm, and joyful. It burst from him, escaping his local-government-official envelope of striped gray trousers, black coat, even spats when I was very young, with a vigor that makes me wonder what emotions were held back, deep inside, by the dam of his normal disciplined behavior. He is ninety-one now and cannot sing anymore, but I still lack the nerve to probe this particular mystery.

He sang loudly in his—cold—bath. He sang at the weekends, taught us songs, while our mother played the piano. Above all he sang at matins when we formed a demure, tidy row in church, about twelve pews back from the choir. Nobody else in the congregation sang very much. They were too refined. He didn't care. I suspect he didn't notice, but if *we* were silent, he would glance at us in a pained way, wondering if perhaps we might be coming down with something. As a young man he had sung in church choirs and knew how to stress the psalms as they were chanted. "My heart is inditing of a good matter . . . Full of grace are thy

49

lips . . . My tongue is the pen of a ready writer . . . O praise God in His holiness, praise Him in the firmament of His power . . . Let everything that hath breath prai-ai-ai-aise the Lord!" And, come Christmas, he taught us how to pronounce choral Latin: "*In dulci jubilo*, Now sing we all *Io, Io* . . . Our heart's joy reclineth *In praesepio!*" emerged from our infant throats without stumble or inaccuracy.

Looking back now, I see that the greatest gift he gave me was not the rules for a good life so sweetly and earnestly instilled, but the unconscious acceptance that music and poetry, especially in combination, are the greatest of man's achievements. At every season, in every event that marks my life, that feeling is there. Words and music well up, comfort, companionship, pain, and delight.

And so it is that we have always begun our Christmas, in my father's way—with carol singing, which by a strange coincidence, for his character was very different, happened to be my husband's way, too. Our Christmas bears no relation to the old rollicking festivities of the distant past, and not even a very close relationship to the Christmas that was invented in Britain by the Victorians. We ignore the pandemonium of the shops until the last few days. Christmas tree, wreath for the front door, decorations never make an appearance until three o'clock on Christmas Eve. We switch on the radio and wait in a tense hush for that first pure note of the boy's voice, "Once in Royal David's City," from King's College chapel.

My father was at Cambridge. So was I. So were all of my husband Geoffrey's family from the sixteenth century to his generation, when he and his brothers went to Oxford and broke the rule. As the choir comes nearer and we hear the red and white robes swishing gently to the sound, we are glad to be busy. That way we can disguise our tears as the Chaplain reads the Bidding Prayer, reminding us of those who rejoice in a greater light and on a farther shore, whose multitude no man can number, with whom we ever more are one. In that language, in that music

we do confer with who are gone,
And the dead living unto counsel call:

and by that language, that music, we know

> *th'unborn shall have communion*
> *Of what we feel, and what doth us befall.*

That is Christmas, our own private but universal start. Our public start in the Wiltshire village of Broad Town is a more hilarious affair, the arrival of the local church choir singing carols, greatly augmented by children from the school, sundry parents, and cheerful hangers-on. For about ten years it was organized by a witty, literate, and musical priest, our vicar, now regrettably called to higher things in a grand parish close to Salisbury Cathedral. One year he persuaded a farmer to clean the dung from his tractor so that a living Nativity tableau could be driven around the village from house to house. Mary sat on a bale of straw, lurching slightly. She clasped not the latest addition to the community, but a big baby doll with a wobbly halo. Joseph clenched his teeth as he tried to keep upright, clinging to a lantern. When they came to our house, everyone else rushed to the door. The two protagonists were quite forgotten. It took a few unholy Wiltshire shrieks before they were helped down over the huge wheels and ushered to the front of the choir that by now was two verses into "Hark! The Herald Angels Sing." We stood in the open doorway, welcomed them as best we could. The children rushed into the candlelit hall to see what this place offered to eat and drink. The grownups sat down. Cakes, biscuits, and other treats were handed round as decorously as anyone could wish. The more daring children sipped a little mulled wine, but soon turned back to orange and lemon squash. The candles guttered, their light catching the raisins in the dark Christmas cake.

One memorable year our caroling was even on television, nationwide. To make a talking point—we were one small item in a food magazine program—I had used Mrs. Beeton's mincemeat for the mince pies. An excellent recipe with rump steak in it, as well as the more usual beef suet. One small neighbor, the cheekiest boy in the village, decided to tease us. The cameras homed in on him. He bit into a mince pie, wrinkled his nose, laughed up at me, and said, "Dis—gus—ting." Which gave life to what might otherwise have been a boring interlude for those inhabitants of

51

Great Britain who did not have the good fortune to be acquainted with the 570 souls of Broad Town parish.

When everything was eaten up, and "Silent Night, Holy Night," sung as always at my husband's request, was over, the BBC team began to take down their tripods and pack up their equipment. The last little girl emerged from the loo. The vicar shooshed his flock out the door. Bidding us goodbye, he swung his long black cloak into place, adjusted the silver clasp, and called back over his shoulder, "Count the spoons! You never know what I may have concealed about my person!" A shame that this best of all priestly exits was uttered off camera.

General advice for entertaining carolers: Keep everything as small as possible, so that it is easy to eat without crumbs everywhere. Don't try to be original. In my experience, clever food is not appreciated at Christmas. It makes the little ones cry and the old ones nervous.

Cheese and Tomato Rolls

My mother used to make these cheese and tomato rolls when we were children. She had the advantage of being able to order proper bridge rolls from an excellent pastry cook. You can try this, but you may find that there is no alternative to the soft rolls of the supermarket; bake them in a hot oven to give them a firmer outside. The ideal length of roll for this sort of thing is 3½ inches maximum, as it is large enough to satisfy people and not too difficult to eat without making a mess. If you are good with your hands, you could use the conventional small rolls, in which case the filling would go further.

12 bridge rolls (or 24 small rolls)
2 medium onions, chopped fine (1 cup)

¾ cup (1½ sticks) butter, divided
1 pound tomatoes, skinned, seeded, and chopped
A little tomato paste, or chopped dried tomatoes
Salt, pepper, and sugar to taste
3 eggs, beaten
1½ cups (6 ounces) grated Cheddar cheese
Chopped parsley and chives to taste
SERVES 12

Cut a small cap from one end of the rolls and hollow them out, leaving a firm wall. Crumble the soft part you have removed, as you will need some of it for the filling.

Soften the onion in about a third of the butter over low heat. Add the chopped tomato, raise the heat, and cook until the mixture is fairly thick and not at all watery. Season to taste with the tomato paste, salt, pepper, and a hint of sugar. Off the heat, stir in the beaten eggs and put back over a low heat, stirring all the time, until the paste thickens. Don't boil it. Stir in the cheese and the remaining butter with some of the breadcrumbs if need be, then check seasoning again, and add herbs to taste. Fill the rolls with this mixture when it is cold.

Cheese Biscuits

A simple processor recipe that has delicious results. Cut up 6 ounces of cheese into cubes, choosing a deep orange Leicester for the sake of its color, if possible, otherwise Cheddar. Reduce the cubes to crumbs in the processor with 1½ cups all-purpose flour. Then add 5 ounces (1 stick plus 2 tablespoons) butter straight from the refrigerator, cut into a dice, and process briefly. You will end up with a stiff dough. Chill in the refrigerator for 30 minutes or longer.

Roll the dough out thin and cut into triangles or fingers. Sprinkle half with cayenne and half with sesame seeds, pressing them gently into the dough. Place on baking sheets lined with parchment paper.

Have the oven preheated to 400 degrees. Put in the baking

sheets, as centrally as possible, and give them about 8 minutes. They will cook rapidly at that temperature, so check them after 6 minutes. They are done when slightly brown.

Sand Biscuits

A roll of this dough is most handy to store in the refrigerator ready for baking several days later. If you freeze the dough, it will keep for several weeks without losing quality. The recipe is adapted from *The Vegetarian Epicure* (1972), by Anna Thomas.

> *½ cup (3 ounces) unblanched almonds*
> *3 cups (12 ounces) all-purpose flour*
> *⅔ cup (6 ounces) sugar*
> *¾ cup (1½ sticks) lightly salted butter, preferably Danish, chilled*
> *1 teaspoon vanilla extract*

Pour boiling water over the almonds, leave them for a moment, and then slip off the skins, putting the almonds into the processor. Whizz them to a sandy powder, adding a little flour as you do so to prevent the nuts from oiling. Incorporate the rest of the flour and the sugar. Cut up the butter into the processor, add the vanilla, and mix to a dough.

Divide the mixture into 2 or 3 equal quantities and form into rolls about 1½ inches in diameter. Wrap in wax paper and store in the refrigerator.

When you want to bake the cookies, slice off circles of dough, put them on parchment-lined baking sheets, and stamp them with the end of a spool of thread to make a pattern. Chill while the oven heats to 325 degrees, then bake for 15 to 20 minutes, or until nicely browned.

Christmas Kringle

An ideal yeast cake from Denmark for those who do not like the rich, fruit-packed mixtures of our tradition. Although in theory you can make the kringle in advance, it tastes best when eaten the same day.

CAKE

2 cups bread flour or all-purpose flour
2 teaspoons active dry yeast
1 teaspoon ground cardamom seeds
4 tablespoons sugar
6 tablespoons lightly salted butter, preferably Danish
1 large egg
5 tablespoons warm milk

FILLING

6 tablespoons lightly salted butter, at room temperature
5 tablespoons sugar
2 teaspoons cinnamon

FINISH

Beaten egg to glaze
5 tablespoons chopped almonds
3 tablespoons sugar
Confectioner's Sugar Icing (see below)

For the dough, mix the flour, yeast, cardamom, and sugar thoroughly. Make a well in the center. Melt the butter and when it is warm (not hot), pour it into the center and add the egg. Mix with a wooden spoon, adding milk gradually. You may not need it all—the dough should be soft but not tacky. Knead it lightly. Oil a warm bowl—the same bowl, if you like—turn the dough in it so that the top is oiled and cover the bowl with plastic wrap. Put in a warm place until doubled in size: this can take 2 to 3 hours, depending on the warmth of the kitchen. These heavy enriched doughs take longer to rise than a plain dough.

Meanwhile, mix the filling ingredients together. Grease a baking sheet and line with nonstick baking parchment or aluminum foil; grease the foil.

Roll the dough out on a lightly floured surface to a strip about 5 by 32 inches. Spread the filling down the center, then flip over the two long ends, one on top of the other, to enclose the filling. Gently fold the long roll of dough into three so that you can transfer it more easily to the baking sheet, then unfold the two ends and bend them around and up to the center to form an enormous pretzel. Think of folding your arms across, so that your hands touch the opposite shoulders.

Tie the whole thing into a giant plastic bag so that it balloons up. The dough needs room to rise without sticking to the plastic. Leave in a warm place for 30 minutes. Meantime, preheat the oven to 400 degrees.

Just before baking, quickly brush the dough with the beaten egg and scatter it with almonds and sugar. Slide it into the oven and bake for 20 to 25 minutes, or until it turns a nice golden brown. Cool, then run trails of icing over the kringle in snowy lines.

Ginger Fruitcake

Although a lot of people do not care for fruitcake, I do find that they will eat this one with its ginger and orange flavoring. It is also worth avoiding currants in favor of sultanas—golden raisins—and black raisins, which have a softer bite to them. You can cover the cake with almond paste and icing in traditional style or you could just cover it with Confectioner's Sugar Icing decorated with bits of ginger and toasted almonds.

> *6 knobs preserved ginger, drained and chopped (reserve the*
> *syrup)*
> *1 cup (4–6 ounces) candied orange peel, chopped*
> *¾ cup (4 ounces) slivered blanched almonds*
> *½ cup (2 ounces) shelled walnuts, chopped*
> *About 3¾ cups (1¼ pounds) mixed seedless black raisins and*
> *sultanas*
> *2½ cups (10 ounces) all-purpose flour*
> *2 teaspoons powdered ginger*
> *1 teaspoon grated nutmeg*
> *Grated rind of 1 orange and 1 lemon*

1 cup (2 sticks) lightly salted butter, preferably Danish, at room temperature
1⅛ cups (8 ounces) light brown sugar, packed
4 tablespoons reserved ginger syrup
5 eggs
½ teaspoon baking soda
1 tablespoon milk
Cointreau or other orange liqueur or brandy
Almond Paste (see below)
Confectioner's Sugar Icing (see below)
Marmalade Glaze (see below)

Grease an 8-inch round cake pan, then line it with baking parchment and grease the paper. Tie a triple thickness of brown paper around the pan, letting it come at least ½ inch above the rim. Fold a pad of newspaper and put it on a baking sheet, with the cake pan on top. Preheat the oven to 275 degrees.

Put ginger, peel, and nuts in a large bowl and add the dried fruit. Mix in half the flour and all the spices and rinds with your hands, breaking up any clumps of peel and fruit. Set aside.

Cream the butter with the sugar and syrup in an electric mixer; beat in the eggs one at a time and then the rest of the flour. Add this to the bowl of fruit and nuts. Dissolve the baking soda in the milk, stir it into the mixture, and add enough alcohol to produce a dropping consistency.

Turn the cake mixture into the prepared pan and make a central depression with the back of a tablespoon. Put it into the oven and bake for 3 hours. Test the cake with a warm skewer, pushing it in diagonally. It should come out clean. Be prepared to give it another 15 to 30 minutes.

Leave the cake to cool in the pan. Turn it out and peel off the parchment. Put the cake upside down on a sheet of brown paper or a brandy-soaked cloth placed on a sheet of aluminum foil. Wrap the paper around the cake, then fasten the foil to enclose the whole thing. Every week or so, open the parcel to expose the base of the cake. Make holes with a skewer and pour in a couple of tablespoons of whatever alcohol you used in the mixture.

If you are giving it the full almond paste treatment, do this about five days before Christmas. If you are just using Confectioner's Sugar Icing, do it one or two days before the carol-singing party is expected, but not much longer. In both cases, before icing the cake, brush it over with the Marmalade Glaze.

Almond Paste

2 cups (8 ounces) confectioner's sugar
1 pound ground blanched almonds
1 large egg, beaten well
3 to 4 teaspoons lemon juice

Sift sugar and mix with almonds. Add the egg and lemon juice and mix to a firm paste, then knead on a hard surface sprinkled with confectioner's sugar. Roll out and use as needed.

Confectioner's Sugar Icing

¾ cup (3½ ounces) confectioner's sugar
3 to 4 teaspoons milk or water

Mix together until smooth and of spreading consistency.

Marmalade Glaze

2 tablespoons marmalade
1 tablespoon water

Bring to a boil in a small saucepan, and strain.

Mincemeat Phyllo Pies

If you are in the habit of entertaining carol singers and first footers on New Year's night, it is worth investing in very small tartlet tins. Miniature mincemeat pies, just a mouthful, are often just enough, especially if the party is moving on to other houses.

Another way is to make mincemeat pies, using sheets of phyllo pastry brushed with melted butter. The top can be marked out in small diamonds and then cut after you have poured on the syrup and let the whole thing cool down a little.

Melted butter
12 sheets of phyllo pastry
1 pound mincemeat (see below)
1 cup (4 ounces) chopped walnuts, or mixed hazelnuts and
  almonds
3 teaspoons cinnamon
¼ teaspoon freshly grated nutmeg
1 cup (8 ounces) sugar
1 tablespoon lemon juice
Fine-shredded zest of 1 orange and 1 lemon
2-inch cinnamon stick

Preheat the oven to 350 degrees. Brush a large oblong baking sheet, about 2 inches smaller than the phyllo sheets and 1½ to 2 inches deep, with some of the butter. Put in 4 sheets of phyllo, brushing each one with melted butter before you lay the next one on top. There is no need to brush the fourth sheet.

Mix the mincemeat, nuts, and spices. Spread a third of this mixture over the pastry. Lay on two more sheets of phyllo, brushing the first with melted butter. Repeat the mincemeat, then top with 2 more sheets of phyllo, then spread with mincemeat again. Tuck over any phyllo edges, then top with the final 4 sheets of phyllo, brushing each with melted butter as before. Tuck down the edges into the baking sheet. Score through the top pastry layer into diamonds as a cutting guide. Sprinkle with water and bake for about 45 minutes, or until golden brown.

Make a syrup by dissolving the sugar with the lemon juice and 2 tablespoons of water and simmering 5 minutes with the orange and lemon zest and cinnamon stick. Strain while hot over the very hot pies. Serve warm—or reheated—in diamond-shaped pieces, cutting down with a very sharp knife.

NOTE: Young carolers may take fright if you sprinkle the pies with rose water, in traditional Middle Eastern style.

Mrs. Beeton's Traditional Mincemeat

A real mincemeat, a dish of medieval origin, from a time when people did not distinguish as they do now between sweet and savory. In fact the steak provides a special moist texture and a particularly good flavor: people not in on the secret would never guess.

3 cups (1 pound) seedless raisins
4 to 4½ cups (1½ pounds) currants, or sultanas, or a mixture
12 ounces lean rump steak, ground
3 cups (1½ pounds) chopped beef suet
2¼ cups (1 pound) dark brown sugar, packed
1 ounce candied citron peel, chopped
1 ounce candied lemon peel, chopped
1 ounce candied orange peel, chopped
½ small nutmeg, freshly grated
1½ pounds sharp apples, peeled, cored, and chopped or grated
Grated zest of 1 lemon
Juice of ½ lemon
½ cup brandy

Mix the ingredients together in the order given, using your hands to turn everything over. Press closely into sterilized jars, or one huge jar. Cover closely and leave for at least 2 weeks to mature in the refrigerator. Like other mincemeats, it will keep in good condition for 2 to 3 months.

Glühwein

A friend of my sister's was at one time in charge of chalet parties at an Austrian skiing resort. She brought back this easy and consoling recipe. You can vary it by using weak tea instead of water, or—for an adult party—by adding up to 2 cups of brandy. The quantity of orange juice and peel and spices is also a matter of individual taste. We make this in large stoneware pots that hold about 1½ quarts and that were originally made in France for storing *rillettes*. They go into pans of water, on a low trivet, so that the wine heats through slowly and keeps warm. It should never come near the boiling point or the alcohol will evaporate and the orange lose its freshness. It's at Christmas time that one realizes how useful a wood-burning stove is, the kind that never goes out, always there for drying clothes, making a stew, or heating up soups and mulled wine.

6 bottles of red wine
1 cinnamon stick
30 cloves
Juice and thinly peeled zest of 1 orange
Juice of 1 lemon
Light brown sugar to taste
SERVES 24

Mix all the ingredients except the sugar with 6 cups water and divide it between the jugs you intend to heat it in. Sweeten to taste as the *glühwein* becomes hot. Orange slices can be floated on top, and the spices varied.

Apple Mull

A nonalcoholic mulled drink that is made by heating together equal quantities of a good apple juice—a cloudy one is fine—and orange juice from a carton rather than fresh orange juice. Add a stick of cinnamon and cloves, less rather than more if the drink is mainly for children, and sweeten to taste with honey.

Martha Kostyra Stewart

CHRISTMAS

COOKIES

With ENTERTAINING *Martha Stewart opened the book on her personal catering style— hospitality with great attention to loving presentation and fine ingredients. Many books and videotapes later, she still recalls her home and the holiday preparations which may have started her career and surely inspired her entertaining.*

IN OUR FAMILY, cooking, baking, eating, and talking about food account for a great part of our collective pleasant memories. I come from a large family—we were six children—and during our growing-up years we all contributed to the culinary history of the Kostyras. We were raised on home cooking and victory-garden produce in a small-town suburb of New York called Nutley, New Jersey. Mother spent most of her long days preparing the meals, baking the cakes and breads and pies we all thrived on, and shopping for the everyday foods at the Co-op, Food Fair, and Shop Rite (which soon after its appearance caused the disappearance of the Co-op and the fish store and the Polish bakery). Exotica—the occasional bean sprouts, Peking roasted ducks, kielbasa, smoked fishes, and sour pickles that graced our table on holidays and special celebrations—came from forays into the local neighborhoods of the ethnic New York that my father loved to explore with one or more of his children in tow. An expedition to Chinatown meant a delicious lunch at a dim sum parlor; a trip to the lower East Side meant hot steaming knishes or a crumbly piece of fresh farmer's cheese; and a trip to First Avenue and Eighth Street promised a pile of sour-cabbage pierogi and a bowl of Polish-style borscht.

For the holidays, especially Easter, Christmas, and Thanksgiving, we put the most effort into creating extraordinary meals for the family and everyone's friends. Our table knew no limits, our china cupboards always had enough plates for all the guests, and the larder was always full enough to provide yet another platter of food. Life is so very different now, and yet my sisters and brothers and I still try to maintain some semblance of our childhoods. My sister Kathy always entertains on Christmas Eve, Rita and George have us all for lunch on Christmas Day, and I always close the festivities with a huge Christmas party—a dinner-buffet-dessert feast.

Perhaps what we remember and like best about our childhood cooking was the cookie-baking time immediately preceding the frantic Christmas holiday. For weeks we would mix and bake and decorate myriad varieties of cookies from recipes that my mother had in her crowded but ultra-organized recipe files. Each year we would try new types of cookies, only to discard most of the recipes as inferior or inappropriate and go back to the old standbys that we all loved.

Batches of cookie dough would be mixed up in huge batter bowls, wrapped in wax paper, and stored in the refrigerator until we had time to roll or press or cut them into shapes. Tins of all sizes were collected over the years and lined each season with fresh wax paper or tissue. These were stored on shelves in the cellar filled with the cookies that seemed only better after a week or two. I remember sneaking downstairs to peek at the tins and sample one or two cookies every now and then. There was a major revolution when Daddy bought Mother her first and only Kitchen Aid mixer, a white 4½-quart model, in 1955. The strong arms of the boys were really no longer required to cream the butter and sugar in the yellowware bowls with huge wooden paddles. I think they felt a bit miffed, but Frank still always appeared when the *Chrusciki* were being rolled and fried, and Erik loved pressing the candied cherries into the butter-nut balls. George, the youngest boy and also the most sensitive, managed to remain a very important part of the baking team. He was extremely neat and could cut out perfect triangles without a ruler, wasting less dough than the rest of us, when we cut out the sugar cookies.

Our father sat at the pink formica table he had designed for the kitchen—it sat the eight of us comfortably with lots of room for several guests and sprouting avocado pits, special seedlings of extra-large tomatoes, and cuttings of holly trees or Christmas cactus in unusual colors—and cracked the nuts for the cookies. One of his pre-Christmas New York visits included a long stopover at the Bazzini nut factory on the lower West Side. There he would purchase in very large quantity walnuts, almonds, pecans, and candied fruits for the cookies and cakes we were about to bake. He had a special cracker for pecans, one for walnuts, and another for hazelnuts and Brazil nuts. Mother chopped the nut meats and stored them in the freezer until we used them, so that their exquisite freshness would be retained.

The baking was not without its highjinks. One year, the year I brought home Andy, my fiancé, my brothers set out a large plate of perfect Noël Nut Balls, pecan-filled balls rolled in a thick coating of confectioner's sugar. Andy immediately popped one into his mouth expecting to taste the wonderful cookie I had raved about, only to discover the cookie was made of plaster of Paris that crumbled into thousands of powdery, chalky bits. Another year we ran out of sugar glitter, and Frank substituted metallic glitter. A whole huge batch of rolled-out elephants, trees, and tiny birds had to be thrown away because of that prank.

My sister Laura reminded me to describe the orderly way we proceeded with all this baking. We had only a single wall oven that accommodated two ordinary-sized cookie sheets. The oven was on for hours at a time. No parchment-lined proofer sheets then, no double-sized Garland ovens or eight-rack convection ovens. And yet everything got done, and got done beautifully.

As we grew up and left home to create our own nests, we took with us the recipes we loved and cherished from childhood. As we set up our own businesses, we tried to make a living, however minuscule, using some of these recipes. If you count on homemade cookies to make your fortune, and I'm talking about this kind of handmade, homemade, complicated cookie, don't count on making a fortune—only lots of friends. Most of these cookies are so labor intensive and so full of expensive nuts and other ingredients that they leave no room for profit!

Laura remembers that in 1977 we made hundreds of gnome gingerbread men to use as tree decorations for a *House Beautiful* article. The photography was in August and none of us thought about the humidity of the day. The gnomes, secured to the freshly cut balsam by millinery-wire ties, fell to an ignominious end as the tips of their red hats broke off in the moist heat.

In 1981 I designed a more economical and simpler cookie tree, one that was completely covered in saucer-sized Alexis chocolate-chip cookies. We set up that tree in my photographer's studio, where it was photographed. A big party followed, with the cookies for dessert. Gluttons for punishment we were and still are. And yet we love it. This past Christmas we baked (the "we" pertains to my professional staff) twenty-three thousand cookies—more than twenty kinds of cookies to pack up in individual batches of ten or twelve. It took five of us fifteen days of untold hours to complete our task. Then it took another five days to wrap the cookies in batches in clear cellophane florist's bags. Twenty-three separate bags of cookies were packed in hundreds of handmade baskets and sent all over the country as corporate gifts for one of our clients. We had to devise special wrappings so that the cookies would not break in transit. For me and my staff the whole thing was a logistical nightmare—for the recipients a joy. I personally can vouch for that, because I'd love to get a bag of Vienna tarts filled with homemade gamay grape jelly or thick peach jam at any time of the year.

We have vowed not to get ourselves into such a cookie nightmare again—unless we want to make a Christmas video or write our own Christmas cookbook. . . . But then we can always stick to gingerbread mansions and brandy-snap cottages.

The Cookie Menu

Chrusciki	*Nöel Nut Balls*
Almond Crescents	*Butter-Nut Balls*
Vienna Tarts	*Almond Spritz Cookies*
Brandy Snaps	*Sugar Cookies*
Butter Cookies	*Cookie-Press Cookies*
Hungarian Filled Crescents	*Anise Cookies*

Chrusciki

A Polish favorite, really a type of fried dough dusted with powdered sugar. If made correctly, they are extremely light and golden
brown. They are shaped into twists. I like to fry them in melted
Crisco or Crisco oil.

2 whole eggs
10 egg yolks
1 tablespoon melted butter
3 tablespoons granulated sugar
½ teaspoon salt
1 teaspoon orange extract
1 teaspoon vanilla extract
1 teaspoon grated lemon rind
1 teaspoon grated orange rind
3 tablespoons whiskey, rum, cognac, or brandy
½ cup sour cream
4 to 5 cups all-purpose flour
Vegetable shortening for deep frying
Confectioner's sugar for sprinkling

In a mixing bowl combine the eggs and yolks, melted butter,
granulated sugar, salt, extracts, citrus rind, whiskey, and sour
cream. Beat until thick and lemon-colored. Add enough flour gradually to produce a thick, fairly stiff dough. Turn out on a floured
board and knead for 8 or 10 minutes, until the dough blisters, is
elastic, and can be handled easily.

Roll pieces of dough very, very thin and cut into strips about
4 inches long and 1½ to 2 inches wide. Cut the ends on a diagonal.
Slit each piece in the center and pull one end through the slot.
Heat the shortening to 375 degrees and fry the dough strips, a
few at a time, for about 1 minute, until lightly browned, turning
once with a long fork or tongs. Drain chrusciki on absorbent brown
paper and sprinkle with confectioner's sugar. Store, tightly covered, in wax-paper–lined tins.

NOTE: This recipe makes an enormous quantity, so it can be
halved if you wish. The amount of flavorings stays the same.

Almond Crescents

Try making these half the size the recipe directs. They will be very delicate moon-shaped crescents. A melt-in-the-mouth cookie.

1 cup (2 sticks) unsalted butter, at room temperature
⅔ cup sifted confectioner's sugar
1 teaspoon vanilla extract
½ teaspoon almond extract
1 cup coarse-chopped almonds
2⅓ cups all-purpose flour
Confectioner's sugar for rolling
MAKES ABOUT 3 DOZEN

Cream butter thoroughly, then add sugar and flavorings. Blend until creamy and smooth. Add the almonds, then the flour. Knead lightly to blend thoroughly.

Divide the dough in two equal portions and form into two long rolls about 1 inch in diameter. Cut off ¾-inch pieces. Roll each piece into a 2-inch length between the palms of your hands. Place on ungreased baking sheets, pressing into crescent shapes. Bake in a preheated 350-degree oven for 15 to 20 minutes, or until tan in color. Cool slightly, then roll in confectioner's sugar.

Vienna Tarts

These are filled cookies with a dough of delicate cream-cheese pastry. For filling use a thick jam or jelly with a strong flavor.

½ cup (1 stick) unsalted butter, at room temperature
3 ounces cream cheese, at room temperature
1 cup sifted all-purpose flour
About ¼ cup stiff, tart grape jelly
1 egg yolk beaten with 2 tablespoons milk
¼ cup fine-chopped walnuts
Confectioner's sugar for sprinkling
MAKES 15 TO 18 TARTS

Cream the butter and cheese together until well blended and fluffy. Add the flour and knead to a smooth dough. Wrap in wax paper or plastic film and chill several hours or overnight.

Roll dough into a rectangle ⅛ inch thick. Cut into 2-inch squares. Place ¼ teaspoon jelly in one corner of each square. Beginning at this corner, fold edge over, completely covering jelly. Press down to seal and roll the square diagonally. Turn into crescent shape. Brush with egg-yolk glaze. Sprinkle with nuts, or dip brushed surface into nuts. Place on greased cookie sheets. Bake in a preheated 400-degree oven for 12 to 15 minutes.

Cool on cake racks. Sprinkle with sifted confectioner's sugar.

Brandy Snaps

These flexible cookies can be used as shingles for a gingerbread cottage, rolled into delicate lacy cookies, or pressed into custard cups to form a tulip-shaped basket for mousse or ice cream.

½ cup (1 stick) unsalted butter
1⅓ cups brown sugar, firmly packed
¾ cup light corn syrup
⅛ teaspoon salt
1½ teaspoons ground ginger
2¾ cups sifted all-purpose flour
MAKES ABOUT 3 DOZEN COOKIES

Place first five ingredients in the top of a double boiler. Heat over boiling water, stirring until the butter is melted and ingredients are well blended. Remove from heat, cool slightly, then add flour. Blend thoroughly.

Chill dough for at least 30 minutes, then divide into four portions. Roll out one portion at a time on a lightly floured board to a very thin sheet, about 1/16 inch thick. Cut into 2-inch rounds and place about ½ inch apart on greased baking sheets.

Bake in a preheated 400-degree oven for approximately 5 minutes. Let rest in pans a few minutes, then remove cookies to a wire rack to cool. Stored in tightly covered containers, these cookies will keep for several months.

Butter Cookies

For cutouts this dough is superb. For additional flavor, substitute brandy for the vanilla. After brushing with an egg-white glaze, sprinkle granulated sugar on the cookies for another texture.

1¾ cups sifted all-purpose flour
¾ teaspoon baking powder
¼ teaspoon salt
⅔ cup (1 stick plus 2⅔ tablespoons) unsalted butter, at room temperature
1 cup sugar
1 egg, well beaten
½ teaspoon vanilla extract
2 tablespoons milk
MAKES ABOUT 24 COOKIES

Sift the flour, measure, and resift three times with baking powder and salt. Cream the butter; add the sugar and continue creaming until well mixed. Stir in the egg and vanilla. Beat in sifted dry ingredients in two or three portions alternately with milk, beginning and ending with the flour mixture.

Chill the dough for at least 30 minutes. Roll out ⅛ inch thick on a lightly floured board and cut into desired shapes. A finish may be made by brushing with slightly beaten egg white, then placing blanched almonds split lengthwise, pieces of candied cherries, chocolate shot, and the like on top. Or sprinkle with granulated sugar.

Arrange on greased baking sheets and bake in a preheated 400-degree oven for 8 to 12 minutes, or until delicately browned. Cool on wire racks. These cookies are excellent for glazing with icing made from sifted confectioner's sugar and egg white after they are baked and cooled.

Hungarian Filled Crescents

Buttery, flaky crescent cookies filled with jelly. I like to use red currant jelly or apple jelly.

½ cup (1 stick) unsalted butter
1 tablespoon lard
2 cups sifted all-purpose flour
¼ teaspoon salt
2 small egg yolks
½ cup sour cream
About ½ cup stiff, tart jelly
1 egg yolk beaten with 2 tablespoons milk
Confectioner's sugar for sprinkling
MAKES 24 COOKIES

In a mixing bowl combine the butter, lard, flour, and salt. Cut with a pastry blender or work with the fingertips until the mixture has the consistency of cornmeal. Drop in the 2 small egg yolks, add the sour cream, and mix thoroughly.

Shape into a patty, wrap in plastic, and chill overnight. Roll out on a lightly floured board to ⅛ inch thick. Cut into 3-inch rounds. Place about ½ teaspoon jelly off-center on each round. Fold over the edge near the jelly, completely covering jelly. Press down to seal, then roll up jelly-roll fashion; turn and shape into crescents. Brush with egg-yolk glaze and place on greased baking sheets.

Bake in a preheated 400-degree oven for 10 to 12 minutes. Remove from pan while warm and place on cake racks. Sprinkle with confectioner's sugar when cool.

Noël Nut Balls

Buttery pecan nut confections rolled into small balls. These are sometimes called Russian tea cakes. I like to roll them in powdered sugar when they have cooled.

1 cup (2 sticks) unsalted butter, at room temperature
2 tablespoons honey
½ cup confectioner's sugar, plus additional for rolling
2¼ cups sifted all-purpose flour
¼ teaspoon salt
1 teaspoon bourbon or orange juice
¾ cup fine-chopped pecans
MAKES 36 SMALL NUT BALLS

Cream butter and honey together in a mixing bowl until soft and fluffy. Stir in the confectioner's sugar, flour, salt, bourbon or orange juice, and pecans. Chill for several hours.

Preheat oven to 350 degrees. With your hands roll 1 teaspoon of dough at a time into balls the size of small walnuts. Place on greased cookie sheets and bake for 12 or 13 minutes. Place on wire racks to cool. When cool roll in confectioner's sugar.

Butter-Nut Balls

Buttery lemon-flecked dough rolled in chopped walnuts and topped with a piece of candied cherry. We make them with red and green decorations.

1 cup (2 sticks) unsalted butter, at room temperature
½ cup sugar
2 eggs, separated
1 teaspoon grated lemon rind
2½ cups all-purpose flour
2 tablespoons milk
1 cup fine-chopped walnuts
12 to 15 candied cherries, halved
MAKES 24 TO 36 COOKIES

In a mixing bowl, cream the butter; add the sugar gradually, beating well. Add the egg yolks and rind and beat until fluffy. Stir in half the flour. Add the milk and beat well, then add the remaining flour. Knead slightly to blend.

Shape into balls the size of small walnuts. Roll in slightly beaten egg whites, then in chopped nuts. Place on greased baking sheets. Press half a cherry in the center of each cookie. Bake in a preheated 350-degree oven for 20 to 23 minutes. Cool on racks.

Almond Spritz Cookies

A very delicate cookie that is put through a cookie press. There are both manual and electric cookie presses, so find one that works well for you.

2 cups (4 sticks) unsalted butter, at room temperature
½ cup sugar
1 small egg
1 egg yolk
2 cups sifted all-purpose flour
¼ cup blanched almonds, grated fine
MAKES 24 TO 36 COOKIES

Cream the butter in a mixing bowl. Blend in the sugar and beat until light and fluffy. Add the egg and egg yolk and beat well. Stir in the flour and almonds, mixing until thoroughly blended. Chill slightly.

Put dough into cookie press and press out into small wreaths onto an ungreased cookie sheet. Bake in a preheated 350-degree oven for 5 to 6 minutes. The cookies should be only delicately brown on the bottom edges. Remove to cake racks while still warm and cool thoroughly. Store in airtight containers.

Sugar Cookies

For rolling and cutting, this dough works very well. We use it for our giant cookie cutouts. They frost beautifully and we like to create one special cookie for each of our friends at Christmas.

1 cup vegetable shortening
2 cups sugar
6 cups sifted all-purpose flour
1 teaspoon salt
1 teaspoon baking soda
1 teaspoon vanilla extract
1 tablespoon lemon extract
1 cup sour cream
Sugar, angelica, or candied fruit for decorating
MAKES 4 TO 5 DOZEN

Cream the shortening and sugar until fluffy. Sift the dry ingredients together and beat into the shortening mixture. Add the flavorings and sour cream. Mix well and chill several hours.

Roll out to ⅛ inch thickness and cut into desired shapes. Sprinkle with plain or colored sugar, or decorate with angelica and fruit (slivered candied peel, slivered or halved cherries). Or leave them plain if you plan to frost them after baking. Bake in a preheated 350-degree oven 10 to 15 minutes. Remove carefully to cake racks to cool.

Cookie-Press Cookies

A very good buttery dough for the cookie press. I especially like to make Christmas-tree–shaped cookies or star- or heart-shaped cookies. Sometimes I will stick two cookies together with melted chocolate.

1½ cups (3 sticks) unsalted butter, at room temperature
1 cup sugar
2 eggs, separated
3¾ cups all-purpose flour
¼ teaspoon salt
1 tablespoon vanilla extract
Chopped nuts, colored sugar, multicolored candies (optional)
MAKES 2 TO 3 DOZEN

Cream the butter and sugar in a bowl until light and fluffy. Add egg yolks, flour, salt, and vanilla. Mix well.

Fill cookie press with dough and shape fancy cookies on an ungreased baking sheet. Brush the top of each cookie with the egg whites, beaten slightly with a little water. Decorate or leave plain.

Bake in a preheated 400-degree oven until the cookies are golden brown on top and done throughout. Test one. Thin cookies take 5 to 6 minutes; thick ones 8 to 15 minutes. Cool slightly, then remove with spatula. When cool, store in airtight container.

Anise Cookies

These cookies, in order to puff, must dry overnight unbaked on the floured and buttered pans. They are wonderfully flavored with anise.

2 eggs
1 cup sugar
1¼ cups all-purpose flour
1 teaspoon anise seed
Anise oil (optional)
Lemon zest or grated rind (optional)
MAKES ABOUT 24 COOKIES

In the large bowl of an electric mixer, beat eggs till very light. Add the sugar and continue beating at medium speed 30 minutes. Add the flour and the anise seed. A drop or two of anise oil can be added as well, and lemon rind, zested or grated. Continue to beat for 5 more minutes.

Drop from a teaspoon onto well-greased and floured cookie sheets, 1 inch apart. Let stand at least 10 hours, or overnight, at room temperature to dry. Bake in a preheated 350-degree oven until the tops puff like meringues and the cookies are pale tan.

When cool, store in airtight container.

Marcella Hazan

CHRISTMAS IN CESENATICO, 1945

Christmas is a time of gifts. For Marcella Hazan's family the greatest gift was the return to their family farm after World War II. Hazan's father rebuilt their plundered home, and her mother and grandmothers pieced together a Christmas dinner made deeply meaningful by being eaten at their own table. Hazan has collected her wealth of knowledge on Italian food in several cookbooks, most recently MARCELLA'S ITALIAN KITCHEN.

THE WAR WAS OVER, and we were home in Cesenatico for the first time in five years. It was Christmas week, and we were waiting for Bajòn, my father's faithful tenant farmer. Bajòn was a nickname which, through constant usage, had erased everyone's recollection of its owner's real given name. In Romagnolo, the dialect of Cesenatico, the word meant easygoing, good-natured, and it fit him perfectly. The mule to which Bajòn hitched his cart also had a nickname: Moto Guzzi. It had been named, mockingly, after the Italian motorcycle because of its disinclination toward any form of guided locomotion, although it would, sporadically, in misguided attempts to live up to its sobriquet, tear off in brief, untimely, and aberrant trots.

In 1940 it had become obvious that Italy would enter the war, and my father, who, in running his own small but productive farm, had shown a talent for getting the most out of both land and farmhands, accepted a post as resident manager of a large agricultural consortium on Lake Garda. We moved there hoping to live out the war in the quiet and safety of the countryside, away from such sites of military interest as our town's harbor. As it turned out, after Mussolini was dismissed from the government, he set up his rebellious Fascist republic on the lake, choosing as his capital a town just ten miles north of us, which also became the Wehrmacht's headquarters. When I recall the Allies' daily raids and the stray bombs that would fall in our yard, I think it incredible that all of us survived. We were rarely able to finish a meal without having to dash for shelter in the basement. Some evenings we didn't even have that much time, and we just dived under the massive walnut dining table. By the end of the war, my father had lost eighty pounds.

We returned to Cesenatico to find our house badly damaged both by the retreating Germans and by the advancing Allies. The former had dynamited a nearby bridge, which, when it blew, carried part of our house with it. Then looters had finished the job, carting away the boiler, the radiators, and all the piping they could rip out to sell for scrap. When General Mark Clark's 5th Army moved in, one of its units camped inside the house, lighting fires on the floor to keep warm and cook by.

Although he had very little cash, my father managed in a short time to make the house habitable again. He found bricklayer friends to rebuild what had crumbled, and he went from farm to farm buying for as little as he could what furniture the peasants wanted to discard. Soon we had beds, chests, and—most important—a dining table and chairs. Replacing the central heating was beyond our means, but there was a terra-cotta stove for the dining room and a wood-fired range in the kitchen.

We heard Bajòn's whoops of encouragement coming from up the path, and soon Moto Guzzi's languorous shuffle came into view. Bajòn was bringing the traditional year-end presents that were part of the crop-sharing arrangement that then governed the relationship between a *contadino*—the man who worked the farm— and the landowner.

When Bajòn pulled into the yard and began to unload the two-wheeled cart Moto Guzzi had so reluctantly drawn, it seemed to me that our own gift-bearing magus had come. He brought a sack of flour milled from our wheat, of the soft variety that is used in Emilia-Romagna for handmade pasta; twenty-four freshly laid brown eggs with wisps of straw from the chicken coop still stuck to them; a long, knobby salami and a couple of yards of sausages; two thick *cotechini*, the boiling sausages made with a large proportion of *coteca*, sweet, tender pork rind; and an earthenware crock of *strutto*, the best shortening for crisp frying, made of the rendered fat of a recently butchered pig.

Then there were the vegetables and fruit. A basketful of small sauce tomatoes had been kept since summer hanging by their branches in the farmhouse. We strung them up from the beams in the kitchen ceiling, next to bunches of golden *albana* grapes. There were cardoons of the variety that in Romagna we call *gobbi*—hunchbacked—because as they grow, earth is piled over them to keep them white, and in the struggle to grow under the weight of the soil, the cardoons hunch over. There was perhaps a bushel of apples, small and of a dull, rose red, their flesh juicy and sugary. And end-of-the-season persimmons, the fall fruit we call by its Japanese name, *kaki*, a dozen or more glossy, orange-red globes.

Last of all, he pulled from the floor of the cart two twitching masses of feathers, a stout capon and a young rooster, live and tied by their legs. My mother deposited them on the kitchen floor, where they heaved and flapped, looking as though they were trying to swim away. When, after having a glass with my father and sharing good wishes with all of us, Bajòn had left, we heatedly began to discuss the Christmas Day menu.

There were five of us—my mother, my father, my two grandmothers, and I. My grandmothers could not be more dissimilar. *Nonna* Polini, my father's mother, born and raised on a farm, had never been outside her native Romagna in her life, except for the war period in Lake Garda, and she spoke only Romagnolo, the local dialect. Ninety and going blind, she did not reach quite five feet, but she was quick-witted, impish, and earthy. My maternal grandmother, *Nonna* Adele, a straitlaced patrician, five feet ten, was fifteen years younger. She had been brought up in Syria and spoke with the round, warm accent common to expatriate Italians from the Middle East and North Africa. Her eyes were large and kind, but museful, as though always turned toward matters removed from immediate circumstances. *Nonna* Polini and *Nonna* Adele's exchanges, entirely in dialect on the part of the former and in Italian laced with Arabic on the part of the latter, had the zany quality of conversations that share the point of departure but soon skid along steadily more divergent tangents.

On the matter of the first course, everyone quickly agreed: we would have *cappellitti in brodo*, stuffed pasta in capon broth. *Nonna* Polini wanted to follow that with *cotechino*, which she had been longing for all the years we had been away. *Nonna* Adele remarked that when her husband had been alive, *cotechino* was what they had for New Year's, together with mashed potatoes. "Mashed potatoes?" said *Nonna* Polini. "I'd rather have it with lentils." *Nonna* Adele replied that she had never had lentils on New Year's Day. "What does New Year's have to do with it?" *Nonna* Polini wanted to know. "We're talking about Christmas dinner."

Father settled the whole thing. Christmas dinner in Romagna meant *cappelletti in brodo* for the first course and boiled capon for the second, and that is what we would have. Moreover, since a holiday meal always called for an extra course, we would also have a chicken fricassee, using the rooster and Bajòn's fresh tomatoes.

We started working on the dinner the day before Christmas. Once the capon was dispatched, plucked, and singed, Mother made the stuffing for the *cappelletti*. She took some of the raw capon breast and sautéed it in a mixture of olive oil and *strutto*, the rendered pork fat. Then she chopped it very fine together with some marvelous mortadella from Bologna she struggled to keep me from pecking at, and mixed it with some soft, fresh cheese, eggs, grated *parmigiano*, and nutmeg. She should have included some veal, according to the classic recipe, but we had none. My father, who was the taster, dipped his pinkie into the mixture and pronounced it perfect, save for another pinch of salt.

There was no question that *Nonna* Polini would roll out the pasta, as she had been doing for nearly eighty years. The skinny pasta pin was nearly as long as she was tall, and she had to climb on a footstool in order to reach the table. In minutes, the motion of her hands, as fluid as the arabesques of a prima ballerina, had produced a transparent sheet of pasta nearly as large as a bedspread. She cut the sheet into squares, my mother dotted the squares with stuffing, and *Nonna* Adele, my father, and I worked quickly to fold and twist each square into *cappelletti*—small hat—shapes before the pasta could become dry and brittle. We lined up the dozens of *cappelletti* like little soldiers on kitchen towels spread on a spare cot, making sure none of them touched; otherwise, by the following day, they would be stuck together and tear when pulled apart. (There are detailed instructions for making *cappelletti* in my *Classic Italian Cook Book*, published by Alfred A. Knopf.)

The last thing to be prepared that day was the dessert, my mother's wonderful bread pudding, with raisins and rum. Actually, there was no rum available then, so she put in some of my father's homemade grappa. This was one of the recipes I set down, years later, when I began to write, and it appears in my first book.

Christmas morning was a morning such as we had doubted, during the last dark years, we could ever live again. Everyone was up early to complete preparations for the meal that was to be the only present any one of us would get that year. As a special gift for my father, Mother rose earlier than anyone else to bake *ciambella*, a breakfast cake *Nonna* Polini had taught her when she was married. It is now my husband's, as it was then my father's, favorite thing to have with a large morning coffee. To make the gift particularly sumptuous, Mother made custard cream, which my father would spread thickly over the *ciambella*.

The capon was boiled with carrots, celery, onions, a potato, and a tomato to produce the fragrant, ruddy broth for cooking the *cappelletti*. My father's task was to trim the cardoons of their tough strings before they too were boiled. They were to be both vegetable and salad, served lukewarm just with olive oil and salt.

Nonna Polini was plucking the rooster, which she did largely by touch, yet flawlessly. It went early into the pot so that it would have time to cook through and through, until the meat came easily off the bone.

We sat down at 12:00 noon, a full hour before our customary midday mealtime. The stirring odors of good things ready to be eaten could no longer be resisted. I had never before, nor perhaps since, experienced such a sense of life being full and right and wholly unblemished.

Marcella Hazan

After dinner, Father brought out the hazelnuts and almonds, the dried apricots, dates, and figs. They were rarities then and had cost a notable part of his small reserve of ready cash, but without them he felt Christmas dinner at home would be incomplete. He poured tumblers full of his own Albana, an amber, lusciously sweet wine. And I listened to the elders reminisce about remarkable Christmases they had had in their lives. I listened wide-eyed and open-mouthed, it not having quite sunk in yet— and it would be some years before I'd be capable of taking in the full sense of it—that this was the greatest Christmas I would ever know, the Christmas that had given me, through the recaptured flavors of our cooking, through the carefree sounds of my mother's and father's voices, through the comforting familiarity of the rooms I had grown up in, the one incomparable gift, the gift of life regained.

La Ciambella di Nonna Polini
(My Grandmother's Pastry Ring)

½ cup (1 stick) butter
4 cups unbleached flour
¾ cup sugar
2½ teaspoons cream of tartar
1 teaspoon baking soda
1 small pinch salt
Grated peel of 1 whole lemon (do not grate deeper than the colored surface skin)
¼ cup lukewarm milk
2 eggs
A heavy baking sheet, lightly buttered and dusted with flour
MAKES 8 TO 10 PORTIONS

Preheat oven to 375 degrees.

Gently melt the butter in a little saucepan without letting it get too hot.

Put the flour into a large bowl. Add the sugar, melted butter, cream of tartar, soda, salt, grated lemon peel, and warm milk.

Add the first egg. As you add the second egg, let the white run into the bowl first. Before adding the yolk, remove a teaspoonful of it, and set it aside. You will use it later to "paint" the ring.

Mix all the ingredients thoroughly, then turn out onto a board or other work surface and knead for a few minutes. Shape the dough into a large sausage roll about 2 inches thick, and make it into a ring, pinching the ends of the roll together to close the ring.

Brush the surface of the ring with the teaspoon of egg yolk you set aside earlier, and score it with a few shallow diagonal cuts.

Place the ring in the center of the buttered and floured baking sheet. Bake in the upper level of the preheated oven for 35 minutes. It should become nearly double in size.

Set on a rack to cool. It tastes best when served the following day.

Pollo in Umido alla Contadina
(Fricasseed Chicken with Tomatoes, Peasant Style)

A 2½-to-3-pound chicken, cut into 8 pieces
3 tablespoons extra virgin olive oil
1 cup thin-sliced onion
2 garlic cloves, peeled and sliced very thin
Salt to taste
Black pepper in a grinder
⅓ cup dry white wine
1½ cups fresh, ripe sauce tomatoes, peeled and cut up, or canned Italian plum tomatoes with their juice

SERVES 4 TO 6

Wash the chicken pieces in cold water and pat thoroughly dry with kitchen towels.

Choose a lidded sauté pan that can subsequently accommodate all the chicken pieces without overlapping. Put in the olive oil and onion and turn on the heat to medium. Do not cover the pan. Cook the onion until it is tender and turns a blond gold color without browning.

Put in the chicken pieces, skin side down, and the sliced garlic. Cook the chicken without turning it until it has formed a light brown crust on one side. Turn it and cook until the other side also forms a crust.

Add salt and several grindings of pepper. Put in the wine and turn up the heat. When the wine has bubbled long enough to become reduced to half its original volume, add the tomatoes, turn the heat down to medium low, and cover the pan.

Cook until the chicken feels very tender when pricked with a fork and comes easily away from the bone. If there should be too much fat left in the pan, tilt the pan and spoon off the excess before serving.

AHEAD-OF-TIME NOTE: The dish can be prepared several hours in advance and kept at room temperature. If preparing it in advance, do not draw off any excess fat when the chicken is cooked. Reheat just before serving over very low heat in a covered pan. When fully reheated, tilt the pan and draw off any superfluous fat with a spoon.

Budino di Semolino Caramellato
(Glazed Semolina Pudding)

½ cup plus ⅔ cup sugar
Generous ⅓ cup small seedless raisins
2 cups milk
¼ teaspoon salt
⅓ cup semolina
1 tablespoon butter
1 tablespoon rum
¼ cup mixed candied fruit, chopped into ¼-inch pieces

Grated peel of 1 orange
All-purpose flour
2 eggs
SERVES 6 TO 8

Choose a 6-cup metal mold. (A simple cylindrical shape is the easiest to work with.) Put the ½ cup sugar and 2 tablespoons water in the mold and bring to a boil over medium heat. Do not stir, but tilt the mold forward and backward from time to time until the syrup turns a light-brown color. Remove from heat immediately and tip the mold in all directions to give it an even coating of caramel. Keep turning until the caramel congeals, then set aside.

Put the raisins in a bowl with enough lukewarm water to cover and soak for at least 15 minutes.

Preheat the oven to 350 degrees.

While the raisins are soaking, put the milk and salt in a saucepan over low heat. When the milk is just about to come to a boil, add all the semolina in a thin stream, stirring rapidly with a wooden spoon. Continue cooking, without ceasing to stir, until the semolina has thickened sufficiently to come away from the sides of the pan as you stir. Turn off the heat, but continue stirring for another 30 seconds to make sure the semolina won't stick.

Add the ⅔ cup sugar and stir, then add the butter and rum and stir. Add the candied fruit and grated orange peel, stirring them evenly into the mixture.

Drain the raisins and dry with a cloth. Put them in a sieve and sprinkle them with flour while shaking the sieve. When the raisins are lightly floured, mix with the ingredients in the pan.

Add the eggs, beating them very rapidly into the semolina mixture. Pour the mixture into the caramelized mold and bake in the middle level of the preheated oven for 40 minutes. Remove from the oven and cool.

When the pudding is cold, refrigerate for 10 minutes to give it extra firmness. To unmold, first very briefly warm the bottom and sides of the mold over low heat to loosen the caramel, then place a dish over the mold, turn the two upside down, and give the mold a few taps and downward jerks. It should lift away easily.

Budino di Pane Caramellato
(Glazed Bread Pudding)

½ cup plus ⅓ cup sugar
2½ cups roughly cut-up stale, lightly toasted, crustless, good-
    quality white bread
¼ cup butter
2 cups milk
½ cup small seedless raisins
All-purpose flour
¼ cup pine nuts
3 egg yolks
2 egg whites
¼ cup rum
SERVES 6 TO 8

Choose a 6-cup metal mold. (A simple cylindrical shape is the easiest to work with.) Put the ½ cup sugar and 2 tablespoons water in the mold and bring to a boil over medium heat. Do not stir, but tilt the mold forward and backward from time to time until the syrup turns a light-brown color. Remove from heat immediately and tip the mold in all directions to give it an even coating of caramel. Keep turning until the caramel congeals, then set aside.

Put the bread and the butter in a large mixing bowl.

Heat the milk, and as soon as it comes to a boil, pour it over the bread and butter. Let the bread soak without mixing and allow to cool.

Put the raisins in a bowl with enough warm water to cover and soak for at least 15 minutes.

Preheat the oven to 375 degrees.

When the bread is cool, beat it with a whisk or a fork until it is an even, soft mass.

Drain the raisins and squeeze them dry in a cloth. Put them into a sieve and dust them with flour while lightly shaking the sieve. Add them to the bowl with the bread mass.

Add the ⅓ cup sugar, pine nuts, and egg yolks to the bowl and mix all the ingredients thoroughly.

Beat the egg whites until they form stiff peaks, then fold them gently into the mixture in the bowl.

Pour the contents of the bowl into the caramelized pan and place it in the middle level of the preheated oven. After 1 hour turn the heat down to 300 degrees and bake for 15 more minutes.

While the pudding is still warm, pierce it in several places with a toothpick. Gradually pour 2 tablespoons of the rum over it. When the rum has been absorbed, place a platter on the pan, turn the pan over on the platter, give it a few sharp downward jerks, and lift it away. Pierce the top of the pudding in several places with a toothpick and pour the rest of the rum over it.

NOTE: Plan to serve the pudding the day after you make it. It improves in texture and flavor as it rests. You can refrigerate it for several days, but always take it out sufficiently ahead of time to serve at room temperature.

Crema Pasticcera
(Italian Custard Cream Sauce)

Crema pasticcera requires the patience to cook it long enough, without boiling it, to give the flour time and just sufficient heat to dissolve in the sauce without leaving a trace of graininess or a pasty, floury taste. There is nothing mysterious about this. When a sauce is lumpy or has a doughy flavor, it means the flour has been cooked too fast or not too thoroughly, or both.

Although I am accustomed to using a heavy-bottomed saucepan for making *crema pasticcera*, if you are worried about how to keep the heat under control, try using a double boiler, but make sure the water in the lower half of the boiler stays at a brisk boil.

3 egg yolks
3 ounces confectioner's sugar
5 tablespoons flour
2 cups milk
Grated peel of ½ lemon
MAKES ABOUT 2¼ CUPS

Put the egg yolks and sugar into a heavy saucepan or in the upper half of a double boiler. Off the heat, beat the eggs until they are pale yellow and creamy. Add the flour gradually, beating in no more than 1 tablespoon at a time.

In another pan bring all the milk just to the brink of a boil, when the edge begins to be ringed with little bubbles.

Add the hot milk very gradually to the egg-and-flour mixture, always off the heat. Stir constantly to avoid lumps.

Put the saucepan over low heat (or over the lower half of the double boiler in which the water has been brought to a boil). Cook for about 5 minutes, stirring steadfastly with a wooden spoon. Do not let the mixture come to a boil; it's all right, however, for an occasional bubble to break slowly through the surface. The *crema* is done when it clings to the spoon with a medium-dense creamy coating.

Remove from heat and stir for a few minutes until the bottom of the pan cools off a little. Mix in the grated lemon peel.

Lee Bailey

A CHRISTMAS REMEMBERED

Graceful and comfortable entertaining has been Lee Bailey's hallmark, advocated in his books, his columns for FOOD & WINE, *and the elegant shop where he established his style. But here we see him as a very young and puzzled boy, about to learn a few hard facts of life.*

''WHAT IS THE EARLIEST Christmas dinner you can remember?'' A group of us, old and good friends, had just finished an especially warm and convivial Christmas meal and were mellowing over coffee. ''Is it a happy memory?''

My thoughts went back to when I was about seven or eight. ''Yes, the memory is happy, but I wonder if that is how I really felt then.'' I was hedging a bit because something happened that particular Christmas that I didn't understand—the impact of which was strong enough to mark the day as Christmases past hadn't been.

Nineteen thirty-five—well into the Great Depression. But I'm remembering a child surrounded and protected by loving parents and relatives, whose bed is warm, who has a dog named Miss Woo, who is allowed to explore freely the narrow world encompassed by the willow tree–lined bayou that runs through the back of the property and the fig trees growing up close to the house, who knows little of the nation's jarring tragedy and its effects. He knows instead about the orange-yellow glow of a radio dial on Sunday nights as he hears the latest from Fred Allen and his gang of zanies. He knows about being awakened with the first light as his daddy goes out to hunt quail, which the next morning will be his breakfast. He knows about beauty parlors and red fingernails from absently eavesdropping on the mostly puzzling conversations between his mother and her sister-in-law. He knows that somewhere there is a place called New Orleans where the family is going to shop for fall clothes, but all this is cold-weather stuff. What he does know best and deepest is summer. And in summer this little boy, me, knows about the special treat of being allowed to spend weeks down at his grandmother's big house, with its kudzu vines reaching up to the second-story porch and wide central hall, there to coax meager breezes from the relentless Louisiana summer heat. Heat that means nothing to him except talcum powder under his chin to keep prickly rash at bay. Midsummer doesn't make him wilt and complain like the grownups in their resigned offhand way. After all, summer sun makes tomatoes red and skin brown and bleaches the small me's already white hair—these are good things, or at least okay things. And besides, there is no school and there is hand-turned ice cream.

The big white house was occupied by two grownups: Mamaw, my grandmother, and Aunt Tee, who was Mother's older sister, probably about thirty-four, who had had a "tragic marriage" and had returned home two years before to teach. Of course, I loved Mamaw—after all, hadn't she had the good fortune to have in me a grandchild whom she considered absolutely faultless?—but it was in Aunt Tee that I found my first adult kindred spirit. She not only liked to draw and was interested in knowing how to grow odd-shaped gourds; she seemed to really understand what I was thinking about and to respond seriously to small puzzling (and thrilling) things like why the first sun's rays hitting a drop of dew resting in a curled leaf looked enough like a diamond to make you think it might really be one.

She knew all about me—I couldn't wait to tell her—but I didn't—couldn't—know all about her. I thought in my child's way that we would be together summer after summer after summer until—when? Forever, I suppose.

But inevitably it was fall, and I returned to home and school, and then it was November and my birthday. I went down to the big white house to be admired and to get my presents from Grandmother and from Tee, who had cut and pasted together a complicated poster-sized card using pictures from magazines we had looked at together that past summer as well as some of my own drawings. I was stunned and intoxicated with my very importance. We ate coconut cake, my favorite, and my mother gave me a cap she had knitted and Daddy told me there was a swing in the shape of an airplane in the backyard waiting for me when we got home. There was also a baby wild rabbit in a cage lined with hay that Parson had caught for me. Parson, the old, old black man whose home was the little newspaper-lined house in the back of my grandmother's garden.

Then sometime just after we had had our cake there was someone else. Mr. Babin. At first I thought it was natural for a perfect stranger to come to wish me happy birthday. But there was something odd about his being there. Everyone was acting too nice and laughing when there wasn't anything funny. I was glad when Mr. Babin left, relieved enough to forgive my aunt for walking out to the car with him to say goodbye.

But by mid-December I knew there was trouble. I had seen Mr. Babin a few more times and had gotten the information that he was someone Tee had gone out with in college before her "tragic marriage" and that he was now courting her—whatever that was. It was worrisome, but I figured it would blow over. I even started asking how long Mr. Babin would be coming to the house—meaning when would he stop showing up at my grand-mother's house. And who knows how many times Mr. Babin had been around that I didn't know about. I don't mean to say Mr. Babin was all I thought about that fall. There was the recent revelation about Santa Claus that I had to deal with. Maybe yes and maybe no. I think I had decided to try to believe just one more year to be on the safe side. Also we would be going out in the woods soon to cut down a tree which we would then try to get into the room we called the library, because it had one wall taken up by glass-fronted bookcases. Years later, while idly going through those shelves, I found a modestly illustrated book about sex, in back of the regular line at the front of one of the shelves. Thereafter I spent many nervous hours searching futilely for others of that sort, but that's another story.

Anyway, four days before Christmas we all went to my grand-mother's house. We were dressed up and there were others there.

Everyone had bourbon or something because the occasion was supposed to be special. I thought at first it was because of the season. But then Tee came in looking really beautiful and behaving in a silly, self-conscious way I had never seen before. Mr. Babin, who came in behind her, was even worse. "Honey, Tee and Mr. Babin are going to get married on Christmas Day," my mother said to me. "What for?" I asked. Everyone thought that was funny. I thought it was logical. For a moment I even let myself hope that maybe after they got married, Mr. Babin would be satisfied and leave for good.

I haven't told you yet that my father loved to cook. Especially for people he knew well and liked. My mother never learned how, but we had a regular cook so that didn't matter. Maybe Mother was intimidated by my father's enthusiasm and talent for it. Whatever, when it came to entertaining friends, he did all the cooking. Guests would crowd in the kitchen and joke while Daddy tended the stove. His food was hearty: wild ducks he and his brothers and their friends had shot, fish they had caught in the murky waterways. Or fresh pork in the fall when the weather first turned chilly and there was occasional frost in the mornings.

It was finally Christmas. That fateful Christmas morning. I was under the tree early and found a wonderful book from which you made pictures by cutting outlined shapes from pages of colored paper in the back and pasting them in similarly outlined places in the front. Also there was a set of miniature logs that you could put together to make a stockade. There was a train—and more. And there was the smell of Christmas already coming from the kitchen.

"How's Daddy's big boy? How's Daddy's cotton top? What did Santa bring you? Let me see. You're not saying much. What's that, a coloring book? Bet you like that, don't you?" I nodded my head yes and handed him the book as he stood in front of the stove, which was sending out waves of warmth and wonderful odors. "That looks like fun. Do you want some milk toast? But you don't want to eat too much. You can smell what's in the oven—yes, sir, that big old bird. And with corn-bread dressing.

Yum, yum. What's the matter, don't you want that good old bird?" I answered yes, but I suppose I was wary or was trying to deal with the new and puzzling feeling of not being able to completely pay attention to what I was hearing or seeing. I had two important things on my mind at once, and that was a new way of thinking for me.

Suddenly Daddy settled down on his haunches in front of me, pulling me toward him as he did, until he could put both arms around me. Finally he said in a steady voice, "What's the matter—you thinking about Tee going away?" I made a little whining sound, looking down. "You should be glad. Tee has had a hard time of it with her first husband, and Mr. Babin is a good man. She's lucky."

"I hate him," I said to his chest. I felt Daddy relax his hold for a second and then pull me closer. "Don't say that, son. You'll see it'll be all right." He was smoothing the back of my head with one hand. "Now come over here and help me with the turkey. You have to keep Daddy company while I baste it. May Pearl will be here soon to cook you a nice breakfast. Come look at the turkey."

As it turned out, Mr. Babin *was* a good man and Tee *was* happy and the turkey that Christmas was the best I had ever eaten. And turkey with corn-bread dressing is still one of my all-time favorite meals, certainly my all-time favorite holiday meal.

I realized some time ago how evocative of happy times and good memories specific odors and tastes can be, which in part led me to set about trying to re-create the flavors from those cherished Christmases I remember best. The following is my reconstructed recipe for the classic turkey with corn-bread dressing. Maybe it will spring some memories for you or start some for your own little boy.

Turkey and Corn-Bread Dressing

Some of you may be puzzled by the term "dressing." That is what we call stuffing in the South.

Before we start, let me give you a few tips that I think help make for a better result here. First, you should order your turkey well enough in advance so that you can get one that has not been frozen and is of the size that you require. Fresh unfrozen birds automatically guarantee a better flavor. Also, be sure to remove it from the refrigerator several hours before you start cooking to let it come to room temperature. When roasting a turkey consider the fact that the legs and thighs are tougher than the breast meat and take longer to be tenderized by the heat. Also, drumsticks and wings tend to dry out in the oven if they are not properly secured, so proper trussing of the bird is important. Simple instructions for doing this may be found in most basic all-purpose cookbooks. My father used to wrap bacon around each drumstick to keep it moist. I don't always do this, but you might give it a try. He also used to soak a torn section of fresh dishcloth in butter and put it on the breast to keep it from cooking too fast. This cloth would then be dampened each time he basted, which was very often. I must admit I don't baste my turkey as often as he did and frankly I can't tell the difference. The cloth on the breast was usually left on through most of the cooking time and then removed so the breast could brown.

After roasting, the turkey should rest for 30 to 45 minutes, to make it easier to carve. Don't worry about it getting cold; if the turkey is covered loosely with foil, you will be surprised how long it remains hot inside. This grace period after roasting will give you ample time to deal with the other elements of the meal.

Incidentally, no matter how quickly and efficiently you carve and get the plates served, the meat will inevitably cool. For this reason it is doubly important to keep the gravy hot, over a warming light if possible.

Now to the main event.

Roast Stuffed Turkey

Skillet Corn Bread (see below)
1½ cups cubed white toast (well toasted)
1 cup (2 sticks) plus 2 tablespoons unsalted butter
3 medium ribs celery, chopped
1 medium green bell pepper, chopped
1 medium onion, chopped
1 cup chopped scallions (about 1 big bunch)
Turkey Stock (see below)
1 cup coarse-chopped toasted pecans (about 4 ounces)
¼ cup minced fresh parsley
2 teaspoons salt
1 teaspoon freshly ground black pepper
¼ teaspoon cayenne pepper
¼ teaspoon thyme
2 raw eggs, lightly beaten
2 hard-cooked eggs, chopped
15-pound fresh turkey, neck and giblets reserved for stock
2 tablespoons all-purpose flour
SERVES 12, WITH LEFTOVERS

Preheat the oven to 450 degrees. In a large bowl, crumble the corn bread and toss with the toast cubes.

In a large skillet, melt 4 tablespoons of the butter over low heat. Add the celery, green pepper, onion, and scallions. Cook over low heat, stirring, until wilted but not browned, about 15 minutes.

In a small saucepan, melt 4 tablespoons of the butter in ¾ cup of the turkey stock. Set aside.

Add the pecans, parsley, salt, black pepper, cayenne, and thyme to the corn-bread mixture. Stir in the wilted vegetables, the raw eggs, and the stock mixture. Toss well to blend. Toss in the hard-cooked eggs.

Stuff the cavity and neck of the bird loosely. (If there is any extra stuffing, wrap it in a buttered foil packet and bake during the last 30 minutes with the turkey.) Sew the openings of the turkey or skewer them shut; truss the bird. In a medium saucepan,

95

melt 1 stick of the butter and soak a 2-foot-long double layer of cheesecloth in it. Place the turkey on a greased rack in a roasting pan and cover the breast with the butter-soaked cheesecloth. Set the remaining 2 tablespoons of butter out to soften.

Put the turkey into the oven. Immediately reduce the heat to 325 degrees and roast, basting with any pan juices every 30 minutes, until an instant-reading thermometer inserted into the inner thigh registers 155 degrees, about 3½ hours; remove the cheesecloth from the breast. Continue to roast, basting, until the thigh temperature reaches 180 degrees, 50 or 60 minutes longer. Transfer turkey to a carving board and let it rest, loosely covered with foil, for at least 30 minutes.

Meanwhile, to make the gravy, mash together the softened butter and flour until blended into a paste. Skim fat off the juices in the turkey roasting pan. Pour in the remaining stock and bring to a boil, scraping up any browned bits from the bottom of the pan. Gradually whisk in the butter paste and boil, whisking, until thickened. Reduce the heat and simmer for 5 minutes. Season with salt and pepper to taste. Strain into a sauceboat.

Skillet Corn Bread

Make this the night before and leave it out, uncovered, to dry out so that it will absorb the stock and seasoning and retain a nice coarse texture.

> ¼ cup safflower or corn oil
> 1¼ cups yellow cornmeal
> ¾ cup all-purpose flour
> 1 teaspoon sugar
> ½ teaspoon salt
> 4 teaspoons baking powder
> 1 cup milk
> 1 egg, lightly beaten

MAKES 1 NINE-INCH PAN

Preheat oven to 450 degrees. Put 2 tablespoons of the oil in a 9-inch cast-iron skillet and place in the oven while it is preheating, about 10 minutes.

Meanwhile, sift together the dry ingredients. In a small bowl combine milk, egg, and the balance of the oil. Pour into the dry ingredients and mix quickly. Do not overmix. Pour into prepared skillet and bake at 425 degrees for 20 to 25 minutes, or until golden and the corn bread has pulled away from the sides of the pan.

Turkey Stock

The stock can be made up to a day in advance. If you buy a turkey neck and giblets separately, you can make it weeks, even months, ahead and freeze it.

Turkey neck and giblets (heart and gizzard; set aside liver for another use)
1 medium onion, chopped
1 large celery rib with leaves, chopped
1 large unpeeled carrot, scrubbed and chopped
3 sprigs parsley
MAKES ABOUT 3 CUPS

Preheat oven to 350 degrees. Put neck and giblets and onion into a small roasting or flameproof baking pan and roast for 1 hour, turning, until browned all over. Transfer browned ingredients to a medium saucepan.

Place the roasting pan over high heat. When the pan drippings start to sizzle, pour in 1 cup of water and bring to a boil, scraping up all the browned bits from the bottom of the pan. Pour this liquid into the saucepan and add the celery, carrot, parsley, and 3 cups of water. Bring to a boil over high heat. Reduce the heat to low and simmer, partially covered, for 1½ hours. Strain, let cool, then cover and refrigerate.

Lee Bailey

Robert Finigan

CHRISTMAS REMEMBRANCES: BOSTON AND LONDON

Charles Dickens created the vision of the perfect Victorian Christmas, redolent of roast beef at the table and lemon oil on it. Robert Finigan, the wine critic, has found authentic versions of Dickens in both Boston and London. God bless them both!

I'VE BEEN FASCINATED by the world of Dickens since early youth, but it wasn't until creeping middle age that I realized how very Dickensian were the Christmases I adored as a child. For me, Santa Claus and Rudolph and the silly post-Thanksgiving songs on the radio were of little interest. I had a special Christmas treat in store. It was all about lovingly polished oak, gleaming crystal, tantalizing aromas from an old-fashioned kitchen, and the company of adults more sophisticated than I could ever hope to be.

The stage was my grandmother's house on the outskirts of Boston, in a neighborhood fashionable then and now once again, but not in between. In current real-estate parlance the house would be called a Victorian, but I'm not sure Bostonians took to that description in the 1940s. It was a house with many small rooms on three floors, and a wonderfully cool cellar, and even a porch. There was an expanse of lawn with, of all things, a bearing peach

99

tree. But especially there was the kitchen, where my grandmother held absolute sway.

Not that my grandmother was a dedicated cook. She was simply a perfectionist, though a jolly one, and she couldn't imagine that anyone else might not be. What she knew about cooking was exactly what the California movement thinks it discovered: buy the best raw materials and treat them with respect, and you'll be just fine.

Yet this approach was not as simple as my description might seem, as I discovered when pressed into service as an apprentice shopper. There was a man for poultry, another for meat, another for fish, and of course another for vegetables. At each station I was told why one choice was better than another, and that sense of discrimination stuck. When backup supplies were needed, there was a larder stocked with the maroon-waistcoated cans of S. S. Pierce, the only grocer my grandmother trusted implicitly.

I always ate well at my grandmother's table and I took it for granted, though I thought her insistence on a wood-burning stove eccentric when we had the latest in electric at home. I wasn't much enamored of being assigned to the ice-cream churn either, though the produce of that strange peach tree yielded the most delicious peach ice cream I've ever tasted.

But the good food I expected in this setting took on a different meaning at Christmas. My grandmother's was of course a perfect Christmas house, and it never shone more brightly than at that season. There was always a Christmas Eve party just for family and the closest of friends; as the only child present, I could focus on the tree only so long, before devoting my attention to the adults, trying to figure them out while staying out of their way so I would not be banished. I thought everyone looked so very elegant in the soft refracted light of chandelier prisms, but I wasn't so sure what they were talking about. Perhaps they weren't either.

I was sure about the appeal of the hors d'oeuvre, however, and about my hopeless crush on my uncle's fiancée (now his widow), whose attention I could never quite command, being of single-digit age. My mind typically wandered to the meal I knew was coming the next afternoon.

From early morning, every corner of the house became perfumed with the most complex aromas of wonderful food. It wasn't just roasting turkey or braising onions, though there were those elements: it was a symphony of Christmas smells, pine and burning logs and the coal furnace along with the intersecting aromas of the meal to come, and it was unique to the season and the place.

But the day had its rituals and pace, and those aromas would tantalize for hours to come. Just as tantalizing were the gaily wrapped presents under the trees, gifts which no one could touch until just before Christmas lunch. Such postponement of pleasure would be difficult for anyone, but for a small boy it was pure torture.

Happily, there were diversions. Mid-morning, my dashing uncle would whisk me away to his fiancée's Back Bay apartment, where they would exchange gifts before he brought her to the family celebration. I thought I had never seen more attractive people, or happier ones. I adopted a diffidence to conceal my affections for Nancy, and I'm sure she saw right through it. I wondered if I would ever have a girlfriend as pretty and charming. I wanted one right then.

Back home, it was time for my annual Christmas visit to my grandfather's den, a little nook on the third floor of the house, perfumed with years of pipe smoke. I loved his shelves of old books, but especially his framed photo of Ted Williams. We discussed school, the prospects for the Red Sox in the coming season, and then, with a shy chuckle, my grandfather gave me an envelope with money, as if it represented a secret between us.

At last, at last, it was time to open presents. Naturally, I was in heaven, but I realized in retrospect that by being the only child in this Christmas setting, I was giving the adults as much pleasure as I was experiencing myself. And difficult as it was to leave new toys and books and such, those aromas from the kitchen were becoming so heady as to be irresistible.

That dining room I knew so well always seemed new and dramatic on Christmas, as it did in different light on Christmas Eve. My grandfather was fascinated by old English furniture, and his gleaming oak table, smelling faintly of freshly applied oil, was one of his triumphs. He delighted in showing me how no nails

101

but, rather, small ebony pegs had been used in its construction. For this meal, the reflections of old silver and crystal shimmered on its surface. Then, at long last, came Christmas lunch.

The turkey was always astonishing to me, since it seemed so very big and yet so manageable by my grandfather, who dissected it expertly with bone-handled cutlery. He did the same with a seemingly mammoth roast of beef. But carving was his only contribution: all else on the table was the product of my grandmother's skill, or that of the help under her direction.

There were platters of mashed potatoes, white and sweet, with rivulets of the freshest butter, and candied yams that were truly candied over a slow fire. There were those onions—real ones, now, not the acidulated product of jars. There was usually puréed squash, the point of which eluded me as a child, and always cranberry sauce with a few of the berries still unpopped. And there were two gravies, a smooth and deeply flavorful one for the turkey, a thinner and more pungent one for the beef and the Yorkshire pudding alongside.

Yes, there was plum pudding for dessert, always from the redoubtable S. S. Pierce and always served with hard sauce, that indigestible mixture of sugar and butter and rum. And I think there was mince pie. I'm certain, though, there was an odd family favorite, an ice-cream bombe smothered in spun sugar. It was a long meal, and a long but lovely day for a small boy.

Inevitably, grandparents died, family members dispersed, and a tradition became a memory. Christmas dinners came to be enjoyed in different circumstances, with different friends, and the "turkey with trimmings" was always a pleasing marker of the season. Yet every now and then I wondered whether the clear memory of my grandmother's excellent cooking really was so clear—or just a recollection romanticized.

I passed into a different tradition when I married a Catalan (just as lovely as my uncle's fiancée) and enjoyed Christmas dinner in Barcelona with my wife's family. No turkey, no cranberry sauce came to the table: the traditional Catalan Christmas meal is *escudella*, a sort of pot-au-feu with assorted meats, vegetables, and pasta. It's just delicious when well prepared, as it was at our table, and I came to look forward to this once-a-year specialty. And the wines which were never part of my grandparents' Christmases were here features of the table, for this family was one of the principal wine producers of northern Spain.

Then, one Christmas, seeming disaster struck. We had overnighted in London on our way to Barcelona, only to find that all the Christmas Day flights to Spain had been canceled because of a labor dispute. It was bad enough to miss the family celebration, but what were we to do by ourselves in London? Christmas reservations in the city's principal restaurants are frequently made a year in advance.

We were staying at the Connaught, that marvelous bastion of all the best that is British, and we threw ourselves on the mercy of the concierge. He seemed doubtful, since the dining room of the Connaught is one of the most prized of Christmas reservations, and it is booked by the same families year after decade. But late in the morning we had a call: there would be a table for two at 1:30.

It was snowing fiercely, and aside from our frustration at not being able to reach Barcelona, we found the Connaught not a bad place to be marooned. A glass or two of Champagne in the hotel's peerless bar put us directly in the holiday spirit, as all around us were multigenerational English families catching up on all that had happened since the previous Christmas. I couldn't help but recall that special glow which seemed to suffuse those at my grandparents' Christmas Eve reception.

Our table was ready precisely as promised—who knows by what means?—and it was a prime table to boot. The warmth of the Dining Room's wood paneling has always seduced me, though the Grill is supposed to be trendier, and never had it been more comforting than on this stormy Christmas Day. We were part of a quintessentially British throng madly popping "crackers" and rearranging the paper hats that are as much a part of English Christmas as they are of American New Year's Eve.

Then came the food. We were happy enough to be where we were, but when the serving carts appeared, I shivered with the feeling of being back at my grandmother's table. Just as had been the case in my childhood, the choices were roast beef or roast turkey, and sampling both, I realized in an instant that I had not

103

tasted their like for a quarter century. Here was turkey that tasted like turkey, a splendid plump bird from Norfolk, and ribs of Aberdeen beef with that mineral beefy flavor I had seldom found since my Christmases in Boston. It would have been senseless to wax ecstatic to the captain, for he took this sort of quality for granted. But the sommelier knew the wine I chose was special indeed: this '61 Corton from Louis Latour's best Burgundy vineyard was supernal, and as it happened, the Connaught's last bottle.

The plum pudding of my childhood was raised to new heights by the Connaught's kitchen, and a final glass of Champagne put the cap on one of the most memorable meals of my life. A special day apparently gone wrong had been transmuted into a trip back in time, complete with the polished wood and crystal and even the aromas of Christmases past.

Prime Rib of Beef (Slow-Roasting Method)

This was the way of cooking prime rib chosen by my grandmother, and the only one she could have chosen, given her preference for a wood stove. She probably relied on touch and smell and experience to make the beef as perfect as it always was, but she was also extremely particular about what she bought.

Select a prime rib roast from an utterly reliable butcher who has dry-aged his beef at least two weeks. There is simply no point in presenting this delectable cut unless the beef itself is of impeccable quality and proper age. With the roast at room temperature, rub it all over with freshly ground pepper, perhaps some rosemary. Insert a few slivers of garlic into the fat at random intervals. Place on a rack, fat side up, in a commodious pan and put to roast in a 250-degree oven.

Assuming you have a three- or four-rib roast, you should let it go for 20 minutes per pound, then check the internal temperature with a reliable meat thermometer. What you are seeking is an internal temperature of 125 degrees for rosily rare. Calculate your further cooking time after this 2-hour checkpoint, and salt the roast lightly before resuming its cooking. At 125 degrees, remove the roast from the oven and let it stand for 15 to 20 minutes. Carve into the thinnest slices you can manage.

Serve with horseradish, fresh if possible, stirred with a little unsweetened whipped cream.

Two-Week Plum Pudding

I tried for years to replicate the plum puddings of my youth, but the much-missed Jim Beard set me on the right track by suggesting long "marination" of the basic ingredients with sequential daily dollops of rum or Cognac. After much tinkering I think I have it right now, and believe me, starting well in advance produces a result you'll never find commercially.

Mix the following ingredients, preferably by hand:

¾ pound beef suet, minced
2½ cups sifted all-purpose flour
3 cups breadcrumbs, mostly from the crust
1½ cups black seedless raisins
2 cups golden seedless raisins
2 cups dried currants
1 generous cup minced candied "Christmas fruits," citron and
    others, tossed with flour
1 cup chopped almonds
3½ cups shredded green apples, peeled first
1½ cups brown sugar, firmly packed
1 teaspoon each ground cinnamon, allspice, and ginger
1 orange, grated rind and juice
1 lemon, grated rind and juice
1 cup rum or Cognac

3½ cups rum or Cognac
6 eggs

When you've had your way with these components, mixing them well indeed, add a cup of rum or Cognac and mix them again. Then put plastic wrap over the bowl and refrigerate. Each

105

day for the next two weeks, add ¼ cup of spirits and work the pudding mixture through your hands (you could have a nip of the rum or Cognac for your efforts).

After two weeks, stir in 6 beaten eggs, mix well a final time, and fill pudding basins or small soufflé molds with the batter, leaving space at the top and then covering with foil preferably secured with twine. Place the containers in a roasting or other pan which will allow you to add boiling water to half their depth, then place in the oven and cook at a slow simmer (about 275 degrees) for approximately 6 hours, replenishing the water as necessary to keep it at half the height of the cooking vessels. After 6 hours test a pudding with a needle or wooden skewer; if it doesn't come out clean, continue cooking for another hour or so.

Serve with a sauce made of 3 parts beaten butter, 1 part fine sugar, and 1 part rum or Cognac, the mixture whipped frothily together.

Carol L. Flinders

THE HOLLY AND THE HAWTHORN: CHRISTMAS AT LAUREL'S KITCHEN

How does wholesome and healthy—and the sunny skies of California—translate into happy holidays? The folks at Laurel's Kitchen, a community in California, have grappled with this question and come up with a fresh mix of tradition, whole food, and frosted cookies on the tree.

LAUREL AND I HAVE BEEN FRIENDS for twenty-three years—early on as students in Berkeley, then later, and now, as members of the large but closely knit circle of friends described in *The New Laurel's Kitchen*. Some of us live together in north Marin County—Laurel's family and mine share a capacious Victorian farmhouse with friends—and others live in nearby towns. At the slightest tug of an invisible cord we converge, for potluck suppers or baby showers, for work parties at Nilgiri Press, or for repair on one of the buildings out of which the press operates.

Christmas is one serious tug on that cord. Whoever among us has chosen to avoid the rigors of wintertime travel and make do with a California Christmas is automatically included in our household's festivities. They are included in the preparations, too, and happy to be so, because Laurel's Kitchen is one all-right place to be about then. Surround yourself with great heaps of figs, dates, spices, nuts, vanilla, and the like, and you can almost forget that the weather is absolutely unsupportive of yuletide sentimentality. (Forgive my churlish slant on all this, but native to the Northwest that I am, I still get disoriented when I walk out of that warm, fragrant kitchen to see green hills and blue skies on Christmas. Indignant even. Every December I say that once too many times, though, and Laurel, native Californian that *she* is, gets a bit fed up. Things usually come to a head at the point when I'm griping at the absence of holly. Brightly, she tries to suggest that hawthorn branches can take their place, and I, in turn, start describing the twenty-foot-high holly tree back home in Oregon and how it looked in the snow with cedar waxwings plundering it. I have to hand it to her—not once has she made the obvious suggestion.)

Years ago, when we first went public about being vegetarians, the question was always the same: "But where do you get your *protein?*" This notwithstanding our visibly robust health and our thriving children. When, gradually, friends realized that we were dead serious about 100 percent whole-grain foods as well—brown rice, brown bread, brown pasta—the question shifted. In effect, now, especially around holidays, it has become, "Where do you get your *fun?*" For truly, isn't Christmas virtually synonymous with a parade of perfectly lethal goodies indefensible on any grounds but pleasure?

Well, we haven't found it necessary to compromise our whole-foods bias for the holidays, but it has taken a few years to get it figured out. We've wanted holiday wonderfuls that our children would look forward to each year, but that we could all enjoy comfortably even though Year Forty was closing in on all of us.

Fortunately, the ante went up gradually. That is, in our early years as vegetarians we were at least not terribly constrained by worries about levels of dietary fat. This was helpful, because we had a lot of basic baking skills to learn. Baking with whole-grain ingredients and natural dried fruits, for instance, *is* different, and it might have been more than we could deal with to have been metering fat calories, too. Today, we know that just because a food is natural and unrefined, it still isn't necessarily healthful in quantity. We are meeting head-on the challenge of preparing vegetarian food that is both appetizing and heart-healthy.

In those early years, however, we tried it all, gamely and optimistically. And we learned a lot. We're here to say that natural dyes made from beets and spinach do not make a frosting that is either convincing or appealing. On the other hand, life goes on without red and green cookies. If the artist in you and your children must express itself in painting cut out cookies with bright (alas) carcinogenic glazes, whale away—only hang them all on the Christmas tree, and don't go near the frosting.

There are dishes we don't attempt because they defy translation. Forget *bûche de Noël* made with carob flour and ricotta cheese. It is *not* acceptable. But fruitcake made with dried instead of glacéed fruit is truly wonderful—a superior product.

Our daily fare tends to be simple—delicious, because we use fresh ingredients and put some time into preparing them, but relatively unadorned. We seldom have desserts, preferring to reserve them for holidays and Grand Gestures. This means that our Christmas feasting really does register as such—much as it must have in times past, when, for a midwinter festival, you would bring out food stored away especially for the occasion. (Those more austere times aren't really so far away—don't others of my generation have parents who remember eating oranges only at Christmas?)

Let me share some of our favorite recipes with you now, and tell you a little more about our own Christmas observances, too.

One of the deep satisfactions of enjoying an extended family of friends like ours is that other people's loved holiday observances become yours by the most natural kind of osmosis.

I'm thinking in particular of Lynne Forester, who has shared with us the beauties of celebrating Advent. Heathen that I am, this beautiful tradition was quite unfamiliar to me, but now the Advent wreath and four candles and the Advent calendar are as intrinsic to the weeks before Christmas as the Christmas tree itself.

Lynne (née O'Brien) is a true Celt. It isn't just that she loves music and poetry; rather, it's that her responses to the changing seasons of the year and to the holy days and weeks that mark those changes come from a great depth. They simply must be expressed—and what better way than through music and poetry?

(Food too, of course—come Easter there must be hot cross buns.) For Lynne, Christmas is truly the center of the year, the still point into which all life flows and out of which it issues forth, renewed, reestablished in hope and sanctity.

From Lynne, then, we have learned beautiful old Christmas carols—unfamiliar, with melodies hard to grasp at first, but, finally, haunting—and we have learned the symbolism of the Advent wreath: a simple circle of evergreen boughs on a table top and four red candles placed around it. We light one candle four Sundays before Christmas—in the evening—sing several Christmas songs, read or tell a story, and enjoy a sampling of whatever Christmas goodies have been baked. Three Sundays before Christmas, the second one is lit, too, and so on until finally all four are ablaze. Way back behind the tradition is an older, pre-Christian one—the yearly return of light from the darkness of deep winter. Hanukkah, the Jewish feast of lights, falls at about the same time of year.

There is more—a "more" that is particularly precious in households where there are children. With the lighting of the first candle, the whole mineral world is said to rejoice in the birth-to-be of the Christ Child. Smooth stones are gathered from a creek or river bed and arranged in a half-circle. On the second Sunday of Advent, the plant world rejoices—pine boughs are placed around and over the rocks. The third candle is lit, and the animals celebrate—carved figures of cows and sheep, a dove, a donkey, and a shepherd's dog are placed within the half-circle of stone. Finally, with the fourth candle, the human world joins in the celebration, and the crèche is completed: Mary, Joseph, the shepherds and wise men, and the angels take their place around the manger and the Baby Jesus.

Once you have taken a child through this beautiful month-long ceremony, I promise you it will be very hard to simply unpack the crèche you've been keeping on the floor at the back of your closet and set it up a few days before Christmas.

Whatever a person's religious beliefs, everyone pretty much agrees that Christmas is a time to reaffirm and strengthen our connectedness with one another. Printed Christmas cards are at the far end of the spectrum for doing this; gifts of home-baked breads, cakes, and other delicacies are at the far *other* end. They carry so much of you with them, and when they can carry a message of good health, too—when they celebrate earth's bounty of fruit, nuts, and grains—they are that much lovelier.

Usually about the time when that first Advent candle is being lit, we are baking fruitcakes to send our friends and family far away. The children come to help. They love chopping nuts in the special kidproof chopper (the kind with a plunger and blades in a jar), and snipping dried fruits with scissors is okay, too—up to a point. We wanted to avoid sulfured apricots this year—in case someone was allergic and because the sulfur flavor can come through—so we presoaked those leathery nonsulfured apricots in hot orange juice. A real coup.

Carol L. Flinders

Christmas Fruitcake

¾ cup unsulfured dried apricots
¾ cup orange juice
1 cup dried figs
1 cup dried apples
1 cup apple juice
2 cups currants
2 cups chopped walnuts or filberts
2 cups whole-wheat flour
1 teaspoon each cinnamon, nutmeg, allspice
½ teaspoon ground cloves
1 teaspoon baking powder
½ teaspoon baking soda
1 teaspoon salt
3 large eggs
⅓ cup safflower or corn oil
Grated peel of 2 lemons and 1 orange
1 teaspoon vanilla extract
½ cup brown sugar, packed
1 cup red wine
Brandy for soaking cakes afterward
MAKES 2 EIGHT-INCH LOAVES

Prepare two 8-by-4-inch loaf pans by greasing them and lining them all the way to the top with parchment paper or brown paper. Grease the paper, too.

Place the apricots and orange juice in a small saucepan. Bring to the boil, then cover the pan and turn off the heat. Let sit for 5 minutes to rehydrate. Meanwhile, chop the figs and apples.

Drain the apricots, reserving juice in a 1-cup measure. Put the figs and apples in the same saucepan along with the apple juice, bring to the boil, then cover the pan and turn off the heat. Let stand for 5 minutes, then drain, adding any extra liquid to the 1-cup measure. Meanwhile, chop the apricots.

Combine the chopped apricots, figs, apples, currants, and nuts in a large mixing bowl.

Preheat the oven to 300 degrees.

Sift the flour with the spices, baking powder, soda, and salt.

Combine the eggs, oil, lemon and orange peel, vanilla, and sugar. Add the wine to the reserved fruit juice in the 1-cup measure, up to the 1-cup mark, and stir into the egg mixture.

Stir the flour mixture into the egg mixture, then stir this batter into the fruits and nuts.

Pour the batter into the prepared pans and bake on the lowest rack of the oven for about 1 hour and 45 minutes. Test by inserting a table knife in the center of the cake. It will come out clean when the fruitcake is done.

Let the cakes cool in the pans on racks until they reach room temperature, then remove from pans. Carefully pour brandy on all surfaces, then wrap the cakes in brandy-soaked cloth and aluminum foil. Once a week during storage, moisten the cloth with more brandy. It will keep at least three weeks.

Come the second week of Advent, I'm usually packaging up gifts of California's wonderful dried fruits and nuts—organically grown, you bet. We've found these to be richly appreciated, and so much simpler than keeping track of sizes of growing nieces and nephews. Had it all become old hat? Did people really *like* the stuff? We sent more conventional gifts one year, and did we hear about it: "We missed the figs!" "We can't get almonds nearly that nice out here!" This year, in support of California's newest agricultural venture, we're including pistachios in the mix.

It's best to clear-wrap nuts and fruits in separate bundles, or the nuts will lose some of their crispness. We arrange the bundles prettily in a flat box and imitate the professionals by tucking special surprises wrapped in colored foil here and there too. The surprises are things like these:

Cashew Cardamom Balls

Cashew cardamom balls have an Oriental ambience. Sophisticated, sweet, and sinfully rich-tasting, they qualify easily as gourmet fare; but they're so easy to make that you can turn them out for lunch-box treats.

Carol L. Flinders

1 cup lightly toasted cashew pieces
Cardamom seeds from 2 to 4 pods (⅛ to ¼ teaspoon ground)
1 cup finely chopped dates
Finely grated peel of 1 orange
½ cup dried coconut, toasted and then powdered in blender
MAKES 18

Chop cashews rather fine (the blender chops them *too* fine). Remove cardamom from pods and grind with a mortar and pestle or between two spoons. Combine cashews and cardamom in a bowl with dates and orange peel. Knead mixture with fingertips until uniform, then roll into balls and coat them with coconut.

Darryl's Almond Truffles

⅔ cup honey
3 tablespoons cocoa powder
1 cup almond or hazelnut butter (available in most health-food
     stores)
½ teaspoon salt (unless almond butter is salted)
1 teaspoon almond extract (if hazelnut butter is used, you may
     substitute orange extract or a drop of Grand Marnier)
½ cup nonfat dry milk (optional)
Cocoa powder to dust truffles
MAKES 5 DOZEN TRUFFLES

Place the honey in a saucepan over medium heat and stir in the 3 tablespoons of cocoa powder. Remove from heat and stir in the almond butter, salt, almond extract, and the powdered milk if you are using it. Chill and form into balls, using about 1½ teaspoons of the mixture in each, and roll in cocoa powder. Like all truffles, these are best stored under refrigeration. Adding powdered milk gives them more of a milk chocolate flavor and helps them keep their shape at room temperature. Better do this if you're mailing them somewhere (and see whether they don't remind you vaguely of Tootsie Rolls!).

Stuffed Prunes

Simply sweeten peanut butter with brown sugar and fill large, soft prunes with it. A simple but winning combination!

Carol L. Flinders

Three candles lit, and Christmas is close at hand. About this time we like to greet our near-at-hand neighbors with loaves of home-baked bread. We live in a dairy-farm region, and neighbors are far-flung, so the distribution of Christmas bread takes several hours—allowing time for talk of weather, gardens, and school-board elections. Our youngest children usually come along, curious to see what the houses are like at the end of those long access roads off the highway, and who lives in them. It's close to inevitable, too, that in several of those old farmhouses they'll walk into freshly baked Christmas cookies.

The breads we bake for Christmas giving are designed to be toasted—the kind of bread that makes any breakfast festive. Sometimes we simply knead dried fruit and nuts into buttermilk bread, but sometimes we go all out with stollen—studded with currants and dried apricots, pineapple and almonds, fragrant with lemon peel and rum. Stollen is a loved German bread that's usually made with staggering amounts of butter so that it will keep for weeks. Our version is leaner, but it keeps well for a full week and makes marvelous toast.

Sometimes, of course, you want to turn out a lovely gift bread on shorter notice. Orange-Cranberry Bread is pretty and fast.

We bake our gift bread in the morning and deliver it in the afternoon. A brown paper bag may be inelegant, but it's the ideal thing to drop a fresh, warm loaf into. A warm loaf wrapped in plastic will "sweat" and be soggy, or worse, moldy, when the otherwise lucky receiver goes to eat it. If you can't deliver your bread the same day, let it cool, and as soon as it's cool, store it carefully—breadboxes are ideal. Quick breads are, of course, too fragile to be dropped into a paper bag; better to let them cool completely, then clear-wrap and deliver on a pretty paper plate.

115

Carol L.
Flinders

My Heart's Brown Stollen

There are perhaps as many traditional recipes for stollen as there are bakers of it. Ours is a new tradition, as good as the old ones but not so wildly rich. The rum is optional, but it does provide a heady dash. (If you prefer a boozier stollen, soak the dried fruit in rum overnight before you proceed.) The cottage cheese makes the bread at once tenderer and a little less reprehensible nutritionally, and is quite traditional in some parts of Germany.

This recipe makes two large stollen or several small ones. It keeps well for over a week, but store in the freezer if you want to keep it longer. It is truly special sliced super thin and served for Christmas tea.

A note here on the baking: Try to use heavy cookie sheets, and keep the bread away from the bottom of the oven if yours tends to overheat there, as most do. It may help to put a second cookie sheet under the first one, especially on the bottom rack. Turn and reverse the loaves halfway through if they are not baking evenly.

4 teaspoons (2 packages) active dry yeast

7 cups whole-wheat bread flour
2 cups whole-wheat pastry flour
2 teaspoons salt
1 cup small-curd cottage cheese
¾ cup honey
¼ cup rum
3 eggs

¾ cup butter (1½ sticks), at room temperature

Grated rind of 2 lemons, about 2 tablespoons
Grated rind of 2 oranges, about 4 tablespoons
1 pound raisins, about 3 cups
1 pound other dried fruits, about 3 cups (include a good amount of apricot plus currants, peaches, pineapple, prunes—or more raisins!)
1½ cup coarse-chopped toasted almonds

Melted butter, about ¼ cup
Confectioner's sugar, about ½ cup
MAKES 2 LARGE STOLLEN

Dissolve the yeast in ½ cup lukewarm water.

Stir the flours and the salt together. Thoroughly mix the cottage cheese with 2 cups of hot water, the honey, and the rum, then blend in the eggs. Add to flour mixture.

Mix the dough and knead about 10 minutes, then work in the butter. Stop kneading when the butter is all incorporated; you will be working the dough more when you add the fruits and nuts.

Put the dough in a buttered bowl, cover with a towel, and let it rise in a warm place. Deflate it after an hour and a half or more, when your wet finger makes a hole in the center of the dough that does not fill in. Return the dough to its warm place to rise again. Meantime, prepare the fruit.

Chop all of the fruit so that it is about the size of raisins. If your apricots or peaches are very leathery, pour boiling water over them and let them stand until they are softer, but not mushy. All the fruit for this bread should be firm in texture so it doesn't get lost in the dough as you knead it in. If your almonds are not very tasty, toast them quite well and sprinkle a tablespoon of almond extract over the nuts when they are chopped.

Work the fruit into the dough on a large surface in a place you can protect from drafts. Flour the surface and turn the twice-risen dough onto it. Press the dough flat, and then with a rolling pin very gently roll it as large as it will tolerate without tearing. Don't be rough.

Cover the dough and let it rest about 10 minutes. Mix the fruits and nuts together and turn onto the dough. Roll or fold them together and in a leisurely way knead in the goodies so that the dough incorporates them uniformly. Divide and round the dough—one round for each loaf you want to make—and let it rest again, covered, for at least 15 minutes. The dough will rise amazingly considering all it has been through. You can make two large stollen or as many smaller ones as you like.

To shape, press or roll each of the rounds into a long oval.

117

Then fold it over lengthwise, not quite in half, and press closed.

Place the shaped stollen on greased cookie sheets and let them rise again in a humid, warm place until the dough slowly returns a gently made fingerprint. Bake in a preheated oven at 325 degrees for about an hour for the large ones, proportionately less for the smaller. Allow plenty of time for cooking, since the fruit holds moisture, but watch closely so that it does not overbake. Paint the loaf with the melted butter as soon as it is baked. When cool, dust with confectioner's sugar.

Orange-Cranberry Bread

Seasonal, of course, and all the more special because of it, this tangy-sweet bread is unique, pretty, and delicious.

¾ cup cranberries, chopped
½ cup raisins, chopped
1 tablespoon grated undyed orange peel
1¼ cups orange juice
¼ cup honey
¼ cup butter or oil

1½ cups whole-wheat pastry flour
½ cup whole-wheat bread flour
2½ teaspoons baking powder
½ teaspoon baking soda
½ teaspoon salt
½ cup toasted wheat germ
½ cup lightly toasted chopped walnuts

MAKES 1 EIGHT-INCH LOAF

Preheat oven to 375 degrees. Grease an 8-by-4-inch loaf pan. Combine in a saucepan the cranberries, raisins, orange peel, juice, and honey. Bring to a boil, stir in the butter or oil, and remove from heat. Allow to cool while measuring and combining the other ingredients.

Sift together the flours, leavenings, and salt, and stir in the wheat germ. When the liquid mixture has cooled to lukewarm, stir in the dry ingredients and fold in the nuts, reserving 3 tablespoons for the topping.

Spread the batter in the loaf pan. Sprinkle the nuts on top and press them down lightly with your hand or the back of a spoon.

Bake for 50 to 60 minutes, or until done. Test with a clean knife or toothpick, but if you should pierce a cranberry, the testing device will come out wet, so try in more than one spot to be sure.

Let the loaf rest in its pan on a wire rack for 10 minutes, and then turn it out on the rack to set for at least half an hour more before cutting. If you can wait longer—it really is worth it—the slices will be less likely to crumble.

Four candles are alight, and the last door on the Advent calendar have swung open. Through the eyes of our children, we gaze once again on the mystery, and the miracle, of the stable and a baby born there. It is for us now to remember and think hard on the words of a medieval mystic: "What good if Christ is born in Bethlehem if He be not born in your heart and mine as well?"

Good, now, to just stop: to wind it all down, and figure whatever's done is good enough. If we didn't get mistletoe hung, well, try again next year. Christmas Eve is the time to draw in very close with family and dearest friends, in a sweetness and intimacy that are paradoxically only enhanced by the presence of one or two who may be there simply because they have no other place *to* be.

Christmas morning is also pretty much family time, but by late afternoon the Nilgiri Press gang comes together for dinner and caroling.

Supper is a wonderful spread—stuffed mushroom caps and creamed spinach last year, with wild rice, Brussels sprouts with chestnuts, sweet potatoes baked in sherry and honey, cranberry relish, light whole-wheat dinner rolls by Laurel, and for dessert— well, that depends on who wins the toss.

A strong contingent favors plum pudding—"You know, like in Dickens's *Christmas Carol*—it's *de rigueur*!" The other just as

Carol L. Flinders

119

vocal crowd insists, " 'Go bake us a figgy pudding,' like the song says!" Truth of the matter is, some like figs and some like plums. Prunes, to be accurate, though no one will ask for prune pudding. Either way, the following recipe is super, and yogurt cheese topping takes it right over the top. Douse the pudding with brandy, light it up, and carry it in flaming—this is high theater.

In case you really can't get a consensus, persimmon pudding is California's sassy and delicious reply to the obsessively British approach to Christmas feasting.

Plum Pudding

2 tablespoons butter, at room temperature
2 tablespoons vegetable oil
½ cup honey
3 eggs
1 cup chopped dried figs or pitted prunes, packed
1 apple, peeled, quartered, and sliced
1 cup apple juice
Grated rind of 1 lemon
1 teaspoon vanilla extract or brandy
1 cup raisins
1 cup fine-chopped walnuts
2 cups soft whole-wheat breadcrumbs
1 cup whole-wheat flour
1 teaspoon baking powder
½ teaspoon salt
¼ teaspoon baking soda
1 teaspoon cinnamon
½ teaspoon nutmeg
¼ teaspoon ground cloves
MAKES 1 PLUM PUDDING

Cream the butter, oil, and honey together. Separate the eggs. Set the whites aside and beat egg yolks until creamy. Add the yolks to the butter-honey mixture. Put the figs and apple through a meat grinder, or simply blend them with the apple juice in a blender or food processor into a jamlike consistency. Combine figs, apple, apple juice, lemon rind, vanilla, raisins, walnuts, and bread crumbs with egg-yolk mixture.

Sift the flour with the baking powder, salt, soda, cinnamon, nutmeg, and cloves. Beat the egg whites until they form stiff peaks. Combine the dry ingredients with the wet ingredients, then fold egg whites in gently. Turn the batter out into a greased 2-quart pudding mold or casserole with a lid. Cover tightly.

Place the pudding mold on a rack inside a pot large enough to provide 2 inches of space all around for steam to circulate. Pour enough boiling water into the pot to come halfway up the sides of the mold.

Cover the pot and let the water boil briskly for a few minutes, then turn it down to low. Steam the pudding for 2½ hours, or until the top springs back when touched. You may need to replenish the water from time to time—check after the first hour.

To unmold, slide a knife around the sides of the pudding and turn it out carefully onto a plate. Splash with brandy if you like, ignite, and serve with a scoop of natural ice cream.

Persimmon Pudding

1 cup whole-wheat flour
½ teaspoon baking soda
¼ teaspoon salt
1 teaspoon cinnamon
¼ cup honey
3 tablespoons vegetable oil
2 eggs
1 teaspoon vanilla extract
1 cup persimmon pulp
½ cup raisins
MAKES 6 SERVINGS

Sift the flour, baking soda, salt, and cinnamon together.

Beat together the honey, oil, eggs, vanilla, persimmon pulp, and raisins. Mix wet and dry ingredients just until smooth and pour into a greased 1½-quart pudding mold or baking dish. Cover the mold tightly. Follow the steaming instructions for plum pudding, above. Steam for 2½ hours.

Serve warm with unsweetened whipped cream or vanilla ice cream.

Yogurt Cheese Topping

1 quart low-fat yogurt
¼ cup honey
Zest of 1 lemon
3 tablespoons Grand Marnier (optional)
MAKES 2 CUPS OF TOPPING—PLENTY FOR 6 TO 8 SERVINGS

To make yogurt into yogurt cheese, line a colander or strainer with a large cloth napkin. Turn a quart of yogurt into it and allow to drain until the cheese is as stiff as you want, anywhere from 6 to 24 hours. Place the colander in a bowl in the refrigerator while it's draining or the cheese will become very tart. One quart will yield about 2 cups of yogurt cheese. Even if it is very stiff, it will liquefy if beaten hard, so handle it gently.

Stir the yogurt cheese gently with a fork and add honey and lemon zest—Grand Marnier too, for special occasions. Serve with plum pudding.

Bert Greene

MEMORIES OF
A NON–CHRISTMAS
LOVER'S CHRISTMAS

Bert Greene was as well known for his stories as for his food. The columnist and author of GREENE ON GREENS *came by his dramatic and culinary talents naturally, as we learn when we meet his memorable mother.*

SOME PEOPLE ARE CHRISTMAS LOVERS. Some are not.

Happily, I am not the non–Christmas lover of the title. Months before the official hanging of holly or the annual house-wrecking search for lost tree ornaments, I find myself collecting odd scraps of carols and rounds in my head the way others accumulate left-over spools of ribbon or tinsel.

"Joy to the world . . ." I will find myself humming inexplicably in early November, ". . . let nothing you dismay." Remembering with tidings of comfort and joy that my favorite season of the year is just beyond the crisping of another leaf.

Definitely, I *am* a Christmas lover.

My mother, however, was not. Her yuletide animus was undoubtedly affected by a traumatic childhood experience. She had been chosen to play Scrooge in a school production of Dickens's *A Christmas Carol* when she was about ten or twelve, and spent the better part of her lifetime, and my own, sneering, "Bah! Humbug!" whenever the first snows fell. She was also a woman who, for one thing, hated shopping and, for another, hated cooking.

"Christmas is one holiday I wouldn't mind taking a long nap

123

through . . . like a bear," she would grumble as the season to be jolly implacably advanced. "Those bears certainly have the right idea."

My mother may have been bearish on the subject, but still she rarely escaped some repercussion of the yuletide. In our family, holiday dinners were divided. Thanksgiving was the exclusive preserve of my grandmother, in whose oven a monumental bird crackled from dawn till dinnertime. Christmas, on the other hand, was the dual responsibility of my mother and her youngest sister, Sally, both of whom, married with homes and children of their own, were expected to alternate as hosts of the festivities.

The plan sounded good in theory, but my Aunt Sally (ten years my mother's junior) was a capricious type at best, rarely up to sharing her part of the prandial bargain. Painters were always coming, or had just left; the kitchen stove had broken down or was teetering on the brink. "So, perhaps, Paula, could we split the costs this year—and you give the party . . . *again*?" My mother never appreciated the honor, but then she never refused it either.

What I remember best of our Christmas dinners are the stratagems and planning sessions that went on for weeks and weeks prior to the actual meal. Surrounded by her family as audience, Paula Greene would sit at the head of the dining-room table, selecting and then immediately discarding scraps of recipes she had collected during the year; dog-earing and then unfolding pages in cookbooks in a fruitless attempt to compose a menu on the back of an early Christmas card.

"Everything is *so* old hat," she would sigh. "How many times can you serve the same old turkey and ham to the same old faces? And *so* many coming this year. Who invited them all?"

The last question was unmistakably directed toward my father, though she knew full well his family never came to our Christmas dinners. And that it was her distant cousins from Ohio who had accepted a casual offer—to come for Christmas when they were in New York sometime—that had swollen the guest list irremediably.

"This dining room is simply not big enough for a family dinner with that mob from Cleveland." She sighed again. "Even with both leaves in the table. Forty people. Forty people are an army!"

My mother gritted her teeth. "It will just have to be a light buffet, a collation. Which still means the end of my *Orientals*, of course. But it won't be anything fancy to eat." And so saying, she folded down a page in the cookbook she'd been perusing—for frozen mousse and Bavarian cream.

For all the litany of complaints beforehand, my mother was no slouch at ostentation on or off the table. For days before Christmas our house was utter chaos. Furniture was rubbed slippery with lemon oil, and the precious Oriental rugs were pulled up and beaten on a cold and icy lawn until the fringes became frozen stiff in the grass. All the silver serving dishes in our dining-room cabinets were polished and then repolished until their gleam rivaled the headlights on our family Nash.

I recall vividly the excitement of those early Christmas parties but very little of the actual dishes my mother prepared except for the desserts. She never served fewer than six or seven to end a meal, and the memories of those towering mousses and velvety custards, the gravity-defying layer cakes and silken fruit tarts haunt my tongue to this very day. Little sighs of pleasure echoed throughout the room as confection after confection was brought to the sideboard by Delia, our Irish "girl" in the kitchen, who was a lady of uncertain age, unsteady step, and unvarnished manner.

Delia always took the prerogative of sticking a finger into everything in the kitchen before it was served.

"De-licious," she would announce in a loud and knowing brogue as she sailed half-tilt through the dining-room doors. "You're going to love it!"

For some time my mother suspected Delia drank a little but she chose not to pursue the clues. Now, the looseness of her tongue and bleary stare confirmed the suspicion beyond a shadow of a doubt. Particularly when Delia lurched into a chandelier while attempting to anchor a precariously sugared strudel on the table.

"I'll serve, Delia." She smiled thinly. "You make coffee. And have some yourself, *dear!*"

My mother was a gracious hostess to the death but far more generous than necessary. She would pile her guests' plates high and then, moments later, ply them with second and third helpings until they begged for surcease.

If she was elated by the party's success, she never showed it. My poor father, basking in reflected glory, made the error of slipping his arm about her waist as the last relative was waved off to Shaker Heights and equidistant parts.

"I think it went very well this year." He nodded. "You should be pleased."

"*Pleased?*" my mother hissed, shrugging his arm aside. "What's to be pleased? That woman" (lowering her voice to indicate Delia, who was soggily trilling "Mother Machree" over the unwashed dishes) "just cracked two of my wedding crystal goblets. There is a cigarette burn on the leather chair. And the needles from that damn Christmas tree are all over my poor rug."

Her last complaint was obviously directed toward me. For it was I who had passionately insisted that our tree be as broad as it was tall that year.

"Christmas is just an aggravation. A headache I can do without!"

I will never know if this was augury on my mother's part or merely a stab in the dark. Because the Depression struck our family resources soon after, and Christmas became expendable.

It was not our only deprivation. In short order we lost our house. And, minus my mother's Oriental rugs, Chippendale table, silver serving dishes, and wedding crystal, we moved to a small apartment, without a "girl" in the kitchen. My mother and sister embarked on a series of diverse employments to help support my father's flagging income while I cooked and did odd jobs after school.

Christmas was not entirely dismissed in my home, but parties for more than four were simply out of the question. And the sense of expectancy along with the hope for some utterly unreasonable largesse—like a bicycle or a motion-picture camera—abated in my breast long, long before the question "What do you want for Christmas this year?" was ever posed.

No longer were closets crammed with a glittery cargo of tinsel and gilt, and no last-minute mystery packages arrived to be sequestered from my view. But I learned how to stuff and roast a turkey, so life did have its compensations, I suppose.

When I was about fourteen or fifteen, it occurred to me the

one ingredient missing from our yuletides was gaiety. My mother, born under the sign of Scorpio (with Scorpio her rising sign as well), was a tenacious and indefatigable survivor, without a doubt, but a pessimist in the matter of unwarranted felicity.

"I don't have the Christmas spirit this year," she announced several weeks into December when I brought up the question of reviving the family party tradition. "Besides, it will cost a fortune."

"Not if I do all the work," I countered. "And the shopping. I even promise to take care of the clean-up, too."

"The truth is, kiddo, I just don't have the spirit," my mother sighed. "But do what you want. I won't stop you."

What my mother meant was that she would not abet me either. Handing me a twenty-dollar bill, like Pontius Pilate, she washed her hands of the entire matter.

On the day before Christmas, with less than half the marketing done, I ran out of money. Precipitously, I had bought token gifts—small boxes of cookies for every member of the family—without realizing how low my funds had dwindled. Cold and wet, I stared into shopwindows fruitlessly, counting and recounting the small change in my pockets. Snow was falling in soft dispiriting flakes that turned to ice once they touched the pavement. As I turned to go, I met my mother on the street coming home from work early.

She looked exhausted by the holidays. By now I had little Christmas spirit either.

"What are you doing here?" she asked as I slipped under her umbrella.

In the past I would have lied or dissembled wildly, but lack of truth seemed utterly pointless at that moment. So I confessed that my overplanned, undercapitalized party was in danger of imminent cancellation.

My mother was sanguine.

"This really means a lot to you, doesn't it?" she said as we huddled away from the last-minute shoppers. Nearby, a very old man was improbably shaking holly wreaths for sale from a damp pile outside a vegetable market. Each scarlet ribbon he held up was lanker and more sodden than the last.

"Yes," I replied honestly. "But I don't know *why*."

127

"It's because you are a Christmas lover. You always were, you always will be! Now, then." My mother always got down to brass tacks sooner than later. "Just how much do you think it will cost to finance this damn foolishness?"

I dreaded to tell her. "Ten dollars."

"Ten dollars?"

Even as I write this, almost fifty years later, it is hard to believe how much that amount of money actually represented. My mother and I stared at each other a long while, weighing the momentous sum before she carefully unbuttoned her coat. There, on the street, without glancing up or down, she quickly removed a bill from her boodle, a small moiré bag that she always wore tucked into the top of her brassiere.

"Make it last," she said wryly. "Try not to come home too late. And for God's sake, don't tell your father!"

I shopped until all the stores closed at nine. When I got home, my sister and I composed appropriate verses to go with each box of cookies before beribboning the boxes. In fact, it was well past midnight before I began my pre–Christmas dinner preparations. I had chopped onions, peeled vegetables, and was drying salad greens when my mother—in a burst of energy or perhaps of insomnia—appeared in the kitchen doorway in her nightgown.

"I feel like making a cake," she said. "Maybe two. You can't have a *single* dessert in this house at Christmas without flying in the face of years of tradition."

While she pulled ingredients off the shelves and out of the refrigerator, I decorated a tiny Christmas tree. Our first in almost six years, it was so minuscule it had to sit on a telephone book and a table to be seen from the window. But the Oriental rugs were safe from its needles, because they had long since vanished with the spoils of the Greenes' other life.

The party was a great success. All the relatives ate well, demolished the desserts, and played games, and those who drank sang dirty songs afterward. All the cookies we made were carried off like Tiffany bibelots.

Both my parents, though proud, were somewhat reserved after the last guest departed.

"I think you did a good thing—for everybody," my father

cautiously allowed as he removed his shoes. "What we all needed around here was a little party. And" (speaking to my mother) "it's a miracle what he managed to *do* on twenty bucks."

"Yes," my mother said evenly, staring at the enormous pile of dishes in the sink. "But if it's all the same to you, some year I'd like to join the bears and sleep through the holidays. Preferably in Florida!"

As I said earlier, some people are Christmas lovers and some are not.

No one but my late mother would possibly serve the following garland of Christmas desserts at the same time or on the same table. Yet each has curious affinities with the others. The very rich chocolate cake complements the delicate vanilla mountain of custard; the frangible nutted strudel is abetted by the wintry bite of a fresh pear tart. The lacy cookies and buttery shortbread are simply after-bites, anodynes for the sweet-toothed (like me) who never want a good thing to come to an end.

My suggestion: Mix and match them all at will. Not just for Christmas but all year round.

La Maxine

FOR THE CAKE

1 cup granulated sugar
1 teaspoon instant espresso powder
6 ounces semisweet chocolate, chopped
1 teaspoon vanilla extract
6 tablespoons unsalted butter, softened
8 eggs, separated
8 ounces ground walnuts
2 tablespoons white-bread crumbs
Pinch of salt

FOR THE ICING

6 ounces semisweet chocolate, chopped
2 teaspoons instant espresso powder
1 cup (2 sticks) plus 2 tablespoons unsalted butter, softened
3 egg yolks
⅔ cup confectioner's sugar
½ cup ground walnuts
SERVES 8 TO 10

Preheat the oven to 350 degrees. Butter two 9-inch round cake pans and line the bottoms with parchment paper. Butter the paper. Flour the pans, shaking out any excess.

To make the cake: Combine the sugar and espresso powder with ¼ cup water in a saucepan. Cook over medium heat, stirring constantly, 5 minutes. Add the chocolate and vanilla; stir until smooth. Remove from heat; let stand 10 minutes.

Beat the butter in a large bowl until light. Add the egg yolks, one at a time, beating well after each addition. Gradually stir in the chocolate mixture, the walnuts, and the breadcrumbs. Mix thoroughly. In a separate large bowl beat the egg whites with a pinch of salt until stiff. Fold into cake batter.

Pour the batter into the prepared pans. Place on the middle rack in the oven and bake until the top is firm to the touch, 25 to 30 minutes. Cool in the pans on a rack for 30 minutes. Remove from pans; continue to cool on a rack at least 2 hours.

To make the icing: Combine the chocolate and espresso powder with ⅓ cup water in a saucepan. Cook over low heat, stirring constantly, until smooth. Remove from heat; let stand until cool. Refrigerate until cold.

Beat the butter in a large bowl until light. Beat in the egg yolks, one at a time, beating well after each addition. Gradually stir in the cold chocolate mixture. Beat in the confectioner's sugar.

Spread the icing over the bottom layer, the sides, and the top of the cake. Press the ground walnuts evenly onto the sides of the cake. Keep in a cool place until ready to serve.

Pineapple Bavarois

6 egg yolks
½ cup granulated sugar
¾ teaspoon vanilla extract, divided
3 tablespoons cornstarch
1½ cups milk, scalded
1 small can crushed pineapple
1 small can pineapple chunks
3 tablespoons kirsch
1½ cups heavy or whipping cream
3 tablespoons confectioner's sugar
1 teaspoon finely slivered orange peel
SERVES 10 TO 12

Beat the egg yolks in a large bowl until light and lemony in color. Beat in the granulated sugar, ½ teaspoon of the vanilla, the cornstarch, and the scalded milk. Transfer to the top of a large double boiler and cook, stirring frequently, over boiling water until thick, about 10 minutes. Remove from heat; let stand to cool. Refrigerate until cold.

Drain the pineapple (both varieties) well in a sieve, gently pressing with the back of a spoon until thoroughly dry. Transfer to a bowl and sprinkle with kirsch. Chill 1 hour.

Drain the pineapple again; fold into the chilled custard.

Whip the cream with the confectioner's sugar until stiff. Beat

131

in the remaining ¼ teaspoon vanilla. Fold the whipped cream into the pineapple custard. Transfer to a serving bowl and sprinkle the top with slivered orange peel. Chill well before serving.

Triple-Nutted Strudel

¾ cup unblanched almonds
¾ cup unblanched hazelnuts (filberts)
1½ cups sugar
3 egg whites
1 teaspoon vanilla extract
4 frozen phyllo or strudel leaves, defrosted, chilled
¼ cup (½ stick) unsalted butter, melted (approximately)
2½ tablespoons fine-chopped walnuts
SERVES 8

Preheat the oven to 375 degrees. Place the almonds and hazelnuts in the container of a food processor fitted with the steel blade. Process until ground fine. Add the sugar; process 2 seconds. Add the egg whites and vanilla; process until mixture forms a paste, about 10 seconds. Set aside.

Place 2 phyllo leaves on a wax-paper-covered damp tea towel. The long side should be parallel to the edge of the work area. Brush the top layer with butter. Sprinkle with 1½ tablespoons of the walnuts. Add the remaining 2 strudel leaves. Brush the top layer with butter.

Using 2 butter knives, spread the nut paste over the bottom quarter of the pastry, leaving 1 inch around the edges. With the aid of the towel, fold the side edges toward the center just enough to cover the filling by ½ inch. Brush the edges with butter. Lightly press the edges down so they do not unfold. With the aid of the towel, roll up the dough away from you and onto a lightly buttered baking sheet. Brush the surface of the dough with butter and sprinkle with the remaining 1 tablespoon walnuts.

Bake the strudel until golden brown and crisp, about 25 minutes. Cool on a rack. Transfer to a serving platter. Serve at room temperature or slightly warm.

Pear-on-Pear Tart

1¼ cups all-purpose flour
⅛ teaspoon salt
Sugar
½ cup (1 stick) unsalted butter
1 egg yolk
2½ tablespoons ice water (approximately)
8 ripe Comice or Anjou pears (about 3 pounds)
1 teaspoon ground ginger
⅓ cup apricot preserves
SERVES 8 TO 10

Bert Greene

Preheat the oven to 425 degrees. To make the pastry: Combine the flour with the salt and 2 tablespoons of sugar in a large bowl. Cut in the butter with a knife. Blend with a pastry blender until the flour has the texture of coarse crumbs. Combine the egg yolk with the ice water and work into the flour mixture to form a soft dough. Add more water if necessary. Knead briefly and press the dough over the bottom and sides of a buttered 10-inch loose-bottomed quiche pan. Trim the edges. Line the pastry with aluminum foil and weight with rice or beans. Bake 10 minutes. Remove foil and rice or beans; bake until the pastry is golden, 5 to 10 minutes. Cool on a rack.

To make the caramel: Combine ⅓ cup sugar with 2 tablespoons water in a medium skillet. Heat to boiling and boil until the mixture turns a light caramel color. Carefully, but quickly, brush the caramel over the bottom and sides of the pastry shell.

To make the filling: Peel 6 of the pears, cut in half, and remove the cores. Cut each half into 4 slices. Place the pears in a large heavy skillet or saucepan. Combine ⅔ cup sugar, the ginger, and 1 cup water and pour over the pears. Heat to boiling; reduce the heat. Simmer, covered, until pears are soft but not mushy, 6 to 8 minutes, depending on the ripeness of the pears. Cool.

Drain the pears, reserving the liquid. Arrange the pears over the bottom of the pastry shell.

Peel the remaining pears, cut into quarters, and remove the

cores. Cut each quarter into thin slices. Arrange symmetrically over the cooked pears.

Combine the apricot preserves with 4 tablespoons of the pear liquid in a small saucepan. Heat to boiling; strain.

Brush the tart with half the apricot mixture. Bake 30 minutes. Remove from the oven and brush with the remaining apricot mixture. Serve slightly warm with whipped cream if desired.

Lace Curtain Cookies

1 egg
½ teaspoon vanilla extract
½ cup (1 stick) unsalted butter, melted
1 cup light brown sugar, packed
2 cups uncooked rolled oats
½ cup walnuts, chopped
MAKES ABOUT 2 DOZEN COOKIES

Preheat the oven to 375 degrees. Beat the egg with the vanilla in the medium bowl of an electric mixer. Slowly beat in the butter and the sugar. Beat in the rolled oats on low speed. Stir in the walnuts.

Lightly butter a foil-lined baking sheet. Drop the batter by generous teaspoonfuls onto the foil; place far apart. There should be only six cookies on each baking sheet. Pat the batter flat and bake until golden brown, about 8 minutes. Cool completely before peeling off the foil. Repeat procedure until all batter is used up.

Christmas Shortbread

1 cup (2 sticks) unsalted butter, softened
½ cup sugar
1 egg yolk
2 tablespoons heavy or whipping cream
1½ teaspoons vanilla extract
½ teaspoon grated orange peel

2½ cups all-purpose flour
½ cup rice flour
SERVES 12

Preheat the oven to 325 degrees. Beat the butter in a large bowl until light. Slowly beat in the sugar, egg yolk, cream, vanilla, and orange peel. Stir in both flours with a heavy wooden spoon. Work with your fingers until a soft dough is formed. Knead briefly and form into a ball.

Butter and flour a shortbread mold and press the dough evenly over the surface. Or, if you do not have a mold, butter and flour the underside of a 9-inch cake pan and press the dough evenly over the top, then invert the dough onto a cornmeal-sprinkled baking sheet, loosening it from the pan with a spatula if necessary.

Bake until the edges of the shortbread begin to brown, 40 to 50 minutes. If baking on a baking sheet, remove from the oven after the first 10 minutes and press lightly in the center with a decorative cutter or butter mold, then score the shortbread into 12 wedges around the pattern, using a pastry wheel or serrated knife. Continue to bake until edges begin to turn golden. Cool on a wire rack.

Marion Cunningham

CHRISTMAS TIME

Marion Cunningham represents California cuisine at its finest. For her elegant holiday celebration she blends the wonderfully fresh produce of her own state with traditional holiday foods. Cunningham draws on her broad background as the reviser of THE FANNIE FARMER COOKBOOK *and the author of* THE FANNIE FARMER BAKING BOOK *and* THE BREAKFAST BOOK.

IN MUCH THE SAME WAY that *The Nutcracker* and *A Christmas Carol* have become staples of the holiday season, I have been directing my own Christmas production for nearly fifty years.

With the beginning of December, I start making little gestures of preparation: a shopping list, a look through several catalogs, baking a few stollen loaves to be frozen. By December 15 our Christmas tree is in the living room, looking green, fresh, and pure. For a fleeting minute I always entertain the idea that I will defy tradition and leave the tree totally natural, but I never do. We fuss, trying to balance the lights on the tree, and by the time we get to hang ornaments, it's a breeze. We also get caught up in rediscovering the favorite old ornaments, and all the stories they represent. And when the tree is done, we always believe that it is the prettiest tree ever. Day by day, the holiday takes shape and form. We give a small dinner or two, a luncheon, and perhaps a dessert afternoon. These are the nicest indulgences, gathering friends that we see too seldom.

Finally, December 25 arrives, and the most important act of the play begins. We start the day with a Christmas breakfast of ruffled ham, butter-basted eggs, sticky buns, and fruit. The gift exchange is next. We carefully open one gift at a time. When the children were younger this more civilized approach was nigh im-

137

possible, but age and acquisition have tempered their sense of urgency. The children were seven and nine years old before we could watch each other open our gifts decorously, following the openings with traditional exclamations of approval.

After this stately unwrapping, we stuff the turkey, prepare the vegetables, and complete all the details so Christmas dinner can be served around 4:00 in the afternoon. We don't lunch, but I satisfy any hunger pangs with our Christmas box of See's chocolates.

When we gather at the table, Christmas dinner looks rich and sumptuous spread before us. The center of attraction is the turkey, which looks perfect, plump and golden, accompanied by a covered dish of fresh sage stuffing, a large bowl of mashed potatoes, a pitcher of dark, rich gravy, buttered string beans, hot angel biscuits, and pretty dishes holding cranberry relish, watermelon pickles, and olives. For dessert, there's a golden-brown pumpkin pie and warm persimmon pudding with whipped cream.

All too quickly, dinner is finished. The Christmas tree lights the room, we listen to Christmas music and visit while the dogs and cats sprawl out in a lulled sleep. Christmas Day is over.

Toasted Walnuts

Beware of nibbling too many of these nuts before dinner. They are seductive, but if you eat too many, you'll spoil what is to come.

2 cups walnut halves
2 tablespoons vegetable oil or peanut oil
1 teaspoon salt
1 teaspoon sugar
2 CUPS

In a bowl, toss the walnut halves with the oil until all are coated evenly. Spread them in a single layer on a baking sheet and toast in a 300-degree oven for about 1 hour.

Remove from oven and sprinkle with the salt and sugar. Toss with a fork to distribute the salt and sugar to all sides. Cool, then slide the nuts onto paper towels to absorb any remaining oil. Place in a serving dish.

Crab and Pink Grapefruit Salad

Marion Cunningham

Dungeness crab and grapefruit are among California's glories. Somehow these good ingredients make up for the state's lack of Christmas snow. We always serve this salad before the turkey dinner; it is clean and light, with a sweet and tangy taste.

2 heads butter or Boston lettuce, washed and dried
3 pink grapefruit, peeled and sectioned
1 pound cooked crab meat, picked over to remove bits of cartilage
1 recipe Grapefruit Dressing (see below)
SERVES 6

Separate the lettuce leaves, using only the choice ones. Arrange a bed of lettuce on six individual serving dishes. Evenly distribute the grapefruit sections and the crab meat over the lettuce, arranging it attractively. Drizzle about 1 tablespoon of the grapefruit dressing over each serving.

Grapefruit Dressing

2 teaspoons grated grapefruit rind
1 shallot, minced
1 tablespoon white wine vinegar
1 teaspoon balsamic vinegar
½ teaspoon salt
8 tablespoons olive oil
MAKES ABOUT ½ CUP

In a small bowl, combine the grapefruit rind, shallot, white wine vinegar, balsamic vinegar, and salt. Whisk in the olive oil slowly. Taste for acid and salt and add more if too bland. Stir to blend before using.

139

Sage Stuffing

Once in a while I've become adventurous and tried different stuffings for our Christmas turkey. One year it was oyster stuffing, another year it was chestnut stuffing. Although both these departures were delicious, we all agreed in the end that simple and traditional sage stuffing rounded out the turkey flavor and juices perfectly.

1 cup (2 sticks) butter, melted
3 cups chopped onions
3 cups minced celery
16 slices white bread, dried and broken
    into small pieces
6 tablespoons minced fresh sage, or 3
    tablespoons dried sage leaves
1 cup minced fresh parsley
2 teaspoons salt, or to taste
1 teaspoon freshly ground pepper, or to taste
1 to 2 cups turkey broth or giblet broth
ENOUGH FOR A 16-POUND TURKEY

Put 4 tablespoons of the melted butter in a skillet. Add the onions and celery and cook, stirring often, over a moderate heat until the vegetables are soft but not browned.

Place the dried bread, sage, parsley, and salt and pepper in a large container. Add the onion and celery mixture and the remaining melted butter and toss until well mixed (using your hands works best for mixing). Add the broth slowly, a little at a time, while tossing the mixture to moisten thoroughly. Take care to add only enough liquid to moisten or the stuffing will become sodden.

To test the stuffing in order to see if the seasonings are correct, melt a little butter in a small skillet. Add a rounded tablespoon of stuffing to the skillet and stir until lightly golden. If it needs a more lively flavor, add more sage, onions, and celery.

Celery Braised in Broth

It seems very strange that celery is overlooked as a cooked vegetable. It has a delicate, light taste that is ideal with turkey, chicken, and fish. We also love to have cooked celery chilled with a mustard dressing on a hot summer day.

3 bunches celery
4 tablespoons olive oil
1½ tablespoons red wine vinegar
2 cups chicken broth
Salt and pepper to taste
SERVES 6

Trim any discoloration from root bottoms of celery but allow the ribs to remain attached. Cut each bunch of celery in half lengthwise. Cut the tops off, leaving the bottom halves about 5 inches long. Reserve some of the celery leaves for garnish.

Place the celery in a single layer in a shallow casserole, cut side up. Drizzle the olive oil evenly over the celery.

Stir the red wine vinegar into the chicken broth. Pour the mixture over the celery. Sprinkle with salt and pepper to taste. Cover the dish with foil and bake at 350 degrees for 1¼ to 1½ hours.

Serve hot or cold. Sprinkle a few of the celery leaves on top as garnish.

Cranberry Relish

Pure and simple, home-cooked cranberry relish, with no other distracting flavors, is the best of all. Tart and sweet, it brings out the rich flavor of roast turkey.

12 ounces fresh cranberries (about 3 cups)
¾ to 1 cup sugar
ABOUT 2 CUPS

Place the cranberries and ¾ cup sugar in a frying pan. Cook over moderate heat, stirring often to avoid scorching, until the sugar has melted and the cranberries are cooked, about 6 minutes. Taste for sweetness and add the remaining ¼ cup of sugar if too tart, stirring in sugar until completely dissolved.

Remove from the heat and cool. Serve when needed.

Angel Biscuits

This is an old-fashioned recipe using three different leaveners—yeast, baking powder, and baking soda combined with buttermilk. In 1868, commercial yeast was available, but people had doubts about its stability; hence recipes often had the backup of at least two leaveners. This dough may be prepared a day in advance, and should rest in the refrigerator at least 8 hours before it is rolled, cut, and baked.

1 package active dry yeast
5 cups all-purpose flour
4 teaspoons baking powder
2 teaspoons salt
3 tablespoons sugar
*¾ cup shortening (preferably solid vegetable shortening), at
    room temperature*
1 teaspoon baking soda
2 cups buttermilk
ABOUT 4 DOZEN TWO-INCH BISCUITS

Sprinkle the yeast over ½ cup lukewarm water in a small bowl. Stir and let stand 5 minutes, or until creamy.

Combine the flour, baking powder, salt, and sugar in a large bowl and stir with a fork to mix. Add the shortening and cut into the flour mixture, using either your fingertips or a pastry cutter, until the mixture looks irregular and crumbly.

Add the baking soda to the buttermilk. Stir the buttermilk into the flour mixture. Add the yeast mixture. Mix well. Cover and refrigerate for about 8 hours.

Turn the dough out onto a lightly floured board. Knead a dozen times. Roll dough out to about ½ inch thickness. Cut the biscuits out with a 2-inch cutter and place them 1 inch apart on greased baking sheets. Loosely cover and let rise for 1 hour.

Bake in a preheated 400-degree oven for about 15 minutes, or until lightly browned. Remove from the oven. Serve warm. Freeze what you are not using right away.

Steamed Persimmon Pudding

There are persimmon puddings and there are persimmon puddings. For me, this one ends the search—it is the best. The color is dark, the texture moist, and the flavor full and spicy. The pudding can be made ahead and reheated; it can even be frozen.

> 1 cup puréed persimmons (about 3 persimmons with skins removed)
> 2 teaspoons baking soda
> ½ cup (1 stick) butter, at room temperature
> 1½ cups sugar
> 2 eggs
> 1 tablespoon lemon juice
> 1 tablespoon rum
> 1 cup all-purpose flour
> 1 teaspoon cinnamon
> ½ teaspoon salt
> 1 cup broken walnuts or pecans
> 1 cup raisins
> Lemon Sauce (see below) (optional)
> SERVES 8

Fill a kettle that is large enough to hold a 2-quart pudding mold with enough water to come halfway up the sides of the mold. Let the water come to a boil over medium heat while you are mixing the pudding batter. The mold must have a lid or be snugly covered with foil while steaming (a coffee can with a plastic lid works well). Also, there must be a rack or Mason jar ring under the mold on the bottom of the kettle to allow the water to circulate freely while the pudding is steaming. Grease the mold.

143

Put the persimmon purée in a small bowl and stir in the baking soda. Set aside while mixing the other ingredients (the persimmon mixture will become quite stiff).

Cream the butter and sugar. Add the eggs, lemon juice, and rum, and beat well. Add the flour, cinnamon, and salt, and stir to blend. Add the persimmon mixture. Beat until well mixed. Stir in the nuts and raisins.

Spoon the batter into the mold, cover tightly, and steam for 2 hours. Remove from the kettle and let rest for 5 minutes. Turn out onto a rack to cool completely, or cool just a little and serve warm. Serve with Lemon Sauce or unsweetened whipped cream.

Lemon Sauce

A good old-fashioned sauce for steamed puddings.

*½ cup sugar
1 tablespoon cornstarch
1 cup boiling water
2 tablespoons butter
4 tablespoons lemon juice
Grated rind of 1 lemon
Pinch of salt*
ABOUT 1 CUP

Mix the sugar and cornstarch together in a small saucepan. Add the boiling water and place over medium heat, stirring constantly. Boil 5 minutes. Remove from the heat and swirl in the butter, lemon juice and rind, and pinch of salt. Serve warm.

Felipe Rojas-Lombardi

CHRISTMAS

IN LIMA

From his writing it sounds as if Felipe Rojas-Lombardi has spent most of his life in the kitchen and enjoyed every moment of it. Rojas-Lombardi, the innovative chef-owner of the Ballroom restaurant in New York City, tells us how it all began, in a blaze of firecrackers and culinary glory.

I RAN THROUGH THE STREETS, trying to find my family, but it was almost impossible to see anything; the smoke-filled air clouded everything beyond three feet. The noise of repeated explosions was terrifying, but mixed with the smell of gunpowder was the irresistible odor of meat cooking over an open fire. People were shouting, and I could feel and hear unseen crowds rushing past me. Where was I? Was this a familiar neighborhood? Panic began to sweep over me and I wanted to cry. I shouted for my mother.

I was seven years old, and it was Christmas in my hometown of Lima, Peru.

Late in the afternoon was when it all started: the fireworks, singing and dancing in the streets, the shouting and laughing, and, most of all, the eating. In Lima, Christmas Day didn't begin the way it does in the United States, with the children coming into the room and seeing the tree all lit up, surrounded by presents. Almost none of us had trees in our houses, although there were always a few decorated trees in squares and parks and even some in the commercial buildings. No, Christmas began weeks before the actual day. Not so much the frantic Christmas shopping, the ads in the paper beginning in mid-October, or Christmas music on the radio. In Lima the preparation for Christmas centered

145

around food. Even before I learned to talk, I could tell it was a special time of year by the smells of cooking that filled every room of the house. And in the streets, too—those delicious chunks of marinated beef hearts, the *anticuchos*, threaded on rough-cut bamboo spears and quickly cooked over open-flame fires on every street corner. It was a romantic time. Young couples would sit, flirting and giggling while they ate their *anticuchos*, always followed by some *picarones*, delicate pufflike fried pastries that were dipped into a sexy fragrant syrup.

At home I knew Christmas was coming by the white corn. The white corn of the Andes is unlike any grown in North America. The kernels are large, as large as your thumb. My grandmother would first soak the dry corn for days. Then it was cooked, and finally peeled, which again seemed to take days. I remember my mother, grandmother, and sisters sitting in the kitchen, catching up on their gossip and, of course, peeling the corn. When it was cooked, ground, and kneaded into the *masa* (dough), it would form the base of the tamales, a great Christmas treat. What a smell! It almost drove me mad with hunger when they cooked the chunks of pork and *aji*—the hot peppers—with the *achiotes*, those wonderful spicy annato seeds. Then another smell, the roasting of the *platano* leaves, the banana leaves that would wrap all those wonderful ingredients to make the tamales. I think of Christmas in Peru as the national day of eating, much as Thanksgiving is in the United States.

Our kitchen seemed busy night and day. When did Grandmother sleep? Everything was so much work. The great miracle grain of the Andes—quinoa—had to be picked free of twigs and then washed several times. Recently introduced to North America, quinoa had for thousands of years kept the Indians of Peru alive and healthy because of its high protein value and the fact that it could be grown in high altitudes. It was a staple at any Peruvian table, and especially welcome at holidays.

Preparing the food took a great deal of time, but the Christmas feast was also a long-drawn-out affair. We could sit at the table for hours, eating, talking, eating, talking. And the talk was mostly about what we were eating. We'd talk about the dishes in front of us and the dishes that were about to come out of the kitchen.

We'd talk about where certain foods had been purchased and how they were prepared. If we were waiting for the goat—the *cabrito* —to come to the table, we'd talk not only about how it was going to be prepared this year, we'd talk about who had raised it! Talking about food was as much a part of the meal as consuming it.

For my grandfather it was not Christmas unless he had his *pichon*. I have never seen anyone eat pigeon or squab the way my grandfather did. I would watch with fascination as he consumed the birds in a methodical way, with a sense of perfection a surgeon would envy. Each bone was picked completely clean, and they had an almost polished look when he was finished. He would arrange them on his plate, again with a perfection that seemed almost architectural. His pigeon made him so happy. A great grin would spread over his face when he was finished, and he would nod to all of us at the table with a look we'd not see again until next Christmas, and his next pigeon.

Sometimes I would try to help out in the kitchen before Christmas, but it was the last place you'd want to be if you enjoyed peace. Mother and Grandmother were natural, if civilized, enemies in the kitchen. Each one's territorial imperative was strong, and to each the other was an intruder. Each staked a claim at opposite ends of the kitchen, not quite armed camps, with her own team of family helpers. At one end my grandmother would be preparing the *cabrito*, butterflied on a table, surrounded by vegetables, the beautiful yellow and blue potatoes of Peru, the *poros* (giant leeks), the *chayotes*, *platanos*, and perhaps a dozen or so other garden delights, a spectacular sight. At the other end my mother would be plucking the feathers off Grandfather's pigeons, or more likely rolling out the dough for the sweet biscuits that would accompany her legendary milk pudding for dessert. Then she'd cut little four-inch circles of the dough and place them on cookie sheets, every once in a while running back to the stove to check on the progress of the pudding. Of course, I'd offer to stir the pudding, but she was on to me and seldom let me do it, knowing my habit of ''tasting'' too much of that delicious stuff and fearing there wouldn't be enough for the dinner. She would put a little bit of pudding between two of the biscuits and sprinkle the top with powdered sugar. And it's interesting, all the years

Felipe Rojas-Lombardi

147

*Felipe Rojas-
Lombardi*

I've worked as a professional chef, I've never been able to duplicate my mother's recipe. It remains a perfect memory, but just that—a memory.

The Incas gave us more than quinoa to help celebrate the Christmas holiday. They gave *chicha de jora*, a wonderful but particularly lethal drink with a base of corn and raw sugar. Since it's fermented it could be likened to beer, but it also has the flavor of an aged cider. Actually, it has a flavor all its own. In the mountains, the Indians share it with their most valuable possessions, their sure-footed llamas, who love it so much that after a few sips they follow their owners around for more, sometimes staggering after a particularly jolly Indian party. Making *chicha* is relatively simple. The kernels of corn are dampened and placed between layers of moistened burlap to allow them to sprout. This takes about ten days, and then the sprouts (or *jora*) are sun-dried (or heated in a very low oven) for five to six hours, then mixed with raw sugar and water, put into an earthen jar, and left to ferment for a few weeks. Sometimes the jar is partially buried in the earth to maintain an even temperature throughout the fermentation. The result is a powerful and delicious drink. Yes, even as a little child I was allowed to share in some *chicha* on very special holidays, none being more special than Christmas.

My most memorable Christmas growing up in the shadow of the Andes was the time my grandmother decided that turkey would be her main centerpiece. A turkey, a *great* turkey, had to be ordered several months in advance. You might say it was grown to order. This particular Christmas, when the turkey arrived, feathers and all, it walked proudly into the house, letting everyone know it was there.

For two weeks Grandmother nursed and cared for that silly bird. She took care of it as she would her own child, giving it corn, chunks of red onion, and any grain left over from the kitchen. I remember that she even fed the bird walnuts, which I loved but wasn't allowed to eat until Christmas Day. She started with one, and each day she'd give him one more, leading up to fifteen the day before he was to visit the kitchen. By now the turkey was really stuffed and ready for his final triumph. Grandmother was very proud of the way she handled things. She wasn't going to let Mr. Turkey suffer. At the magic moment he never knew what hit him. Grandmother gave him a huge dose of *pisco*, one of Peru's great contributions to inebriation, and he just staggered around, dropped, and never got up again. I like to imagine that he was a very happy bird by the time he fulfilled his destiny.

My grandmother's nursing and fussing over the turkey might seem excessive, but to this day I've never tasted a better one, so tasty and tender, with an incredible flavor. In fact, the whole dinner that year was spectacular, and around four in the afternoon the fireworks began. Stuffed, feeling the effects of the *chicha de jora* (I had managed to sneak a bit too much of it), I rushed out of the house to join the fun. The family followed, but we seem to have separated. Smoke filled the air and clouded everything beyond three feet—and that's where we started.

Christmas is still my favorite holiday. But it's different now. My grandmother is no longer in the kitchen.

Felipe Rojas-Lombardi

Picarones

The simple doughnut form of the original *picarones* is very humble, but technically this is not a simple pastry to shape. Dropping this sticky and flavorful dough into the hot oil while shaping it into a circle and leaving a hole in the middle requires both skill and experience. At home, however, my mother always made ball-shaped *picarones*, which are easier. Just dip a spoon into the dough and, with the help of another spoon, scrape the dough into the hot oil. Fry until the balls puff up and become crisp, right in front of your eyes. The procedure is quite quick.

1 cup dark brown sugar, packed
1 cup plus 1 tablespoon granulated sugar
2 (4-inch) cinnamon sticks
1 dry red chili pepper, seeded
4 to 6 whole cloves

1 cup lukewarm milk
1 tablespoon active dry yeast
2 tablespoons cornstarch
1 cup Puréed Butternut Squash (see below) or sweet potatoes
2 cups all-purpose flour
⅛ teaspoon coarse salt
1½ quarts (6 cups) vegetable oil
MAKES 28

For the syrup, in a small saucepan combine the dark brown sugar, 1 cup granulated sugar, cinnamon, chili pepper, and cloves with 1 cup of water. Simmer over a low flame for 20 to 25 minutes, stirring occasionally, until the mixture thickens into a syrup. Set aside to cool.

In a small mixing bowl, combine the milk and yeast with 1 tablespoon of sugar and allow to sit for 5 to 10 minutes, or until creamy. Stir in the cornstarch and allow to sit a few minutes longer.

Place the puréed squash or sweet potatoes in a large bowl. Add the yeast-cornstarch mixture and blend thoroughly. Stir in the flour and salt and continue to stir vigorously to make a runny, soft, well-blended dough. Place the mixing bowl in a draft-free place, cover with a dampened cloth or plastic wrap, and let rise for about 2 hours, or until double in bulk. Deflate the dough with a wooden spoon. (At this point the dough should be soft and somewhat elastic.)

In a deep fryer or heavy saucepan large enough to hold the 6 cups of oil, heat the oil to 325 degrees. Dip out 1 tablespoon-ful of the dough and, with the help of another tablespoon, scrape the dough into the hot oil and fry until golden. As soon as they are cooked, remove the *picarones* from the oil with a slotted spoon and drain on paper towels.

To serve, arrange the *picarones* on a platter and pour the syrup over them.

Puréed Butternut Squash

1 butternut squash (about 3 pounds)
Olive oil

Preheat the oven to 400 degrees. Cut the squash in half lengthwise, scoop out the seeds, and rub the inside and outside with the olive oil. Place in a baking pan along with 1 cup water, cover with foil, and bake for 20 minutes. Remove the foil and bake for another 35 minutes, or until the squash is soft when pierced with a fork.

Remove the peel and press the flesh through a food mill or a fine sieve.

Anticuchos

Of course, the open flame is the real flavor when making *anticuchos*. *Anticuchos* must be made with beef hearts; however, the marinade can be used for other cuts of beef. When preparing *anticuchos*, it is important that the fat from the heart is trimmed off and the membranes and veins are removed. A good sharp knife is necessary to keep the surface of the meat even and smooth. In Peru the skewers are roughly cut from bamboo and soaked before using so they add a wonderful flavor to the finished *anticuchos*. Sharply pointed at one end, they are long enough to allow a substantial amount of room to use as handles for turning while the meat is searing in the open flame and then later so you are able to hold them. But you don't need a skewer to make marvelous *anticuchos*. A good frying pan will do. Just sear the chunks of meat quickly on both sides in a very hot broiler, placing the meat as close to the flame as possible.

151

Felipe Rojas-Lombardi

1 beef heart, about 4 pounds
3 large cloves garlic, peeled
1½ tablespoons coarse salt
⅛ teaspoon freshly ground black pepper
2 teaspoons ground cumin
3 dry red chili peppers, seeded
1 dry ancho pepper, seeded
¾ cup red wine vinegar
⅓ cup Achiote Oil (see below)
2 or 3 strips bacon (2 ounces)
8 bamboo skewers, about 8 to 10 inches long
SERVES 6 TO 8

Trim any fat from the heart and remove veins and membranes. Cut into 24 cubes. Place in a bowl and set aside.

With a mortar and pestle pound the garlic and salt to a paste. Add the pepper and cumin and continue pounding. Set aside.

Place the seeded red chili and ancho peppers in a bowl, add the vinegar, and let soak for about 10 minutes, or until the peppers are soft.

Place the softened peppers with the vinegar in a blender and purée until liquid. Add this mixture to the garlic paste and stir thoroughly. Allow to sit for 10 minutes. Add the Achiote Oil and pour the mixture over the cubed meat, stirring to coat all the pieces. Let marinate, covered, at room temperature for 6 to 8 hours, or in the refrigerator overnight.

Thread 3 pieces of the marinated cubes of beef heart on each of the 8 skewers, reserving the marinade, and set aside.

There are two ways of cooking the beef hearts. Both methods require quick searing.

1. If barbecuing or broiling, heat ¼ cup of the reserved marinade with 2 or 3 strips of the bacon in a saucepan over medium heat until all the liquid has evaporated and only the Achiote Oil and the fat from the bacon remain. Discard the bacon or reserve for another use. Brush the skewered meat cubes with the flavored oil from the saucepan and barbecue them over a light layer of coals in a charcoal broiler (the coals should be burned until white ash has appeared on the surface). Or broil them in a preheated

broiler (about 3 inches from the heat source) for 1 or 2 minutes on one side. Brush the beef cubes again with the flavored oil, turn the skewers, and broil for another minute or two.

2. If using a 12-inch cast-iron skillet, heat ¼ cup of the reserved marinade, add the bacon, and cook until the bacon is golden. Discard the bacon or reserve for another use. Place the skewered meat cubes in the pan and cook over high heat, while turning them, until the meat is seared on the outside but remains medium rare on the inside. This will take about 5 minutes.

Serve the *anticuchos* hot.

Achiote Oil

1 cup vegetable or olive oil
½ cup annato seeds
1 dried serrano pepper, crumbled
1 bay leaf
MAKES 1 CUP

Place the oil, annato seeds, serrano pepper, and bay leaf in a saucepan. Allow to sit at room temperature, stirring now and then, for 30 minutes. Place the saucepan over low heat, while stirring, and bring gently to a boil. Remove from heat and cool thoroughly. Strain through a fine sieve or several layers of cheesecloth. Discard the seeds, bay leaf, and pepper. The oil will have become a bright red-orange and can be kept refrigerated, tightly covered, for up to 1 year.

Cabrito

A *cabrito* is a young goat. It has always been a holiday food for me. It is very hard to describe the delicious taste of the *cabrito*. Of course, if a *cabrito* is not available, a lamb will do. Just choose the smallest one available.

6 cloves garlic, peeled

2 tablespoons coarse salt

8 ounces fresh spearmint leaves, or 2 tablespoons dried

2 tablespoons ground cumin

½ teaspoon ground cloves

½ teaspoon ground white pepper

¼ cup red wine vinegar

¼ cup Achiote Oil (see above)

¼ cup olive oil

1 kid, about 15 pounds (reserve head, heart, neck, and innards, except liver, for Cabrito Stock, see below)

1 bouquet garni (fresh mint, thyme, and parsley)

2 tablespoons semisweet sherry (Amontillado, if possible)

SERVES ABOUT 10

With a mortar and pestle pound the garlic and salt to a paste. Add the mint, cumin, cloves, and white pepper and continue pounding. Dissolve the paste with the vinegar, and then stir in the Achiote Oil and the olive oil. Set aside.

Have the butcher prepare the kid by removing the head and neck and butterflying it (splitting it lengthwise down the middle and opening flat). Wipe the meat clean with a damp cloth and rub it inside and outside with the garlic paste. Allow to marinate at room temperature for 8 hours, or in the refrigerator overnight.

While the kid is marinating, make the stock according to the directions below. Chill and set aside until needed.

If the meat has been refrigerated, allow it to sit at room temperature for at least an hour before roasting. Preheat the oven to 475 degrees.

Place the goat on a rack in a roasting pan and roast for 45 minutes to 1 hour. The goat should be an even golden color.

Remove from the oven, transfer to a platter, and allow to sit in a warm place while you make the sauce. Deglaze the roasting pan with the prepared stock, stirring in the pan juices. Strain through a fine sieve into a clean saucepan and add a bouquet garni of fresh mint, thyme, and parsley. Bring to a boil, lower the heat, and simmer until the liquid is reduced to about half its volume. Discard the bouquet garni. Add the sherry and correct seasoning with extra salt to taste.

Cabrito Stock

1 leek, cut in half and cleaned thoroughly to remove sand
5 stalks celery, each cut into 3 pieces
1 carrot, scraped and sliced
1 whole head garlic with skins, sliced horizontally in half
1 large unpeeled onion, quartered
2 fresh jalapeño or serrano peppers, seeded and sliced
1 bay leaf
2 whole cloves
1 teaspoon dried thyme
½ teaspoon dried oregano
1 kid's head, neck, heart, and other innards (no liver)
3 tablespoons all-purpose flour

Place all the vegetables, herbs, and spices in a large pan or on a baking sheet. Arrange the head and heart on top, sprinkle with the flour, and roast in a preheated 400-degree oven for about 30 minutes or until brown. Remove from the oven, put all the ingredients into a large stockpot, add 8 quarts of cold water, and bring to the boil. Lower the heat and simmer, uncovered, for 3 to 3½ hours, or until the liquid is reduced to about 3 cups. Strain and degrease the stock.

Quinoa

I like quinoa so much that I am including two recipes so you can see the versatility of this grain. Cooked and without any preparations, it can be kept in the refrigerator for a long time and makes a good quick meal. I use it in stews and ragoûts, as a salad, as a dish for lunch, as an accompaniment for a sumptuous dinner, or even as a major ingredient for desserts. Quinoa is properly cooked in plain water with no salt or any other flavorings. If you have

Felipe Rojas-Lombardi

cooked quinoa on hand, you can add it to almost anything you cook. It's wonderful and adds taste and texture to most dishes. Quinoa can be found in many specialty food shops and health-food stores.

Quinoa en Salpicon

¼ cup fresh lime juice
¼ teaspoon ground white pepper
1 fresh jalapeño pepper, seeded and minced
1 teaspoon coarse salt
½ cup olive oil

3 cups raw quinoa (15 to 16 ounces)

1 cup cucumber, peeled, seeded, and diced
1 cup tomato, seeded and diced
½ cup scallions, white only, sliced thin
⅓ cup chopped Italian parsley
⅓ cup chopped fresh mint
SERVES 6 TO 8

Make a vinaigrette by whisking together the lime juice, white pepper, jalapeño pepper, and salt, then gradually adding the olive oil. Set aside.

Place the quinoa in a fine sieve and wash under running water, rubbing the quinoa with your hands, for a few minutes. Drain. In a pot large enough to hold the ingredients comfortably, combine 2 quarts of water and the cleaned and drained quinoa. Bring to the boil, lower the heat, and simmer, uncovered, for about 10 minutes, or until the quinoa is barely tender. Do not overcook. Remove from the heat and pour through a strainer. Drain thoroughly, and let cool. (Do not rinse.)

Place the cooled quinoa in a serving bowl with the cucumber, tomato, scallions, parsley, and mint and toss. Add the reserved vinaigrette and toss again. Correct seasoning with extra salt and white pepper to taste, and serve.

156

Croquetas de Quinoa

¾ cup raw quinoa
¼ cup all-purpose flour
3 tablespoons grated Parmesan cheese
1½ teaspoons coarse salt
⅛ teaspoon white pepper
½ cup fine-chopped scallions (4 to 5 medium-sized stalks, white
    part only)
3 tablespoons chopped Italian parsley
1 egg
1 egg yolk
¾ cup vegetable oil

Lemon wedges for garnish
MAKES 18 TO 20 CROQUETTES

Place the quinoa in a fine sieve and wash under running water, rubbing with your hands, for a minute or so. Drain. Place the quinoa in a 2- or 2½-quart pot and cover with 4 cups water. Bring to the boil, lower heat; simmer, uncovered, for about 10 minutes, or until just tender. Drain the quinoa thoroughly (do not rinse), then set aside.

In a bowl, using your hand or a spoon, combine the cooked quinoa, flour, Parmesan, salt, and pepper. Fold in the scallions, parsley, egg, and egg yolk until all ingredients are thoroughly mixed. The mixture should have the consistency of a soft dough.

Heat the oil in a heavy skillet until medium hot and, with the help of a soup spoon, form the mixture into egg shapes. Drop them gently into the hot oil and let cook until golden on all sides. Remove the croquettes from the oil and drain them on paper towels.

Serve the croquettes warm, garnished with lemon wedges.

Pichon

Squab (pigeon less than 4 weeks old) is a red-meat bird, like wild duck. It is lean and should be cooked like beef, as rare as possible in the center. When roasting or broiling, try to sear the bird as quickly as possible with strong heat for a short time to color the skin and trap the juices and flavor of this luscious creature.

To broil the squab, butterfly the bird and flatten it as much as possible for even cooking. Place it under a hot broiler, about 6 inches away from the heat source, and broil it, skin side up, for about 5 to 6 minutes. Then turn the squab and finish broiling for another 6 to 7 minutes.

> 3 cloves garlic
> 1 tablespoon coarse salt
> ⅛ teaspoon cayenne pepper
> 2 teaspoons ground coriander seeds
> 1 teaspoon ground cumin seeds
> 2 tablespoons aguardiente, pisco, or light rum
> ⅓ cup olive oil
> 6 to 8 squabs
> SERVES 6 TO 8

With a mortar and pestle pound the garlic and the salt to a paste. Add the cayenne, coriander, and cumin and continue pounding. Add the aguardiente, pisco, or rum; let sit for 15 minutes to dissolve the paste. Blend in the olive oil and set aside.

Prepare the squabs by wiping them clean with a damp cloth outside and inside. Rub the outside and inside of each bird with the garlic paste and allow to marinate at room temperature for about 4 hours, or in the refrigerator overnight.

Place the birds on a rack, breast side up, in a shallow roasting pan and bake them in a preheated 475-degree oven for about 20 minutes, or until the birds are golden on the outside but medium rare inside. Remove from the oven, transfer to a platter, and serve.

Tamales

In South America banana leaves are not the only wrappings used for tamales; dried or fresh corn husks are used to wrap not only savory tamales but sweet ones, too.

A short variation of *Tamales Peruanos* is *Tamal de Fuente*, a gigantic tamale invented by my mother, much to the disgrace of my grandmother. A 10-by-10-inch baking dish is lined with "smoked" banana leaves and then filled with a delicious mixture of ground hominy, chicken or pork, olives, jalapeño peppers, and peanuts. The dish is covered with the overlapping leaves and then baked in a bain-marie in the oven.

*Felipe Rojas-
Lombardi*

Tamales Peruanos

1 pound boneless pork shoulder
3 cloves garlic, peeled
1 tablespoon coarse salt
2 teaspoons ground cumin
¼ teaspoon ground white pepper
¼ teaspoon ground cloves
2 tablespoons pisco or light rum

2 dried mirasol peppers, seeded
6 cups Spicy Chicken Stock (see below)
¼ cup Achiote Oil (see page 153)
4 thin slices bacon
1 large onion, chopped fine (1½ cups)
1 bay leaf
3 (16-ounce) cans whole hominy, drained

12 banana leaf pieces, each measuring about 12 by 13 inches
    (2 1-pound packages of banana leaves)
1 hard-boiled egg, sliced
6 black olives, pitted
1 hot pepper (mirasol, jalapeño, or serrano), seeded and cut in
    6 slices
1 large roasted pimiento, cut into 6 strips
8 or 20 roasted peanuts, shelled
MAKES 6 TAMALES

Cut the meat into 6 cubes.

With a mortar and pestle pound the garlic and salt to a paste. Add the cumin, pepper, and cloves and continue pounding. Add

159

the pisco and stir to dissolve the mixture thoroughly. Pour the marinade over the cubed pork pieces and mix. Allow to marinate for a few hours at room temperature, or overnight in the refrigerator.

Soak the dried mirasol peppers in 2 cups of the chicken stock for about 30 minutes, or until the peppers are soft. Purée them in a blender until the peppers are liquid. Set aside.

In a skillet, heat the Achiote Oil, bacon, and pork pieces and any leftover marinating juices. Cook over medium heat for 10 to 15 minutes, or until golden on all sides. Add onion and bay leaf and continue cooking until the onion is totally translucent.

Add the puréed pepper mixture along with the remaining 4 cups of chicken stock to the sautéed pork and onion. Bring to the boil, lower the heat, and simmer, uncovered, until all the liquid has evaporated and the pork is tender, about 1 hour and 15 minutes. Drain all the fat from the pan and set aside. Remove the pork and onion mixture and set aside. Press the extra juices from the bacon into the fat. Discard the bacon and bay leaf. You should have about ⅓ cup of the flavorful red-orange oil.

Purée the hominy in a food processor or meat grinder. Place it in a bowl and add the ⅓ cup of flavored oil. Knead this mixture into a dough until smooth. Set aside.

To prepare the banana leaves, gently wipe them along the grain with a damp cloth. Pass the leaves rapidly over an open flame to soften them and to bring out their flavor. Place two banana leaves (double wrapping) lengthwise on the table in front of you.

Divide the dough into 6 equal portions. Take one of the portions and divide it in half. Place one half in the center of the leaves and flatten it into a 4-by-3-inch rectangle. Arrange on top of the rectangle: 1 chunk of pork with some of the onion and seasoning, 1 slice of hard-boiled egg, 1 olive, 1 slice hot pepper, a few pimiento slices, and a few peanuts. Cover the filling with the other half of the dough, pressing gently to seal the edges. Repeat this process until all 6 tamales are assembled.

Using the banana leaves as wrapping paper, fold one side of the leaves over the dough to cover it completely, then fold the opposite side of the leaves over the already-covered dough. Then fold the remaining ends of the banana leaves toward the center of the tamale to form a neat, compact package. Stretch out a long piece of string, place the tamale in the center, lengthwise, over the string and bring the string toward the middle of the tamale; twist, and wrap the string around the middle of the tamale. Tie in the center as you would a package. Repeat this process until all the tamales are assembled.

Place the tamales in a steamer basket and steam, tightly covered, for about 1 hour. Cut and discard the strings, and serve at once in the banana leaves, opened.

Spicy Chicken Stock

4½ pounds chicken backs, wings, necks, gizzards, and feet
2 stalks celery, including leaves, cleaned and chopped
2 medium carrots, chopped (1½ cups)
2 unpeeled medium onions, cut in half
3 unpeeled garlic cloves
1-inch piece fresh ginger, sliced
6 to 8 sprigs fresh thyme or ½ teaspoon dried
6 to 8 sprigs fresh parsley
1 or 2 fresh hot peppers (jalapeño or serrano) or dried red chili peppers
2 or 3 whole cloves
2 teaspoons coarse salt
MAKES ABOUT 2½ QUARTS

Rinse the chicken parts, pulling off obvious clumps of fat. Put into a 6- to 8-quart stockpot with the remaining ingredients and cover with a generous amount of cold water (about 5 quarts).

Bring to the boil, continuously skimming off the scum that rises to the top. Lower the heat and simmer, uncovered, for 2 to 3 hours, until reduced by half. If you keep the stock at a gentle simmer, never letting it boil hard, it will be quite clear.

When it is done, let it cool. Strain and skim off any fat that rises to the surface. Or you can pour the stock into a large pot, refrigerate overnight, and then lift off the hardened fat with a spoon.

NOTE: To make the *Tamal de Fuente*, use four to six 15-inch smoked banana leaves. Line a 10-by-10-inch baking dish, overlapping them in the center. Cover the dish with almost half the leaves reaching over the rim of the pie dish. Spread half the dough, then the filling, then the remaining dough over the leaves resting in the dish. Fold the overhanging leaves over the dough. Place a sheet of waxed paper and a sheet of aluminum foil over the dish and bake in a bain-marie in a preheated 400-degree oven for 1 hour.

Remove the dish from the oven and the bain-marie, open the leaves, and serve at once.

Alfajores

These delicate little dessert sandwiches made of egg-enriched sweet biscuits are filled with milk pudding and dusted with confectioner's sugar.

Although endless time goes into making milk pudding, evaporating the liquid, it is worth it when you end up with this wonderful and deliciously textured sweet.

There is no reason that the pudding cannot be made in advance; it keeps well in the refrigerator for 10 days. (If there is anything left over, spoon a bit on some toast, use a little bit as a garnish, or sneak a spoonful for a quick snack.)

The pastry, which is delicious by itself, should be made fresh the day you plan to serve this dessert. It is quite simple.

Alfajores Pastries

3¼ cups all-purpose flour
½ teaspoon baking powder
5 tablespoons (2½ ounces) lard
20 egg yolks
3 tablespoons pisco or light rum

5 (14-ounce) cans (8½ cups) sweetened condensed milk, or 2 quarts fresh milk
1 (4-inch) stick cinnamon

¼ cup confectioner's sugar for garnish
MAKES 8 TO 10 FOUR-INCH PASTRIES

Sift 3 cups of the flour with the baking powder into a bowl and set aside.

Melt the lard in a small saucepan.

In a separate bowl lightly beat the egg yolks, while slowly adding the melted lard and the pisco or rum. Add all of the sifted flour and baking powder and mix well until the dough is very smooth.

Roll out the dough on a floured pastry board to a thickness of ⅛ inch. Cut with a cookie cutter into 4-inch circles. Place the circles on a parchment-covered baking sheet, prick them all over with a fork, and bake them in a preheated 375-degree oven for 15 to 20 minutes, or until barely golden. Remove from oven and place pastries on rack to cool.

In an enameled saucepan heat the condensed milk; add the cinnamon stick and bring to the boil while stirring. Let simmer over very, very low heat for 2½ hours, stirring with a wooden spoon every 10 to 15 minutes. If the milk sticks and has slightly burned the bottom of the saucepan during the simmering process, do not stir, but pour the milk into a clean enameled saucepan and continue simmering with the cinnamon stick. The pudding is done when the milk coats the back of a wooden spoon and has a pudding-like consistency. Remove from heat, discard the cinnamon stick, and beat for a few minutes with a wooden spoon until smooth and light in color.

To assemble the *alfajores*, place 2 tablespoons of the cooled milk pudding in the center of the flat side of the pastry round and put another pastry, flat side down, on top, sandwich-fashion. Lightly sprinkle with confectioner's sugar and serve.

Felipe Rojas-Lombardi

Fresh Milk Pudding

2 quarts (8 cups) fresh whole milk
2 cups granulated sugar
1 (4-inch) stick cinnamon

In an enameled saucepan heat the milk with the sugar and the cinnamon stick while stirring. Allow to simmer over very low heat for 4½ hours, stirring every 5 minutes for the first 2½ hours and continuously for the remaining time. Continue to cook until the milk coats the back of a wooden spoon and has a pudding-like consistency. Remove from heat, discard the cinnamon stick, and beat for a few minutes with a wooden spoon until the pudding is smooth and light in color.

Chicha de Jora

Most often our drinks in South America are rum, aguardiente, or something more refined, pisco. But what excites me most is the *chicha*, the unique drink of the Andes. *Chicha* is as old as the Incas. *Jora*, as *chicha*, is the name in Quechua, the language of the Incas, for beer and dried corn sprouts, respectively, that not only carry the taste but also add thickness and sugar to produce this remarkable drink.

Jora is very simple to make at home. However, in Spanish-American markets you can buy it in packages already prepared. All you have to do is open the package and follow the instructions to make the *chicha*.

> *1 pound (4 full cups) Maiz de Jora, purchased or homemade (see below)*
> *2 cakes (15 ounces) chancaca, or 1 cup white sugar and 2 cups packed brown sugar (see Note, page 166), plus additional for sweetening*
> *8 whole cloves*
> *1 dried hot chili pepper*

1 fresh stalk (about 36 inches) sugarcane (1½ pounds), cut into
*   pieces and crushed*
1 lemon, sliced, for garnish
MAKES 4 QUARTS

Felipe Rojas-Lombardi

In a stainless-steel stockpot large enough to hold 2½ gallons of liquid, combine the *jora, chancaca* or sugars, cloves, pepper, and crushed sugarcane with 8 quarts of cold water. Allow to soak for 1 hour. Place over high heat and bring to a boil, stirring now and then with a wooden spoon and scraping the bottom of the pot to prevent sticking and burning. When the mixture comes to a full boil, lower the heat and gently simmer, covered, for 4½ hours, stirring now and then.

Remove from heat and allow to rest for about 2 hours undisturbed. Pour through a strainer. Press liquid from the sugar cane and discard the pulp. Strain the mixture again through a double layer of cheesecloth into a ceramic, porcelain, or glass container and store in a dark, cool place, covered tightly with cheesecloth or a kitchen towel. Allow to sit from 3 to 8 days, depending on how strong and how thick you want the *chicha* to be. The longer the *chicha* sits, the higher the alcohol content and the thicker it will get.

To serve, add the additional sugar to taste, chill thoroughly, and garnish with lemon slices.

MAIZ DE JORA

Soak 2 pounds of yellow corn kernels overnight in cold water. Drain.

Line the bottom of a baking tray with a moist piece of burlap or a double layer of cheesecloth. Spread the soaked kernels evenly over the cloth and cover the entire surface of the baking tray with another piece of moist burlap or cheesecloth. Place in a dark, cool spot.

Keep cloth moist, but not wet, at all times until the corn has sprouted. This will take about 8 to 10 days. Remove all the sprouted corn, which at this point is called *jora*, to a baking tray and dry it in the sun for a full day.

If the *jora* is to be stored for future use, make sure that it is

165

thoroughly dry. If one day in the sun is not sufficient, retrieve the baking tray, keep it indoors overnight, and expose it to the sun the next day. Repeat this operation until the *jora* is dry. Store in an airtight container in a dark, cool place.

NOTE: *Chancaca* is a Peruvian term that refers to raw cane sugar, unrefined and unbleached. Dark, with a pronounced flavor, it is hard and shaped like a coffee cup. Each cake weighs about 7½ ounces. You will need 2 cakes for this recipe. You can substitute a mixture of 2 cups of brown sugar and 1 cup of white sugar.

Jenifer Lang

CHRISTMAS WITH
SAUERKRAUT

Her Catholic-Jewish Irish–East European background has given Jenifer Lang a broad outlook, broad enough for the staple dish of her Christmas dinner to be a family-developed sauerkraut with giblet gravy. Lang, American editor of the newly revised LAROUSSE GASTRONOMIQUE, *writes extensively on food.*

HAVING A QUIRKY FAMILY CAN BE TRYING; one thing you can say—it's never dull. Mine was full of drama and intrigue, laced with a certain schizophrenia.

Take my paternal grandparents, for instance: my grandmother was an Orthodox Jew and my grandfather a superstitious Irish Catholic. This lifelong love affair between two strong-willed people produced profound cultural and religious influences in my childhood. Usually, I tended to identify with the grandparent I had spoken to last, and the end result is that today I feel both Catholic and Jewish to the same degree, especially when it comes to the kitchen.

Because my parents were in their teens when they married, my five siblings and I spent much of our growing-up time in the company of Mimi and Boppa, as we called our grandparents. Whenever we moved—and heaven knows, we moved a lot, to Florida, Pennsylvania, California, Indiana—they followed along and set up house just next door to us. Maybe my grandparents wanted to stay close because they saw a chance to inculcate into another generation their separate beliefs.

Whatever the reason, we accepted these two wildly different ways of thinking quite comfortably. We dutifully went to the local Catholic church every Sunday with Boppa, learning the Baltimore

167

catechism and the Latin Mass (and invariably behaving so disgracefully during the service that the priest regularly ended his sermon with ". . . and the Lonergan children must come to see me in the rectory directly after Mass!").

I was taken to the Holy Land by my grandfather at the age of eight to see the real-life Stations of the Cross, and as a neat balancing act my older brother learned from my grandmother to light candles every Friday night, as her family had done from time immemorial. We all learned a great deal of Yiddish, which was my grandmother's first language; little did I know that it would come in quite handy when I moved to New York.

One of the side benefits of my grandparentage was that we all got to celebrate twice as many holidays as anyone else, all of those on the Jewish calendar and all of those on the Christian calendar, clearly the dream of every child.

Christmas was the highlight of the year for all of us; it was not only one of the most worshipful days of the Catholic year but it was also full of the kind of secular revelry that appealed to the immigrant entrepreneur in Mimi and Boppa. So all the kids in my generation had more presents under the tree than we could open in five hours at breakneck speed.

Included in the festivities was a massive Christmas dinner that was Norman Rockwellian in its American correctness—turkey, of course, with a bread stuffing; mashed potatoes; sweet potatoes with a toothachingly sweet marshmallow topping; Day-Glo–green spiced pears and red pickled crabapples; a relish tray with radishes, scallions, carrots, celery sticks, and black pitted olives; soft Parker House rolls; and two kinds of pie: mincemeat and pumpkin (we kids never went *near* the mincemeat but devoured the pumpkin with loads of freshly whipped cream).

The one oddity in this feast was a testament to the fact that my grandparents had come to détente in the culinary sphere of their lives. Served at dinner right alongside everything else, in an ornate sterling-silver Victorian vegetable dish, was a somewhat unusual family specialty: sauerkraut with giblet gravy. It never seemed unusual to me, of course. In fact, it was always my favorite part of the dinner.

The sauerkraut was put up every fall, first by Mimi's mother (called Nanna by everyone, she never learned to speak English), then by Mimi herself; it was made from fresh cabbage and pickled for weeks in stoneware crocks in the basement of my grandparents' house. Mimi and her family had come to America via Ellis Island around the turn of this century from a part of Eastern Europe that is now in the Soviet Union; for her people, sauerkraut was as much a staple as potatoes were to the Irish. The way Mimi made sauerkraut, from scratch, it bore little resemblance to the salty, sour, canned or packaged supermarket version; it was truly a vegetable, and it spoiled me for sauerkraut for life.

For everyday meals, Mimi cooked her sauerkraut with beef ribs, which we all loved. At Christmas, she made giblet gravy just as Boppa remembered it from his childhood. Unfortunately, she never had the chance to learn it directly from Boppa's mother, as my great-grandmother never spoke to her son after he married a "heathen"—her loss, as she never got to taste Mimi's sauerkraut or her mellow gefilte fish, for that matter.

I don't know whether the giblet gravy came from Ireland or from Broken Bow, Nebraska, where my grandfather's family settled, as it's a traditional gravy for poultry in both the British Isles and in Midwestern America, but it's a fine way to moisten the innocent components of a holiday dinner. No one in my family can tell me how or when someone first decided to put the giblet gravy on top of the sauerkraut as well as the mashed potatoes, but as with the person who was brave enough to try the first oyster, his or her descendants are forever grateful for the original audacity.

The sauerkraut gives a teasingly piquant touch to an otherwise somewhat bland and good-natured series of traditional holiday dishes. If the turkey is wild, as it should be, then the sauerkraut is an essential counterpoint to the slightly gamy taste of the bird.

All of Mimi and Boppa's many descendants serve sauerkraut with giblet gravy as part of our Christmas dinners. Those who marry into our family think this is a little odd at first, but invariably they are converted to the custom.

Our spouses hear many stories about the larger-than-life patriarch and matriarch of the Lonergan clan, and I'm sure most of them are sick of the anecdotes, which tend to be told again and again. No doubt it's easier to take the sauerkraut with giblet gravy, which lives on from year to year on all of our Christmas tables, deliciously confirming Mimi's and Boppa's idiosyncratic personalities and proving that romance and love of good food can overcome seemingly improbable marriages.

Mimi's Homemade Sauerkraut

10 pounds firm white cabbage
6 tablespoons kosher salt
MAKES ABOUT 3½ QUARTS

Remove the tough outer leaves from the heads of cabbage; cut the heads into quarters and remove the cores. Using a sharp knife or a food processor, slice the cabbage as thin as possible.

Using your hands, mix the sliced cabbage thoroughly with the salt. If it's easier, mix half the cabbage with half the salt, repeat with the second half of cabbage and salt, and then mix the two batches together. Allow the salted cabbage to rest for about 15 minutes so the wilting process can begin.

Pack the salted cabbage firmly and evenly into a large clean ceramic crock or glass jar, large enough to hold all the cabbage. (You can often find large glazed jars in flea markets.) Using your hands, press down firmly on the cabbage until the juice rises and covers the surface of the cabbage.

Weigh down the sauerkraut. Mimi weighed down hers with a dinner plate and some tin cans, but I use a more modern method: Half-fill a sturdy plastic bag with water and close the bag tightly. (If you don't think the plastic bag is strong enough, put one plastic bag inside another.) Place the bag on top of the cabbage so that the entire surface of the cabbage is protected from the air. The weight on the cabbage also helps bring out its juices. Add enough water to the bag so that the brine exuding from the cabbage just covers the surface.

Allow the cabbage to ferment. Cabbage ferments best at a temperature of 68 to 72 degrees; therefore, it should not be kept in a refrigerator but in a cool cellar, pantry, or back porch (depending on the season). At that temperature, the fermentation should be completed in 5 to 6 weeks. Taste it after about 5 weeks, and if it is too crisp, let it ferment for another few days.

If you're not using all of it right after it has finished fermenting, put up the remaining sauerkraut and process in a water bath. (See any basic cookbook for canning instructions.)

Jenifer's Sauerkraut Cooked with Apples

3 slices bacon, diced
¾ cup chopped onion
*4 cups drained sauerkraut (about 2 pounds undrained), either
    made from scratch or packaged*
1¼ cups chopped apple (cut into ½-inch pieces)
1½ cups Champagne or white wine
10 juniper berries, put into a tea ball or a piece of cheesecloth
MAKES ABOUT 8 SERVINGS

In a heavy non-aluminum saucepan, place diced bacon and onion and sauté over medium heat, stirring frequently, for about 15 minutes, until the onion is translucent.

Add the remaining ingredients and partially cover the saucepan. Adjust the heat so that the liquid simmers and cook for 40 minutes, stirring occasionally. Discard the juniper berries and serve sauerkraut in a covered vegetable dish.

Boppa's Giblet Gravy

STOCK

1 whole medium-sized unpeeled onion
1 pound chicken or turkey giblets (see Note), rinsed and drained
2 cups chopped celery
2 cups chopped carrots
1 cup chopped onion (with skin)
4 cups broth
1 teaspoon whole black peppercorns
5 whole cloves
1 bay leaf

GRAVY

½ cup fat poured from the roasting pan after turkey has roasted,
    or ½ cup (1 stick) unsalted butter
½ cup all-purpose flour
4 cups stock
Salt and freshly ground pepper
Giblets reserved from the stock

MAKES ABOUT 8 SERVINGS

To make stock: Heat a dry heavy skillet over high heat for 3 minutes. Cut the whole onion in half and place, cut surfaces down, in the hot skillet. Heat the onion pieces until the cut surfaces are completely blackened, about 3 to 5 minutes. Place charred onions in a heavy large stockpot. Add the remaining stock ingredients to the stockpot along with 4 cups of water; bring to a boil, stir, and lower heat so that the stock simmers slowly. Cook, uncovered, for 2 hours, stirring once or twice. Pour the stock through a strainer; reserve liquid. When solid ingredients are cool enough to handle, remove the giblets and reserve. Discard remaining vegetables and seasonings.

To make gravy: In a heavy medium saucepan, heat ½ cup fat from the roasting pan (or butter) over medium heat and stir in the flour. Cook, stirring constantly, until the mixture has turned a golden brown color, about 5 minutes. Pour in the hot stock and whisk while bringing to a boil. Add salt and freshly ground pepper to taste, reduce heat to a slow simmer, and cook gravy uncovered, stirring occasionally, for 15 minutes. In a food processor or by hand, chop giblets into very small pieces, about ⅛- to ¼-inch dice. Add to the gravy and heat for 2 more minutes. Serve in a gravy boat at the table, to be used on turkey, mashed potatoes, and especially on the sauerkraut.

NOTE: You can collect poultry giblets—gizzards and hearts, but no livers—in the freezer and defrost them for this recipe, or buy the whole lot from a butcher.

Jenifer Lang

Jacques Pépin

A FAMILY CHRISTMAS: MIXED TRADITIONS

In his monumental ART OF COOKING, *Jacques Pépin demonstrates his vast knowledge of food and its preparation. With his family now spread over three continents, Pépin takes pleasure in bringing his relatives and their traditional dishes together for the holidays.*

FOR US THE CHRISTMAS HOLIDAYS are always one of the most festive times of the year—a time for our scattered family to come together. Usually, either my mother or one of my brothers visits from France or our whole family goes to Europe to be with them. Some years, instead, we go to Puerto Rico to spend time with my wife Gloria's mother. It is a time of togetherness and serenity, and nothing expresses our joy in these happy times more than a table laden with great food.

Some of our Christmases have been very elegant, black-tie events, replete with Baccarat crystal and fine linen on the table; this fit our mood and went well with the guests we had on those occasions. However, I remember just as fondly more casual Christmases when everyone enjoyed hot wine and an earthy menu around a roaring fire. Whatever the menu for the holiday, we always think its main purpose is to satisfy and make people feel happy and comfortable.

175

The food of Christmas or the holidays for me has to be savory. It is family food, well accented with taste and a certain panache. It has to be presented nicely but, more important, the food should carry the smell and taste of the holidays. It must have taste memory, to bring back happy times as well as to enrich and sustain the memories of children as they grow up.

From my childhood comes the food of France. For Christmas it is traditional to serve goose-liver pâté, oysters, a bird—either turkey, capon, or goose—and the Christmas yule cake. In some parts of France, like Provence, there are the twelve desserts of Christmas, among them cookies, macaroons, dried fruits, and so on, placed on the table much as we in the United States serve dried fruit and nuts at Thanksgiving.

Although a French Christmas dinner kindles holiday feelings for me, the other members of my family also have dishes that mean Christmas for them, and we always make some of these during the holiday season. For Gloria, it's a highly seasoned fish dish and traditional roast turkey, reflecting her combined Caribbean and American heritage. Claudine, our daughter, looks forward to the cheese fondue, a melted Gruyère, garlic, and white-wine mixture consumed with chunks of crusty French bread. She expects hot cider and roasted lamb, while I look forward to the smell and taste of roasted chestnuts and Champagne.

The dishes in my Christmas menu must please everyone—children as well as older people. This cooking of love has more to do with taste than with presentation and it is not a time for experimentation with new dishes but rather a time of recollection.

Even though we sometimes visit family abroad during Christmas, our favorite place during the holiday season is at our own home in Connecticut. It may be the only time of year when we are looking for and happy to see snow to get the real feeling of Christmas. We cook up casseroles, stews, soups, gratins, and chocolate truffles. This is the type of cooking where the smell of the food mixed with the smell of the snow and the wood-burning fireplace creates a wholly new smell of its own.

There is always Champagne for Christmas, as it is the most festive of all drinks for us. Along with Champagne, which may be served through the whole meal, we always have a sweet wine for dessert, occasionally great Sauternes like Château d'Yquem, or a great port wine. However, in between, we usually serve red and white wines. For the menu here we recommend a beautiful white Robert Mondavi Sauvignon Blanc 1984 and, for a red, a Saint Joseph 1981, which is a spicy, well-built, and assertive wine from the Rhône valley. There are also strong coffee and petits fours with chocolate truffles and, in addition, candied orange, lemon, and lime peel that we eat and also give as gifts to family and friends.

Oyster and Spinach Soup

Fresh oysters are much better in this dish than preshucked oysters, which tend to be washed and less flavorful. There is also less liquid when you buy the oysters already shucked, and in addition the shucked oysters are usually the very large ones. The fishmonger can shuck the oysters for you or you can shuck them yourself.

The oyster stock is brought to 4 cups with the addition of water and clam juice if there is not enough oyster juice. If you have some fish stock handy, you can add that instead of or in addition to the water and clam juice.

The leeks and garlic are sautéed with the juice; this can be done ahead. However, the final cooking of the spinach and oysters should be done at the last moment. The oysters will toughen and the spinach yellow if they are prepared too far ahead. Their finishing takes only a few minutes and the result is much better.

3 dozen freshly shucked oysters (about 1½ pints), juice reserved
Clam juice, mussel juice, or fish stock, if needed
1 tablespoon butter
1 tablespoon good-quality virgin olive oil
1 large leek, cleaned and sliced thin
2 cloves garlic, peeled and chopped
¾ pound spinach, with stems removed, cleaned and dried (about
8 ounces when completely cleaned)
2 cups heavy cream
Salt to taste
1 teaspoon freshly ground black pepper
SERVES 8

Place the oysters with their juice into a large pot and "wash" the oysters in the juice. Lift the oysters up out of the juice and, if they are very large, cut them in half with scissors. (Medium-size oysters should not need cutting.) Place the oysters in a bowl and refrigerate until needed. Strain the oyster juice through paper towels into another bowl. (You should have approximately 2 cups of juice; if not, supplement with clam juice, mussel juice, or fish stock.) Add 2 cups of water to the juice to make 4 cups of stock; set aside.

Heat the butter and olive oil in a large saucepan. When hot, add the leeks and sauté over medium to high heat for about 2 minutes. Add the garlic and sauté for about 30 seconds, then add the 4 cups of stock, bring to a boil, and remove from heat. Set aside until serving time. (This can be done up to 8 hours ahead of serving.)

At serving time, bring the stock back to a boil, add the spinach, and return the stock to the boil. Boil over high heat for 1 minute, then add the cream, salt, and pepper. Bring back to the boil, add the oysters, stir gently, and heat to just under the boil. Divide among 8 soup plates and serve immediately.

Roast Capon with Date-Nut Dressing and Chestnut Sauce

The dressing for this capon is made with little cubes of French bread and a garnish of onions, garlic, scallions, celery, and so on. It is flavored with cumin powder and cayenne. The pistachios add crunchiness and a nice color and the dates lend a sweetness and mellowness to the dressing that cut the richness of the capon.

The bread for the dressing can be browned ahead but should not be combined with the other dressing ingredients until just before serving or it will get soggy. It is better to finish the dressing at the last moment, after the capon is cooked, so you can use the fat the bird renders as well as some of its drippings to moisten the dressing. If there is any dressing left over, it can be reheated in a skillet, sautéed with a couple of eggs on top, and served for lunch the next day.

It involves a bit more work, but fresh chestnuts are much better in this dish, although unflavored chestnuts in cans or jars can be added to the sauce instead. Be sure to cut through the skin of the fresh chestnuts along their whole length on both sides. That will make them very easy to peel after they are roasted.

Fresh capons are much better than frozen. Notice that the capon is cooked here breast side down most of the time so the juices run into the breast without basting and only the back is exposed. This yields a very moist capon. The same cooking technique can be used for small turkeys.

SERVES 8

179

Date-Nut Dressing

6 ounces French bread, preferably a baguette, cut into 1½-inch
     dice (about 6 cups)
2 tablespoons good-quality virgin olive oil
1 large onion, peeled and chopped (about 1 cup)
3 to 4 cloves garlic, peeled and finely chopped
4 ribs celery (whitest possible), cleaned and peeled if fibrous
     and cut into ¼-inch dice, yielding 1¼ cups
About 10 scallions, cleaned and minced (about 1 cup)
1 teaspoon crushed dried sage leaves
1 teaspoon powdered cumin
¾ teaspoon salt
⅛ teaspoon cayenne pepper
¼ teaspoon freshly ground black pepper
1¾ cups chopped dates (about ½ pound)
½ cup shelled pistachios
Approximately 1¼ cups fat (with drippings) from Roast Capon
     (see page 182)

Arrange the bread cubes in a roasting pan and place in a 400-degree oven until nicely browned, about 8 to 10 minutes. Set aside.

Heat the olive oil in a saucepan and, when hot, add the onion and garlic and sauté for 1½ to 2 minutes. Add the celery, scallions, and ½ cup of water. Bring to a boil, cover with a lid, and cook for about 2 minutes. Then add the sage, cumin, salt, cayenne pepper, black pepper, dates, and pistachios, and toss gently. (The mixture will be quite wet.) Cover with a lid and set aside without stirring further until ½ hour before serving time. (The dressing can be prepared a few hours ahead to this point.)

Remove the fat from the drippings in the roasting pan. Leave the defatted juices in the pan and reserve 1¼ cups of the fat (containing a little of the drippings. No more than ½ hour before serving, bring the dressing mixture to a boil again and add the reserved fat (with drippings) from the capon. Toss with the bread mixture, mix lightly, spread on a gratin dish, and place in the oven (turned off but still hot from cooking the capon) for 10 to 15 minutes to warm while making the sauce.

Cooked Fresh Chestnuts

1 pound fresh chestnuts (about 40)
1½ teaspoons salt

Score the chestnuts on both sides, cutting through the length of the shells on both sides with the point of a sharp knife. This will make them easier to peel.

Arrange about half the chestnuts on a baking sheet and place in a 400-degree oven for 12 to 15 minutes. The chestnuts will pop open slightly where slit. While they are still hot, press on the chestnuts to open them further, and remove both the outer shell and the skin beneath it. While you are peeling the first batch of chestnuts, place the remaining chestnuts in the oven at the same temperature and for same length of time and then peel them. (It is better to prepare the chestnuts in two batches, as they are much harder to peel when cool.)

When the chestnuts are all peeled (it doesn't matter if they are broken, since they should be in pieces in the sauce), place them in a saucepan with 3 cups of water and ½ teaspoon salt. Bring to a boil, cover, and boil gently for approximately 30 minutes, or until tender. (Most of the liquid will have been absorbed.) Set aside. (This can be done several hours ahead.)

Chestnut Sauce

Defatted juices from cooked capon (see Roast Capon, below)
½ cup full-bodied red wine
1 cup brown stock (or, if unavailable, chicken stock can be substituted)
1 teaspoon potato starch or arrowroot
1 pound Cooked Fresh Chestnuts (see above)
Salt and freshly ground pepper

In the pan containing the defatted juices, vegetables, and trimmings from roasting the capon, place the red wine and the stock. Bring to a strong boil over high heat, scraping the pan with a wooden spatula to melt the solidified juices. Boil for 2 minutes, then strain through a fine strainer.

Dissolve the potato starch or arrowroot in 1 or 2 tablespoons water and add to the strained juices. Bring just to the boil to thicken the sauce lightly. Add the chestnuts. (If there is only a small amount of liquid with the chestnuts, add it also. Otherwise, pour some of the liquid off so it doesn't dilute the sauce too much.)

Bring the mixture to a boil, reduce the heat, and simmer gently for 4 to 5 minutes. Add additional dissolved potato starch if the sauce needs a bit more thickening; season with salt and pepper to taste.

Roast Capon

1 large onion, peeled and quartered
2 to 3 carrots, washed and cut into 1-inch pieces
Large pieces of fat from inside the capon, cut into ½-inch dice
Capon neck, gizzard, and heart, chopped into 1-inch pieces
½ teaspoon salt
1 capon, preferably fresh, 7½ to 8 pounds

Spread the onion and carrot pieces and the capon fat, neck, gizzard, and heart pieces in a roasting pan with shallow sides (no more than 2 inches high or the capon will have a tendency to steam rather than roast). Sprinkle a little of the salt inside the cavity of the capon and truss it with a piece of string so that it holds a nice shape with a puffed-up breast. Sprinkle the remaining salt on the outside of the capon and place it, breast side up, on top of the bed of vegetables and trimmings in the roasting pan. (The capon can be prepared up to this point 5 to 6 hours ahead. If done ahead, however, do not salt the outside of the bird. Cover it with plastic wrap and refrigerate.)

At cooking time, place the capon in a preheated 400-degree oven and roast for 20 minutes. Then turn the bird over (so it is breast side down in the pan) and roast for 40 minutes longer. Turn breast side up again and continue cooking for 30 minutes, or until the capon is nicely browned and an oven thermometer inserted into the inner thigh reads 175 degrees. Baste once during this period. The bird should be moist. Remove the capon from the oven and place it breast side down (so the juices run into the breasts) on a platter. Set aside in a warm place, while finishing the sauce.

To serve, cut the capon into pieces so each person gets a little white and a little dark meat. Arrange the dressing on the individual serving plates and place the meat on top. Coat with the chestnut sauce and serve with the gratin of pumpkin on the side.

Field Salad with Mushrooms and Walnuts

This is an excellent winter salad, as the expensive but quite flavorful field salad (mâche, lamb's tongue, doucette) is a winter green. If unavailable, a mixture of other greens could be substituted, from arugula to romaine lettuce or Boston lettuce.

The mushrooms can be prepared up to 8 to 10 hours ahead in the marinade. The dressing for the salad can also be prepared in advance and the greens washed ahead of time, but the salad should not be tossed until the last moment so that it doesn't wilt.

The roasted walnuts can also be prepared up to 8 to 10 hours ahead but should not be done any sooner, as they taste much better when fresh.

6 cups field salad, or a combination of greens (see above)
4 tablespoons good-quality virgin olive oil
1 tablespoon good-quality red wine vinegar
Freshly ground black pepper
Salt
2 cups sliced mushrooms (about 4 or 5 ounces), preferably large
3 tablespoons peanut oil
2 teaspoons lemon juice
1 tablespoon Dijon mustard
1 cup walnut meat pieces
1 tablespoon butter
SERVES 8

Thoroughly wash and dry the greens. Mix the olive oil, vinegar, and ¼ teaspoon each of pepper and salt and set aside.

Slice the mushrooms, stack the slices together, then cut slices into sticks. Combine the oil, lemon juice, ¼ teaspoon each of salt and pepper, and the mustard and toss with the mushrooms. Set aside.

Place the walnuts in a roasting pan with the butter. Heat on top of the stove until the butter melts, then toss with the walnuts. Sprinkle lightly with salt and place in a preheated 400-degree oven until lightly browned, about 12 to 15 minutes.

At serving time, toss the dressing with the greens and arrange them on individual plates. Spoon some mushrooms into the center and arrange some of the walnut pieces on top. Serve immediately.

Gratin of Pumpkin

A savory rather than sweet gratin of pumpkin may seem unusual, since pumpkin is generally used as a dessert in the United States. The flesh of pumpkin is excellent in a gratin, however. If pumpkin is not available, butternut squash, acorn squash, or the like can be substituted. Although the same recipe can also be made with frozen or canned pumpkin purée, it is better when done with fresh pumpkin.

The mixture of purée, cream, milk, nutmeg, salt, pepper, eggs, and Swiss cheese can be assembled a few hours ahead or even the day before, but the gratin should not be cooked more than a few hours before it is served.

This recipe can also be cooked in individual gratin dishes. The same preparation technique applies but the small gratins will cook in about 20 minutes.

3½ cups pumpkin purée (see below)
1 cup heavy cream
1 cup milk
⅛ teaspoon grated nutmeg
2½ teaspoons salt
¾ teaspoon freshly ground black pepper
6 eggs

½ cup grated Swiss cheese
2 tablespoons grated Parmesan cheese
SERVES 8

In a large mixing bowl, combine the pumpkin purée, cream, milk, nutmeg, salt, and pepper. Beat in the eggs, one at a time, and stir in the Swiss cheese. Pour into a buttered 6-cup gratin dish.

Place the gratin dish in a pan containing enough boiling water to come halfway up the sides of the dish. Sprinkle the Parmesan cheese on top. Bake at 375 degrees for 40 to 45 minutes. Serve immediately, spooning the gratin onto individual serving plates.

Fresh Pumpkin Purée

4 pounds fresh pumpkin
MAKES 3½ CUPS

Seed, peel off skin, and cut pumpkin flesh into 2- to 3-inch chunks. Place in a saucepan and cover with cold water. Bring to a boil and boil gently, covered, until tender, 25–30 minutes. Drain well while still hot and purée in a food processor.

Bacalao Gloria

This traditional Spanish recipe reflects my wife Gloria's Caribbean background. Although Gloria was born in New York, her mother is Puerto Rican and her father Cuban. Traditionally served at Christmas, bacalao is cooked both with potatoes, as I have done it here, and in a lighter version served on toast. The assertive taste of this dish works well, I feel, with the rest of the menu, served between the rich cream soup and the capon.

1 pound salted codfish

¼ cup plus 2 tablespoons good-quality virgin olive oil

2 onions, peeled and sliced thin (2 cups)

4 to 5 cloves garlic, peeled and sliced very thin (about 3 tablespoons)

1 potato, peeled and cut into ½-inch dice (1 cup)

1 pound plum tomatoes, peeled and seeded, cut into 1-inch dice (2 cups)

1 yellow pepper, peeled with a vegetable peeler and cut into ½-inch strips (1¼ cups) (see Note)

½ teaspoon freshly ground black pepper

⅛ teaspoon cayenne pepper

Salt to taste

About 18 oil-cured olives, pitted and cut into ½-inch pieces (about ⅓ cup)

8 slices whole-wheat bread

½ cup fresh coriander leaves

SERVES 8

There are different types of codfish and some are drier than others. The drier and more salted the codfish is, the longer it must be soaked. Wash the codfish under cold water to remove any salt from the surface, then place it in a bowl with 8 to 10 cups of cold water. Let soak for 6 to 8 hours, change the water, and let soak again for 6 to 8 hours or up to a full day. Taste a small piece of the codfish to test for saltiness; it should taste just mildly salty when it has soaked long enough.

Wash the fish under cold water, place it in a pot with 4 cups of cold water, and bring to a vigorous boil. Remove from heat, drain in a colander, and cool under cold water. Flake the fish, trimming and discarding any pieces of sinew or skin. One pound of codfish should yield about 2½ cups (about 14 ounces) of flaked fish. Set aside.

Heat ¼ cup of oil in a saucepan. When hot, add the onions and cook over high heat for about 2 minutes. Add the garlic and cook about 30 seconds longer, then add the diced potato and the fish and stir about 1 minute over high heat to raise the temperature. Lower the heat to very low, cover, and cook slowly for 15 minutes. (The dish can be done a couple of hours ahead up to this point.)

Just before serving time, reheat the ingredients in the saucepan and add to them the tomato and yellow pepper, the 2 tablespoons of olive oil, black pepper, and cayenne pepper. Heat the mixture until it boils, then cover and cook over low heat for 4 to 5 minutes. Taste for salt, adding it if needed. Add the olive slivers and stir them in.

Toast the bread and trim off the crusts. Arrange the toast on individual plates and top with a scoop of the bacalao. Garnish with coriander leaves and serve immediately.

NOTE: Yellow pepper tastes much sweeter when the skin has been removed. Although the skin is removed conventionally by blistering it under the broiler and then peeling it off, raw peppers (especially thick-fleshed varieties) can be peeled with a vegetable peeler. To remove the skin from the pleats or recesses of the pepper that you can't reach with the peeler, cut directly through the center of the recesses of the partially peeled pepper to separate it into wedges. Then peel the skin from the areas that were not accessible before. Discard the seeds and cut the pepper into thin strips. Prepared in this manner, the peppers don't have to be cooked very long and are very mild in taste.

Frozen Praline Meringue

This frozen praline meringue is done in the round shape of a cake, but for Christmas it could be done in the shape of a yule log, making two strips of meringue with the same amount of meringue as used here. Ice cream and cream should then be piled up between the strips and they could be shaped and decorated to look like the branch or trunk of a tree.

The advantage of this dessert is that it can be prepared several weeks ahead. Be sure, however, that after it is decorated with the rosettes of whipped cream, it is frozen long enough so the rosettes are hard before you wrap it. Then use plastic wrap and two layers of aluminum foil so it doesn't pick up any tastes or rancidity in the freezer.

187

The longer the meringue is frozen and the colder the freezer, the more time it should stay in the refrigerator to soften before serving. Generally, after it has been in the deep freeze for more than a couple of days, it should stay in the refrigerator for ½ hour before serving.

Making this recipe from scratch requires an ice-cream machine. However, the same dessert can be made with only whipped cream—flavored in different ways—frozen in the center, or commercial ice cream can be substituted for the homemade version here.

The meringue is cooked so that it is very brittle and hard, maybe even a little beige in color. The sugar is incorporated into the egg whites quite fast, which yields a mixture that is still slightly granulated but, after cooking, will make a very tender meringue.

> 5 egg whites
> Granulated sugar
> 2 cups half-and-half
> 5 egg yolks
> 1 tablespoon vanilla extract
> 1½ cups sliced almonds
> 3 cups heavy cream
> 4 tablespoons confectioner's sugar
> 1½ tablespoons dark rum
> Crystallized violets or rose petals
> SERVES 8

Butter 2 pieces of parchment paper and place them, buttered side down, on 2 aluminum cookie trays.

Beat the egg whites with an electric mixer at medium-high speed for about 6 minutes, until the whites are firm but not grainy. Add 1 cup of granulated sugar over a 10-second period, turn speed up to high, and continue beating for no longer than 10 seconds. (Some of the sugar will remain slightly granulated in the whites, making a very tender meringue.)

Place the meringue mixture in a large pastry bag fitted with a plain tip with about a 1-inch opening. Starting in the center of one of the parchment paper–lined cookie trays, pipe out larger and larger adjoining rounds of meringue to create a disk about 10 inches in diameter by about ½ inch thick. Repeat this procedure to create a disk of the same size on the other cookie sheet. Place the meringues in a preheated 200-degree oven and bake for approximately 4 hours, until cooked and hard. Turn off the oven and let the meringues cool in the oven. They will be slightly beige in color.

To make the ice-cream custard, bring the half-and-half to a boil. Meanwhile, combine the egg yolks and ¼ cup granulated sugar in a bowl and mix well with a whisk, beating for about 1 minute to lighten the mixture. When the half-and-half is boiling, pour it all at once into the egg yolks and whisk for 8 to 10 seconds to mix well. The boiling half-and-half will cook the egg yolks and the temperature of the mixture should still be about 180 degrees. Immediately strain the mixture through a fine sieve to remove any curdled yolk. Add the vanilla to the strained mixture and set it aside while you make the praline.

To make the praline, lightly oil a cookie tray. Place ½ cup granulated sugar in a dry saucepan and cook over medium to high heat, stirring occasionally with a wooden spatula as the sugar closest to the sides of the pan begins to melt. Stir the melting sugar into the dry sugar in the center. After 6 or 7 minutes, the mixture will turn a rich caramel color. (Don't worry about some crystallization of the sugar during this procedure; it will melt when the sugar caramelizes.) Add the sliced almonds. This will solidify the caramel a little. Continue cooking about 2 minutes longer to remelt the sugar and brown the almonds. Pour onto the oiled cookie tray and cool for at least ½ hour. Break into pieces and process in the food processor until finely ground.

Combine the powdered praline with the ice-cream custard and prepare according to the ice-cream machine manufacturer's instructions.

Spoon the ice cream onto a plate lined with plastic wrap. Cover with another piece of plastic wrap and flatten the ice cream until it is in a circle about the size of the meringue disks (about 10 inches in diameter) and close to 1 inch thick. Place in the freezer until hard. (This dessert can be made several weeks ahead and the finishing done several days ahead.)

For the whipped cream filling, combine the heavy cream, confectioner's sugar, and rum and beat until stiff but not dry.

To finish the cake, cut a piece of cardboard the size of the meringue disks and wrap it with aluminum foil. Trim the meringues to make them the same size and uniformly round, reserving the trimmings for use in the cake. Place one of the meringue disks, flat side down, on the cardboard. Arrange the ice-cream round on top of the meringue. Spread a fourth of the whipped cream filling on top, smoothing it gently with a spatula. Sprinkle the crumbled meringue trimmings on top and place the second meringue disk on top with the flat side up. Lightly coat the sides and top with half the remaining whipped cream filling. Spoon the rest of the filling into a pastry bag fitted with a star tip and decorate the top and around the cake with rosettes of cream. Gently press pieces of crystallized violets or rose petals into the rosettes and place the dessert in the freezer, uncovered, for at least 3 hours, until hard. Then wrap with plastic wrap and aluminum foil and place back in the freezer.

At serving time, remove from the freezer and unwrap before the mixture softens. Place, unwrapped, in the refrigerator for ½ hour to soften slightly before cutting and serving.

Beatrice Ojakangas

A SCANDINAVIAN

ROUNDTABLE

Beatrice Ojakangas has written extensively on Scandinavian food and presents here a smörgåsbord of memories built around the sturdy Scandinavian roots of the Midwest. These are the foods of a long northern winter enlivened with the love of family and friends working together.

'' 'TWAS THE NIGHT BEFORE CHRISTMAS . . .'' The line brings back childhood memories of my farm home in northern Minnesota. Preparations for the holiday were extremely simple. Christmas Eve seemed pretty much like any Saturday. We'd clean the house all day and take a sauna in the evening in the special outbuilding intended just for bathing. As on every other day of the week, the cows had to be milked at five o'clock. Christmas Eve was usually bitter cold, and the cows got an additional bed of straw or extra hay. The evening meal would be a simple one of fish stew and bread. However, when we came into the house after sauna, we'd see the Christmas tree lit with real candles and we'd have a cup of hot cocoa and a "gingerbread" bun my mother had made for each of us. It wasn't really gingerbread but a light cardamom-flavored yeasted coffee-bread dough, shaped in the form of a person.

We read the Christmas story, which I loved because it put our evening into perspective. "And Mary gave birth to her first-born son and laid him in a manger." This seemed perfectly normal to me, as all ten of us except for one were born at home in that same farmhouse and the idea of being born anywhere else was remote to us. That the birth happened in a place other than a bedroom wasn't all that strange either, for I remembered hearing

191

that my grandparents were born in the sauna. The idea of a manger for a birthing place seemed equally good. Mangers were always warm from the body heat of the cows, and fresh straw has a pleasant, clean aroma.

Mom's Cardamom Yeast Rolls in the Shape of Gingerbread Boys

Mom used to make these little dough people for each of us. She didn't have a cookie cutter, so she used her all-purpose kitchen knife to slash pieces of dough to shape them. I have tried shaping them with a large gingerbread cookie cutter and that works well, too, so I am including two different directions for shaping the dolls. You may choose to chill the dough or not, depending on your time schedule, but the dough shapes more easily if it is chilled.

> 2 packages active dry yeast
> 1 cup milk, scalded and cooled to lukewarm
> 1 teaspoon freshly crushed cardamom seeds
> ⅓ cup sugar
> 1 teaspoon salt
> 3 eggs
> 5 to 5½ cups all-purpose flour

⅓ cup butter, melted
1 egg beaten with 2 tablespoons milk
Raisins for decoration
MAKES 12 DOLLS

In a large bowl, dissolve the yeast in ½ cup lukewarm water. Allow it to stand for 5 to 10 minutes, or until creamy. Stir in the milk, cardamom, sugar, salt, and eggs; beat until eggs are blended. Mix in 2½ cups of the flour; beat until smooth. Beat in the melted butter and continue adding more flour until dough is stiff. Cover with a towel and let stand 15 minutes.

Turn dough out onto a lightly floured board and knead until smooth and elastic, about 10 minutes. Wash the bowl, lightly grease it, and return the dough to the bowl. Turn it over to grease the top. Cover and let rise in a warm place until doubled, about 1 hour.

Punch the dough down, cover with plastic wrap, and chill 2 hours, if desired and if it is convenient on your schedule. Otherwise, you may continue with the shaping immediately.

Turn the dough out onto a lightly oiled board. Roll or flatten the dough to about 1 inch thickness. With a large gingerbread cookie cutter, cut out gingerbread people. Or cut dough into 12 parts. Roll each part into an oblong about 6 inches long. With the tip of a knife, cut out snips of dough where the doll's neck would be, shaping the head. Then make slashes to shape the arms, and on the opposite end slash the dough to shape the legs. With fingers smooth out the body of the doll and place on a lightly greased cookie sheet. Roll out 2 little snips of dough (from the neck) into a ball. Make a little hole where the doll's nose would be and fit it into the hole. Roll out the other snip of dough into a skinny strand and place it over the top of the head to simulate hair. Let rise 45 minutes or until puffy.

Preheat oven to 375 degrees.

Beat the egg and milk together until blended. Brush the gingerbread people with the mixture and press raisins into the figures to make eyes, mouth, and buttons.

Bake for 12 to 15 minutes or until lightly browned. Remove from oven and cool on racks.

193

Many years later, curious about the Christmas memories of other families, I invited a group of my friends and their mothers over for lunch one eve of Christmas Eve. I asked each of them to tell about what Christmas was like where she grew up. The first reaction of each guest was that her story was not "different," but as each guest lit a candle, she recounted a Christmas memory, and the result was a smörgåsbord of stories, none of them alike.

The special effect of this lunch was that it gave me a sense of what had been happening in other homes while we were bedding our cows down in clean straw. Friends we hadn't yet met were "having Christmas" in different ways. Yet, among Scandinavians, there was a similarity in the memories and the food.

"Oh," said Emma Swanson, "we never did anything unusual. Christmas was pretty simple. Typically Norwegian. We'd have Christmas Eve at one of the grandparents' and Christmas Day at the other." But Marj, her daughter, said she remembered how Grandpa played the violin and mouth organ, and she always remembered his "long prayer" and how glad she was when it was over. Then everyone in the family would join hands and sing as they danced around the Christmas tree. Emma said she remembered that one year they decided to go to church with the Swedes at 5:00 in the morning on Christmas Day. "Once was enough," she said. "It was cold!" She said she preferred going to Christmas Eve services. Emma said that as a child they had a simple Christmas Eve meal of rice pudding, and each person had a candle. Marj has continued that tradition with her family.

Marj's Christmas Eve Rice Pudding

There is an almond buried in the rice pudding, and the person who gets it is "Santa" in the Bergeland family and distributes the gifts from under the tree. Depending on the number of people, Marj doubles or triples this recipe.

¾ cup raw medium-grain rice
½ teaspoon salt
4 eggs

⅓ cup sugar
3 cups milk, heated to lukewarm
1 teaspoon vanilla extract
⅓ cup light or dark raisins
1 whole almond
Cinnamon sugar and cream
MAKES ABOUT 6 SERVINGS

In a saucepan, combine the rice with 1½ cups of water and the salt. Bring to the boil, stir, and reduce heat to low. Cover and simmer 20 minutes, or until the rice has absorbed the water.

In a bowl, whisk together the eggs, sugar, warmed milk, and vanilla. Add the rice and raisins. Turn into 2-quart buttered baking dish. Bury the almond in the pudding.

Place the baking dish in a larger pan of boiling water. Bake at 350 degrees, uncovered, for 1 hour or until the pudding is set. Stir once or twice during baking and before serving.

Serve hot in bowls with cinnamon sugar and cream.

Beth Storaasli remembered that it was one of her parents' Christmas Eve traditions to deliver food gifts to the needy. She always had to go along, and although at the time she didn't think it was so wonderful, it was still exciting because it indicated to her that Christmas was "beginning." She realizes now, of course, that she was learning something about sharing and caring for those outside the immediate family, especially those who were not so fortunate.

For many Swedish families, Christmas season begins on December 13—Lucia Day. Although families celebrate in different ways, Ethel told of a Hedman family tradition. At six in the morning, by the light of the Christmas tree and candles, the youngest daughter, who had to be at least three years old, wearing a crown of lighted candles and decked in a white robe. She descended the staircase to the family, all of them awaiting the little "Lucia." They sang the St. Lucia song and Grandpa Hedman told the story of Lucia. They then enjoyed the traditional Lucia Day breakfast of golden saffron bread, ginger cookies (*pepparkakor*), and steaming

195

hot coffee from a copper pot. The menu ᵥvas often augmented by rice pudding, fruit soup, and a Swedish omelet.

The tradition of Lucia Day developed during the ninth century, but no one knows its true origin. Some say it began with a young girl who brought food and a light of hope to starving people in western Sweden. Other legends tell of a young girl on the island of Sicily who was martyred on December 13 in the year 304 because she embraced Christianity. Another legend holds that during a famine in Värmland and other parts along the shores of Sweden, a large ship came across Lake Vänern with a white-robed maiden, encircled by light, at the bow. At her command the ship landed and distributed food to the starving people. Throughout the variations of the legend, the theme of candles, light in the darkness, sacrifice, good food, and the central message of Christ bringing light to the world is constant.

Golden saffron-flavored bread is a tradition at Swedish Christmas, and it makes its first appearance at the St. Lucia breakfast. It seems strange that this exotic, expensive spice from Spain should become part of the tradition of this northern country. Swedes may not be wealthy people, but like other Scandinavians they believe in "going all out" on Christmas, making it special for friends, family, and all those around them.

As one of the friends at lunch said, "We could do nothing, and ignore the season, but it's so much more fun to go all out, to light every candle and do all you can to make the holiday special for everyone—especially the children, who really *do* remember despite apparent disinterest." "Nothing is special unless you make it special!" exclaimed one of the guests. When events have value, we want to repeat them. They become tradition.

Swedish Saffron Bread
(Saffransbröd)

This yeast dough is easy to make because it is simply mixed with a spoon, then refrigerated, eliminating the kneading step. The chilled dough is very easy to handle. You can refrigerate the dough for 2 hours or up to 4 days, and you can pull off just a portion, to bake a little at a time if you like. The directions that follow are for shaping *lussekatter*, the special buns served for breakfast on Lucia Day. In the variation, we tell how to make a Lucia wreath.

Beatrice Ojakangas

> 2 packages active dry yeast
> ⅛ teaspoon powdered saffron
> ½ cup melted butter
> ½ cup sugar
> 6 egg yolks or 3 whole eggs
> 1 teaspoon salt
> ½ cup golden raisins, plus additional for decorating rolls
> 3½ to 4 cups all-purpose flour
> 1 egg beaten with 2 tablespoons milk
> MAKES 16

In a large mixing bowl, dissolve the yeast in 1 cup of lukewarm water. Let stand 5 to 10 minutes, until yeast is creamy. Stir in the saffron, butter, sugar, egg yolks or whole eggs, salt, and ½ cup raisins. Beat in the flour a cup at a time until dough is too stiff to mix but all the flour is moistened. Cover the bowl with plastic wrap and refrigerate at least 2 hours or up to 4 days.

LUSSEKATTER
Turn dough out onto a lightly floured board. Cut dough into quarters. Cut each of the quarters into 4 parts. Divide each part into 2 parts. You'll end up with 32 pieces of dough.

Shape each piece into a strand 7 inches long. Place 2 strands together in pairs and pinch along the centers to join them; curl each end up. Press a raisin into each curl and place on a lightly greased baking sheet.

Cover with a towel and let rise in a warm place for 45 minutes or until the rolls appear puffy.

Preheat the oven to 400 degrees.

Beat the egg and milk together to make a glaze and brush the buns with the mixture. Gently press raisins back into the rolls if they have popped out during the rising period.

Bake for about 10 minutes or until just golden. Do not overbake or rolls will be dry.

Beatrice Ojakangas

ST. LUCIA WREATH

Divide refrigerated dough into 3 parts. On a lightly floured surface, roll each part out to make a strand about 48 inches long. Braid the strands. Join the ends to make a wreath and pinch ends together to seal. Place on a lightly greased baking sheet. Cover with a towel and let rise in a warm place for 45 minutes to 1 hour or until the braid appears puffy. Preheat oven to 400 degrees. Brush wreath with the glaze (eliminate the raisin garnish). Bake for 25 minutes or just until a wooden skewer inserted in the center of the braid comes out dry. Do not overbake or the bread will be dry. The wreath is often presented with ginger cookies clustered in the center.

Frukt Soppa
(Norwegian Sweet Soup)

The Gildseths, as a young couple, ran a little general store in Iowa with three apartments upstairs. One was occupied by an elderly Norwegian couple, the Gregorsons, the second by the organist for their little Norwegian church, and the third they lived in themselves.

Church bells had rung out over the snow-blanketed countryside at three in the afternoon, but the Gildseths were in their store, busy into the evening wrapping gifts for their customers, when the young organist came into the store in tears; she would be alone for Christmas, she said. The Gregorsons and the Gildseths also were alone.

"Come and have Christmas with us!" Leona Gildseth offered. So the occupants of the three apartments became family because "we all needed each other." Mrs. Gregorson, a talented caterer, cooked *lutfisk* and brought in a punch bowl filled with sweet soup. That Christmas began a new tradition in the Gildseth family—inviting somebody who is alone to share the holiday with them. Christmas is a time for family—and an extended family too. Mrs. Gregorson's sweet soup has become the traditional holiday punch in the Gildseth household. This is the recipe as told me by Leona Gildseth, and I'd have named it after her except that she insists that it is Mrs. Gregorson's. It makes a lot, and is best served warm. Although it is excellent served right after it is prepared, you can make it up to a week ahead of time and reheat it before serving. Sometimes we serve it for dessert with a dollop of whipped cream, or spooned over a creamy rice pudding. But I like Leona's idea—of serving it as a punch. You need to provide spoons! I served it this year after cross-country skiing with *goro-kakor*, a Norwegian cardamom-flavored cracker which I make using a special iron that impresses a design into each one as it cooks on top of the range.

6 cups cranberry, cranberry-apple, or cranberry-raspberry juice
4 cups grape juice
1 pound frozen pitted dark sweet cherries
1 pound frozen sliced peaches
1 (12-ounce) package pitted prunes
2 apples, peeled, cored, and chopped
½ cup each dark and golden raisins
½ teaspoon whole cloves
1 stick cinnamon
4 thin slices orange, with rind on
4 thin slices lemon, with rind on
⅓ cup minute tapioca
½ to 1 cup sugar
¼ cup grenadine syrup (optional)
Thin-sliced lemons for garnish
MAKES ABOUT 16 SERVINGS

In a large non-aluminum pot, combine the juices, cherries, peaches, prunes, apples, and raisins. Place the cloves in a tea ball or wrap in cheesecloth and add to the mixture along with the cinnamon stick and the orange and lemon slices. Stir; then heat to simmering and simmer 1 hour or until the prunes are soft. Remove the cloves, cinnamon, and orange and lemon slices.

Pour 2 cups of water into a bowl, sprinkle the tapioca over it, and let stand 5 minutes. Stir into the soup and simmer until the soup is thickened, about 20 minutes longer. Taste and add sugar. Add grenadine syrup, if desired (it adds color and a fruity

Beatrice Ojakangas

199

flavor to the soup). Before serving, garnish with thin lemon slices. If the soup is made ahead, cover and refrigerate, then reheat, if desired, before serving.

Ethel Hedman's Dopp i Gryta
(Swedish "Dip in the Pot" Soup)

My Swedish friends were in agreement about Christmas Eve. It was the time for an important meal. Originally, the first course was served in the kitchen for lunch on the day before Christmas, when the ham was cooking in plenty of broth and the bread was fresh. Chunks were dipped in the pot (*dopp i gryta*) as a snack to stave off hunger pangs.

Today, Ethel makes a special broth using three kinds of meat. The "doppa" is the first course of the meal, served in a big iron kettle in the middle of the table much like a fondue. Everybody dips in chunks of fennel-flavored rye bread.

3 pounds meaty short ribs of beef
2 pounds pork steaks with bone
1 pound boneless stewing veal
3 stalks celery, cut into 1-inch pieces
4 medium-sized carrots, cut into 1-inch pieces
2 medium-sized onions, chopped coarsely
1 tablespoon whole allspice
1 tablespoon whole black pepper
Salt to taste
MAKES 12 TO 16 SERVINGS

In a large heavy soup pot, brown the meat slowly over low to medium heat a few pieces at a time. When all pieces are browned on all sides, add the celery, carrots, onions, allspice, and black pepper to the pot. Add water to cover and simmer for 5 to 6 hours, or until the stock has a meaty flavor and the meat shreds easily. Remove the meat from the pot. Shred the meat and reserve; discard the fat and bones. Strain, discarding the vegetables, then chill the stock. Remove the fat from the top and reheat. Add salt to taste. If the stock needs a meatier flavor, simmer until it is reduced and flavor is concentrated. (Sometimes, Ethel said, she adds a can of beef consommé, undiluted.) Before serving, return the meat to the broth. (Extra soup can be frozen for serving later.)

Gorokakor

This traditional Norwegian cookie/cracker is baked in a special iron, has a mild cardamom flavor, and isn't very sweet. The *goro* iron makes one large wafer which separates into three crackers about 2 by 4 inches each. They are about the same thickness as the Italian *pizelle*. *Krumkake*, another Norwegian cookie baked in a round iron, are much thinner and more delicate. (You can order a *goro* iron from Maid of Scandinavia in Minneapolis, Minnesota, by calling 1-800-328-6722.)

> *1 egg yolk*
> *⅓ cup whipping cream*
> *⅓ cup sugar*
> *½ teaspoon freshly crushed cardamom seeds*
> *3 to 5 tablespoons ice water*
> *3 cups all-purpose flour*
> *1 cup (2 sticks) butter, firm and preferably unsalted*
> *Melted shortening for greasing iron*
> MAKES ABOUT 36 CRACKERS

In a small bowl, mix together the egg yolk, cream, sugar, cardamom, and 3 tablespoons of the ice water.

Measure the flour into a large bowl or into the work bowl of a food processor with the steel blade in place. Slice the butter ¼ inch thick and add to the flour. Cut into the flour using a pastry blender, or by using on/off pulses of the food processor, until butter is in pieces about the size of small peas. Combine the flour mixture with the egg mixture and stir with a fork until the dough holds together in a ball. Add more ice water if necessary. The dough should feel like pie pastry. Wrap in wax paper and chill 30 minutes.

Turn out onto a lightly floured board. Roll out to about 12 inches across. Fold into thirds, making a long, narrow strip of dough. Roll out to about ¼ inch thickness. Fold from the ragged ends into thirds to make a square. Roll out again to make a sheet no thicker than ¼ inch. Cut into 4-by-6-inch rectangles.

Place *goro* iron on a burner over medium heat. Continue heating, turning the iron over to heat both sides. When a drop of water dances on the inside of the grid, the iron is ready for baking. Brush lightly with melted shortening or unsalted butter.

Transfer a rectangle of dough onto the heated iron. Close the iron and cook about 2 minutes on each side, or until golden. Remove from iron and cool on a rack. Before serving, separate into individual pieces.

Mormor's Meatballs

Cecile Swenson said, "Oh, we have to have Mormor's meatballs on Christmas Eve!" Grandmother to the Swenson children is "Mormor," and this meatball recipe is unusual because the meatballs are seasoned with a brown-sugar glaze. They're served after the *lutfisk* and mashed potatoes, along with lingonberries and a cooked vegetable. These meatballs are also great served as appetizers.

> ½ *cup dry breadcrumbs*
> ½ *cup milk*
> ½ *pound ground beef*
> ½ *pound ground pork*
> *Salt*
> ½ *teaspoon ground allspice*
> ½ *teaspoon ground ginger*
> *1 small yellow onion, chopped fine*
> *1 egg, slightly beaten*
> *6 tablespoons brown sugar, packed*
> ½ *cup concentrated beef broth*
> *2 tablespoons melted butter*

MAKES 36 MEATBALLS, 4 TO 6 SERVINGS

In a bowl, mix the breadcrumbs and milk; let stand a few minutes until milk is absorbed. Add the beef, pork, 1 teaspoon salt, allspice, ginger, onion, and egg and mix until blended. Shape mixture into balls about 1 inch in diameter.

Bring 2 quarts of water to a boil in a large saucepan and add 2 teaspoons of salt. Drop the meatballs into the water and simmer, covered, for 15 minutes.

Meantime, preheat the oven to 350 degrees. In a small saucepan, combine the brown sugar, broth, and melted butter; stir and heat until the brown sugar is dissolved to form a glaze.

Drain meatballs and place in a single layer in a 13-by-9-inch baking dish. Spoon the glaze over the meatballs and bake, uncovered, for 30 minutes, turning the meatballs by shaking the pan after each 10 minutes of baking.

Danish Cabbage

Martha and Johannes Aas, carrying out Danish tradition, butcher a whole pig before Christmas and make all their own pâtés, sausages, and cold cuts. On Christmas Eve it is time for goose or duck, red cabbage, and caramelized potatoes, but for lunch during the holidays they enjoy *smorrebrod* with their homemade specialties. On the second day of Christmas, December 26, their traditional meal is homemade sausage served with their own special Danish white cabbage. This is an unusually simple and delicious dish that starts out with cabbage that is cooked, puréed, and drained like cheese. Martha likes the cabbage heated with just salt and pepper, and Johannes likes to top it with cinnamon sugar.

2 large heads white cabbage, 3 to 3½ pounds each
½ to 1 cup whipping cream
Salt and pepper to taste
MAKES ABOUT 8 SERVINGS

Trim the cores off the cabbages and discard. Shred the cabbages, put into a large pot, and add boiling salted water to cover. Simmer, covered, for 1½ to 2 hours, or until the cabbage is very

203

tender. Drain well. Put cabbage through a meat grinder, or purée in a food processor fitted with the steel blade.

Line a strainer with 4 layers of cheesecloth and add the puréed cabbage. Gather the corners of the cheesecloth and hang the bag of cabbage until no more liquid drips from the bottom.

Refrigerate until ready to serve. Before serving, turn into a heavy pan and add enough cream to give the cabbage the consistency of mashed potatoes. Add salt and pepper to taste and reheat slowly on top of stove. Serve accompanied by braised, fried, or broiled sausages.

The Minnesota countryside was filled with Scandinavian tradition during my childhood, but the American English in the city of Duluth celebrated on a different schedule. In the early 1900s, Duluth had more millionaires per capita than any other city in the country. They made their money as executives and owners in the iron ore and timber industries, shipping, and the railroad.

The Congdons were one of these families. Their home, nestled on the shore of Lake Superior, was named Glensheen. A Christmas tea was always scheduled there for the middle of December, setting the cooks and helpers in the house into a swirl of busyness and creativity.

The tea was served in the living room of the mansion on a big round table with a cloth that went to the floor. Decorations were purposely made from simple natural ingredients—pine boughs and pink carnations arranged on a polished silver tray, cedar branches on the sills of leaded glass windows, simple and tasteful handmade garlands over the many fireplaces. The whole house was filled with a fragrant Christmas mood. Nothing was to be overdone, after all; the Congdons believed that with wealth comes responsibility not to flaunt it.

When Vera Dunbar, the personal secretary to one of the Congdons, came home with a three-tiered German crèche that revolved when the candles were lit, it was the hit of the household. It was added to a growing collection of crèches from many countries in the world.

Christmas dinner was served at two o'clock on Christmas Day.

The centerpiece was a roast, ordered by the cook, who had called the meat man and asked him to take the "best roast beef out of the vault." Besides the beef, roasted, Christmas dinner included Yorkshire pudding and gravy, vegetables that had been grown in the Congdons' garden, and mashed potatoes. Plum pudding and mince pies were served for dessert.

Later on in the evening the "extended family" was invited for a holiday supper and there were lots of people. It was served buffet style. Guests started with Glensheen wassail, followed by a buffet of turkey, vegetables, cranberry mold, mince pies, cheese, fresh fruit, and coffee.

Beatrice Ojakangas

Glensheen Wassail

2 cups sugar
2 tablespoons chopped crystallized ginger
4 whole allspice
12 whole cloves
2 cups fresh orange juice
2 cups fresh lemon juice
2 quarts apple cider
Thin orange slices for garnish
MAKES 20 SERVINGS, 6 OUNCES EACH

In a large pot, combine the sugar with 4 cups of water, the ginger, allspice, and cloves. Heat to simmering, stirring until the sugar is completely dissolved. Remove from the heat and allow to stand until ready to serve. Just before serving add the orange juice, lemon juice, and apple cider and reheat to serving temperature. Garnish with a few thin slices of orange with the rind on. Ladle hot wassail into punch cups.

Glensheen was later donated by the Congdon family to the University of Minnesota, Duluth. It is now open year round to the public for touring, and during the Christmas season is decorated in the Congdon family tradition.

Maida Heatter

AH, THERE'S GOOD NEWS TONIGHT

Maida Heatter's name has been synonymous with dessert since the publication of the first of her five dessert books, THE BOOK OF GREAT DESSERTS, *in 1974. But she was baking long before that, making rich and chewy cookies for her holiday gift-giving. For ten years she made all the desserts for her husband's two restaurants.*

THE YEAR WAS 1943. The country was at war. Dwight Eisenhower, Supreme Commander of the Allied Forces in Europe, was preparing for the invasion of Normandy. German submarines were sinking ships along the eastern coast of the United States; burning vessels could be seen from the Atlantic shoreline. In the South Pacific, battles were fierce; the brutal struggle for Guadalcanal was one of the worst.

The whole country had one determination—to win the war as soon as possible. Fifteen million brave men and women were in the armed services, and in one way or another, every single American was deeply involved in the war effort. Ordinary men and women were performing extraordinary feats. Automobile factories built tanks and other armaments, shipbuilders launched a ship a day, aircraft factories turned out one hundred thousand war planes in a year. Too many homes had a gold star or two hanging in the window, each star an indication that a member of the family had died in the service. Telegrams brought the terrible news: "Wounded, missing, or killed in action." Many women

207

worked in war production factories. Housewives rolled bandages for the Red Cross and baked cookies for the local USO, the United Service Organization, which had clubs all around the country for the servicemen who were away from home.

My husband was in the army and my brother was in the navy. My year-old daughter and I lived with my parents on Long Island. My father, Gabriel Heatter, was one of the country's best-known radio news commentators. He did his broadcasts from home, where we had set up a broadcasting studio in an upstairs bedroom as well as a stand-by studio in the basement air-raid shelter. To make an ordinary room into a studio it was necessary to hang heavy drapes (even a few blankets) and to use thick rugs and upholstered furniture so that the voice did not echo or bounce off the walls. Associated Press and United Press news tickers installed in our home brought my father worldwide news twenty-four hours a day. Although an engineer came every night to handle the technical aspects of the broadcast, he taught both my mother and me what to do in an emergency if he didn't get there. Happily, we were never called upon. The broadcasts were carried across the country by about four hundred radio stations and to the armed forces overseas. A personal representative of Winston Churchill and another who was President Roosevelt's man came to lunch several times a week, every week, and they stayed, often, through dinner and through the broadcast at 9:00 P.M.

Those were nervous times—exciting, tense, scary, wonderful, and terrible.

Professionally, I was a fashion illustrator. But my hobby was cooking. Especially baking cookies. I had always baked cookies, but now that there was a war on, there were a whole army and navy to bake for. I sent packages to everyone I knew in the service, and although I would have continued to bake and mail out cookies without any thank yous, when the grateful letters came in from overseas, I was totally inspired; the oven hardly ever had a chance to cool off.

When, that fall, I heard that the New York City USO wanted cookies for a big Christmas party, it was music to my ears. I baked those cookies from early until late every day for weeks. My only problem was getting enough boxes to pack them in. Food shortages and rationing (butter and sugar were strictly rationed) didn't bother me, as there were always friends and neighbors who wanted to help. They gave me their ration coupons, they shopped for me, and they helped pack the cookies. The filled boxes lined the entrance hall and the dining room flowed over into the living room.

The day before Christmas a neighbor piled the boxes into his truck and my mother and I went along to deliver the cookies to the USO at Times Square. Gasoline was rationed but *this* was a priority delivery.

My father always searched the news for any little item that might give hope to a worried wife or mother, and to everyone listening to his broadcast. One night when the news was especially grim—the Allied forces were losing several large battles—he found a few words on the ticker implying that the Allies might have sunk a small German ship (maybe not much more than a shrimp boat). Exaggerating a bit, he opened his broadcast with "Ah, there's good news tonight." The country needed that. Everyone listening slept better that night. Those words became his slogan. Even today, when I meet someone new, they might smile and say, "Ah, there's good news tonight." If they're old enough to remember.

On that Christmas Day—the day after we delivered the cookies—the phone rang. I answered it. And I heard the whole USO clubroomful of people all yell in unison, "Ah, there's good news tonight." I loved it, and so did my mother and father. And over the next few months I received mail from many of the men who had been there telling me how much homemade cookies meant to them. They said it was the next best thing to a trip home. I think I received more happiness out of it all than they did. That often happens with cookies; the giver gets as much as, or more than, the receiver.

If I counted the number of cookies, or the number of recipes, that special Christmas, I don't remember it now. One thing I do remember is that none of those cookies was dainty. I was baking for the army and the navy and the marines. They were all he-man cookies. The ones that had raisins or nuts had lots of them. The chocolate cookies were very chocolate. The spice cookies were very spicy. In a way, I think that one baking experience influenced everything I have baked since.

There have been many times since then when I have baked cookies in tremendous quantities. I baked cookies for hundreds of girls at a Girl Scout Christmas party. I baked cookies for President Reagan and six other heads of state and their staffs of hundreds at the economic summit in Colonial Williamsburg in 1983. I baked a cookie buffet for one of Craig Claiborne's sumptuous New Year's Eve parties and another for one of his monumental birthday parties. All memorable events, since to me happiness is baking cookies. But that one particular time, during the war, baking for the servicemen, was like a first love affair. Special.

All of the following cookies are, in fact, among those that I made that special Christmas (with minor changes and updating). They all pack well, they store well (when wrapped airtight), and they travel well. They may be frozen (thaw before unwrapping). Correct oven temperature is essential for cookies. Please always check your oven with a portable mercury-type thermometer, available in hardware stores, before baking.

Merry Christmas.

My Mother's Gingersnaps

Maida Heatter

These are the cookies that my mother and I made together probably more often than any other. They are Christmas cookies, but we made them all year. Many famous people left our house carrying a bag or a box of these. They are crisp, chewy, large and thin, spicy and peppery but mellow. The dough should be refrigerated overnight before rolling, cutting, and baking.

⅔ *cup (3½ ounces) loosely packed candied ginger*
2 cups unsifted all-purpose or unbleached flour, plus additional for rolling out dough
1½ teaspoons baking soda
¾ *teaspoon salt*
¾ *teaspoon black pepper, ground fine*
1½ teaspoons ground ginger
8 ounces (2 sticks) unsalted butter, at room temperature
1 cup sugar
¾ *cup dark molasses*
1 egg graded ''large''
1¼ teaspoons cider vinegar (see Note)
1 cup unsifted all-purpose whole-wheat flour
35 LARGE COOKIES

Adjust two racks to divide the oven into thirds. Preheat the oven to 350 degrees. Line cookie sheets (preferably the kind with only one raised rim) with aluminum foil, shiny side up.

Cut the ginger into pieces ¼ inch or less and set aside.

Sift together the all-purpose flour, baking soda, salt, pepper, and ground ginger and set aside.

In the large bowl of an electric mixer beat the butter until it is soft. Add the sugar and beat to mix. Beat in the molasses, egg, and vinegar (the mixture might look curdled; it is okay). Then beat in the cut candied ginger. Add the sifted dry ingredients and the whole-wheat flour and beat on low speed until incorporated.

Spread out three lengths of wax paper or foil. Place one third of the dough on each paper. Wrap and refrigerate overnight. (If you can't wait, put the packages in the freezer for about an hour.)

To roll the dough, generously flour a pastry cloth and rolling pin. Place one piece of the chilled dough on the cloth, press down on it a few times with the rolling pin, turn the dough over to flour both sides, and roll out the dough until it is ¼ inch thick. Work quickly. Do not leave the dough unattended; it becomes sticky and gooey if it is allowed to reach room temperature (which seems to happen quickly). Reflour the cloth and the pin as necessary.

With a round cookie cutter measuring 3⅛ inches in diameter (or any other size), cut out the cookies; start cutting at the outside edge of the dough and cut the cookies just barely touching each other. Reserve the scraps and press them together (the dough will be too sticky for you to press the scraps together with your hands—it is best to put the scraps in a bowl and mix them together with a spatula). Wrap and rechill.

With a wide metal spatula quickly transfer the cookies to the foil-lined sheets, placing them 2 inches apart (if the cookies are 3⅛ inches wide, I place only 5 cookies on a 15½-by-12-inch sheet—they spread).

Bake two sheets at a time, reversing the sheets top to bottom and front to back once during baking to ensure even baking. As they bake, the cookies will rise and then settle down into thin waferlike cookies. They will take about 15 minutes to bake; if you bake only one sheet, use a rack in the middle of the oven—one sheet might bake in slightly less time.

When the cookies are done, remove the sheets from the oven and let stand until they are just barely cool. (If you have used the sheets with only one raised rim, slide the foil off the sheet and slide the sheet—which may still be hot—under another piece of foil already prepared with cookies on it, and continue baking.)

Then lift the cookies away from the foil, or transfer the cookies with a wide metal spatula (if the cookies stick to the foil they were not baked long enough—return them to the oven).

Place the cookies on racks to finish cooling or just turn them over to allow the bottoms to dry.

Store airtight.

NOTE: It is best to pour some vinegar into a cup and spoon out the amount you need. If you pour it into a spoon held over

the mixing bowl there is a good chance you might pour more than
you want.

Espresso Brownies

Dark, rich, incredibly chocolate. Bittersweet. The sour cream in
these is most unusual in brownies; it makes the brownies divinely
moist and fudgelike. Variations of this recipe have been with me
all my life. These are great brownies either with or without the
espresso.

2½ cups (10 ounces) walnuts
5 ounces unsweetened chocolate
6 ounces (1½ sticks) unsalted butter, plus additional for greas-
   ing pan
4 eggs graded "large"
2 cups sugar
⅔ cup sifted unbleached flour
⅓ cup sifted unsweetened cocoa powder (preferably Dutch
   process)
½ teaspoon salt
5 teaspoons instant espresso powder (I use Medaglia D'Oro)
1 teaspoon vanilla extract
⅓ cup sour cream
24 LARGE BROWNIES

Adjust an oven rack one-third up from the bottom and preheat
the oven to 400 degrees. Prepare a 10½-by-15½-by-1-inch jelly-roll
pan as follows: Place the pan upside down on a work surface.
Place a 19-inch length of 12-inch-wide aluminum foil shiny side
down over the pan, centering it carefully so the borders are all
the same. Fold down the sides and corners to shape the foil.
Remove the foil. Run cold tap water into the pan to wet it all
over. Pour out excess water, but do not shake or dry the pan.
Place the shaped foil in the wet pan (the wet pan holds the foil
in place). To butter the foil, place a piece of butter in the pan and

place the pan in the oven to melt the butter. Then spread the butter with a piece of crumpled plastic wrap or wax paper to coat the foil all over. Set the prepared pan aside.

To toast the nuts: Spread them in a single layer in a large shallow pan and bake for 8 to 10 minutes in a 400-degree oven until the nuts are just about too hot to touch. Cool. Break into large pieces and set aside.

Place the chocolate and the butter in the top of a double boiler over hot water on moderate heat. Cover and let heat until the chocolate and butter are almost melted. Then uncover and stir until smooth.

Remove the top of the double boiler and set aside.

In the small bowl of an electric mixer beat the eggs to mix. On low speed gradually add the sugar. Increase the speed to high and beat for 15 minutes.

Meanwhile, sift together the flour, cocoa, salt, and espresso and set aside.

In a small cup stir the vanilla into the sour cream. Add to the egg mixture and mix only briefly. Transfer the egg mixture to the large bowl of the electric mixer. Then, all at once, add the warm chocolate mixture and the sifted dry ingredients and beat together on low speed—scraping the bowl frequently with a rubber spatula—only until just barely mixed, no longer.

Remove the bowl from the mixer, add the walnuts, and fold them in with a rubber spatula.

Turn into the prepared pan and spread as smooth as possible.

Bake for about 20 minutes, or until a toothpick gently inserted in the middle comes out dry—do not overbake or underbake.

Remove the pan from the oven. Let stand for 5 minutes. Then cover the pan with a large rack and turn the pan and the rack upside down. Remove the pan and the foil. Let the cake cook upside down.

When cool, chill the cake for about 45 minutes in the freezer or longer in the refrigerator.

Cover the cold cake with a large rack or a flat-sided cookie sheet and turn upside down, leaving the cake right side up. Transfer the cold cake to a cutting board and, with a ruler and toothpicks, mark it into quarters. With a long-bladed sharp knife or a serrated bread knife cut into quarters—and then cut each quarter into 6 brownies.

Wrap individually in clear cellophane or wax paper.

Blondies

This non-chocolate brownie (a.k.a. Butterscotch Brownie) is made with an unusual technique—the eggs and sugar are cooked together before the other ingredients are added. The cookies are deliciously chewy.

Butter for greasing pan
1½ cups (6 ounces) pecan halves
4 eggs graded "large"
1 pound lump-free light brown sugar (strain if necessary)
2 cups triple-sifted unbleached flour (sift before measuring)
1 teaspoon baking powder
½ teaspoon salt
1 teaspoon vanilla extract
24 BARS

Adjust a rack one-third up from the bottom of the oven and preheat the oven to 375 degrees. Prepare a 13-by-9-by-2-inch pan as follows: Place the pan upside down on the work surface. Center a 17-inch length of aluminum foil shiny side down over the pan. Fold down the sides and corners of the foil to shape it. Remove the shaped foil. Pour a little cold water into the pan and then pour it out; do not dry the pan. Place the pan right side up and place the shaped foil in the pan; press it into place gently and carefully. To butter the foil, place a piece of butter in the pan, place the pan in the oven to melt the butter, and then carefully brush the butter all over the foil or spread it with crumpled wax paper or plastic wrap. Set the pan aside.

To toast the nuts, place them in any shallow pan in the oven for about 10 minutes until very hot. Cool, then break into coarse pieces and set aside.

In the top of a large double boiler whisk or beat the eggs to mix them. Add the sugar. Place over warm water on moderate heat. Stir with a rubber spatula until the ingredients are mixed. Then let cook over hot water for 20 minutes, stirring and scraping the sides occasionally.

Meanwhile, sift together the flour, baking powder, and salt, and set aside.

After cooking the egg mixture for 20 minutes, transfer the mixture to the large bowl of an electric mixer. Without cooling the mixture, add the vanilla extract and then, on low speed, add the sifted dry ingredients, scraping the bowl and beating only until incorporated. Remove the bowl from the mixer. Stir in the nuts. Turn into the prepared pan and smooth the top.

Bake for 20 minutes, or until the top has a hard golden-colored crust and a toothpick gently inserted in the middle comes out only slightly sticky.

Let stand at room temperature until cool. Then cover with a cookie sheet and turn the pan and the sheet upside down. Remove the pan and gently peel off the foil. Cover the cake with a length of wax paper and another cookie sheet. Carefully turn both cookie sheets and the cake upside down again, leaving the cake right side up.

These will cut much better if the cake is chilled. Place it in the refrigerator for at least an hour or in the freezer for a shorter time.

Mark the cake into quarters. With a serrated bread knife cut it into quarters and then cut each piece into 6 bars. Wrap individually in clear cellophane or wax paper. Or pack in an airtight box with wax paper between the layers.

Raisin Oatmeal Cookies

Huge, soft, and chewy—with peanut butter, raisins, oatmeal, and no flour.

1½ cups (8 ounces) raisins
4 ounces (1 stick) unsalted butter, at room temperature

1¼ cups (12 ounces) smooth peanut butter (I use Peter Pan)
1 teaspoon vanilla extract
1 teaspoon light or dark corn syrup
1 cup granulated sugar
½ cup dark brown sugar, packed.
3 eggs graded "large"
2 teaspoons baking soda
½ teaspoon mace
4 cups old-fashioned rolled oats (not "instant")
22 TO 24 LARGE COOKIES

Adjust two racks to divide the oven into thirds and preheat the oven to 350 degrees. Line cookie sheets with parchment paper or with aluminum foil, shiny side up. Set aside.

Place the raisins in a vegetable steamer over hot water on high heat, cover, and steam for about 10 minutes. Uncover and set aside.

In the large bowl of an electric mixer beat the butter until soft. Add the peanut butter and beat until mixed. Beat in the vanilla, corn syrup, and both sugars. Then add the eggs one at a time, beating until mixed. Through a fine strainer add the baking soda and mace. Then on low speed add the oats. Remove the bowl from the mixer and stir in the raisins.

Place a length of aluminum foil on the counter next to the sink. Use a ¼-cup measuring cup (the kind intended for dry ingredients) to measure the dough, and place the mounds any whichway on the foil. Wet your hands, just shake off the water, pick up a mound of dough, shape it into a ball, and then press it to about ½-inch thickness and 3 inches in diameter. Place the round of dough on the lined cookie sheet. Keep your hands wet, continue to shape the cookies, and place them on the sheets at least 2 inches apart (these spread—place only 4 on a sheet).

Bake two sheets at a time, reversing the sheets top to bottom and front to back once during baking. Bake for about 18 minutes or until the cookies are golden but not until they feel firm when gently pressed with a fingertip. Do not overbake. These will firm up as they cool, and they are best if they are soft.

Let the baked cookies stand on the sheets for about a minute to firm up a bit. Then with a wide metal spatula transfer the cookies to racks to cool.

If these are not to be served soon they should be wrapped individually in plastic wrap, wax paper, or foil. Or box them with wax paper between the layers. Just don't let them dry out.

VARIATION: *Chocolate Chunk Raisin Oatmeal Cookies*
You should use about 12 ounces of semisweet chocolate— preferably the kind that comes in thin bars like Tobler Tradition or Lindt Excellence. Cut the chocolate into pieces about ½ inch in diameter. I use an ice pick rather than a knife to break up the chocolate. The pieces will be uneven. Follow above recipe, and add the chocolate after adding the raisins. Shape as above. (If the cookies tend to crack on the edges press the cracks together and, if necessary, move some of the pieces of chocolate from the edges to the top.) Bake as above. Serve while the chocolate is still soft or let the cookies stand until the chocolate hardens before wrapping.

Pennsylvania Dutch Chocolate Cookies

Plain, very dark, and intensely chocolate wafers. This is one of only very few chocolate recipes that are traditional Christmas recipes. It is customary to serve these after dark on Christmas Eve.

> *1 cup sifted whole-wheat flour*
> *1½ cups sifted unbleached flour*
> *1 teaspoon baking soda*
> *1 teaspoon cinnamon*
> *Scant ½ teaspoon salt*
> *1 cup unsifted unsweetened cocoa powder (preferably Dutch process)*
> *8 ounces (2 sticks) unsalted butter, at room temperature*
> *1 teaspoon vanilla extract*
> *2 cups granulated sugar, plus additional for sprinkling cookies*
> *1 egg graded "large"*

ABOUT 15 HUGE COOKIES OR 36 MEDIUM-SIZE

Adjust two racks to divide the oven into thirds. Preheat the oven to 400 degrees. Line cookie sheets with parchment paper or with aluminum foil, shiny side up; or if you wish these can be baked on unlined sheets—they will not stick. Set aside.

Sift together both flours, the baking soda, cinnamon, salt, and cocoa, and set aside.

In the large bowl of an electric mixer beat the butter until soft. Beat in the vanilla and the 2 cups of sugar. Then beat in the egg and 1 tablespoon of water. On low speed gradually add the sifted dry ingredients, scraping the bowl as necessary and beating until incorporated. Turn the mixture out onto a large board or a counter-top and knead it until it is perfectly smooth. Then work with half of the dough at a time.

On a lightly floured pastry cloth, with a floured rolling pin, roll out the dough just a bit. Then, to flour both sides, turn the dough upside down and roll the dough until it is ¼ inch thick (no thinner).

Traditionally these are cut with a very large plain round cutter about 5 inches in diameter. These are gorgeous when large, but make them any size or shape you want.

Cut out the cookies right up against the edge of the rolled dough, and cut them just touching each other. Use a wide metal spatula to transfer them to the cookie sheets. Place them about 1 inch apart. If the cookies are 5 inches wide, place only 3 or 4 on each sheet.

Reflour the cloth only slightly before rolling the second half of the dough. Reserve the scraps from both halves of the dough, knead them together, and reroll. Do not incorporate any more flour than is necessary.

Sprinkle the tops of the cookies generously with additional sugar.

Bake for 9 to 10 minutes, reversing the sheets top to bottom and front to back once during baking to ensure even baking. Do not overbake; these are so dark that they can burn and you wouldn't know by looking. These will not be firm to the touch when they are done, but they will become firm when they cool.

With a wide metal spatula transfer the cookies to racks to cool. Store airtight.

Maida Heatter

219

Edward Giobbi

CHRISTMAS EVE—
SEVEN FISH
SEVEN WAYS

Artist and author Edward Giobbi has combined both his vocations in an unusual Christmas Eve custom—seven fish served seven ways—a custom that may have grown from the observation of a fast day. Dining on family-crafted dishes and place mats, the Giobbis have created a warm and festive evening that reaches out to friends of all faiths. Giobbi has written ITALIAN FAMILY COOKING *and* EAT RIGHT, EAT WELL THE ITALIAN WAY *(with Dr. Richard Wolff).*

CHRISTMAS EVE is the most important holiday of the year for our family and has been since my childhood in Waterbury, Connecticut. It was always wonderful, even during the Depression, when there were very few gifts and very little money for food. The mystery of the Nativity and a feeling of good will were still strong and steadfast, and somehow my parents always managed to scrape together a wonderful dinner on Christmas Eve despite the hard times.

As a boy I delivered Christmas trees for our neighbor, who sold them; on Christmas Eve he would pay me for my work with a tree. Excitedly I would drag it home. My father would make a stand for it and my sisters and I the decorations. We loved our tree.

That night, in particular, the house always smelled special. Even though my father was a very fine cook in his own right, on Christmas Eve my mother, another superb cook, did all the cooking. She had already prepared the Christmas pastries—turnovers filled with an exotic combination of cooked chick-peas, honey, and toasted almonds that were deep-fried, then dusted with powdered

221

sugar, and unforgettable crispy rounds filled with a reduction of grapes, saved from my father's wine-making, chopped chocolate, orange rind, and walnuts. These pastries were dear to us. The ingredients were expensive and hard to come by and were reserved especially for Christmas. To this day, they remain singularly special to me.

My mother came from a small town in the central part of Italy near the Adriatic, by the name of Centobuchi. There the tradition was to serve fish on Christmas Eve. She had brought her traditions with her to this country, and despite the Depression we ate fish, marvelous fish, served different ways on Christmas Eve. It was a magical time. We ate in the kitchen, which was heated by a cast-iron kerosene stove, just my mother, my father, my two sisters, and me. The table was bountiful, and there was a tangible, reverberating joy of being surrounded by the mystery of the Nativity.

Gifts were a very small part of our holiday. I used to receive one of the forerunners of comic books called Big Little Books, or a box of crayons or a coloring book. My sisters would get a small doll each. We didn't believe in Santa Claus, because he had never visited us. What enthralled us was the mystery and magic of Christmas. My parents were not religious people, but they were spiritual, and they expressed this by breaking bread together. Indeed, there was a very strong emphasis on the food in our household. Despite the Depression and our poverty, the food was nearly always suitable for the occasion.

As the years progressed and life became easier, more gifts appeared under our tree, my mother made more sweets, and more fish came to our table. It reached a point in the late 1930s when the tradition of serving seven different fish cooked seven different ways took hold. My mother had a friend from a fishing village in southern Italy, where the tradition existed. I was told that the seven fish represented the seven sacraments. For my sisters and me, these seven courses were utterly captivating. And although, as with most children, fish was not our favorite food, we looked forward to the dinner with jittery anticipation and actually counted the courses to make certain seven, not six or five, appeared. We also ate everything on our plates, as unexpected as that might sound for children; we wanted to play a part, equal parts, in the joyous occasion.

During World War II the tradition of our very special Christmas Eve dinner continued. Fish was plentiful, being unrationed. Then during my student days in Italy in 1951–54, I spent Christmas with my relatives on their farm in Centobuchi. Interestingly, they did not observe the tradition of serving seven different fish cooked seven different ways. We did have fish, but it was served as an antipasto, with pasta, then broiled, and finally fried. Of course, it was delicious, but it didn't hold a candle to the way we prepared it at home.

When I got married, my wife and I continued the tradition of my family's Christmas Eve dinner, and our children—like my sisters and me—though not especially fond of fish, eagerly awaited the holiday, counting the fish dishes to be certain there were seven. Our children are now adults and the custom lives on through them. Tradition is a form of constancy and it seems to me that constancy of a pleasurable experience is something everyone quietly hungers for, and needs.

Fish is consumed on Christmas Eve in Italy perhaps because of the importance of the symbolism of fish in the Catholic Church. Our dinner is difficult to prepare, but my mother looked forward to making it, as do I. To prepare each fish properly, it should be cooked just before serving, unless the recipe indicates otherwise. This means your selection of recipes and timing has to be very accurate, especially since the majority of the recipes should not be prepared ahead of time.

The following menu is a typical Christmas Eve dinner served in our home. Final decisions for the menu depend upon whatever fish are available at that time.

Antipasto
Baked Stuffed Littleneck Clams
(a recipe my mother always made on Christmas Eve)
Grilled Long Island Scallops
Fried Whitebait with Lemon Wedges
Shrimp and Artichoke Hearts San Benedetto Style

Edward Giobbi

Linguine with Crab Sauce

Baked Cod with Broccoli di Rape
Cuttlefish with Fresh Peas

Desserts
Ellie's Pecan Pie and
Almond Biscotti
Ellie's Bread

Espresso
My best homemade wines reserved for Christmas Eve
Grappa   Brandy

You will need to be organized, particularly in readying and serving the antipasto. Begin by opening the clams and stuffing them ahead of time. Keep them refrigerated. Have the scallops and whitebait rinsed and ready for cooking. The shrimp and artichoke combination can be fully prepared in advance. So, while the guests are seated, bake the clams as you grill the scallops and fry the whitebait. It sounds difficult, but I assure you it is not. When everything is ready, present each antipasto on a platter and serve small portions of each dish on the same plate. As a postscript to this most challenging part of the dinner, I do not recommend having helpers in the kitchen. Maybe one other person, but that is all. Otherwise the cooking and control of finishing each dish gets away from you, and you have a dinner that is probably fine but not done quite the way you might have done it had you remained in charge. No question, working alone, you do have to keep your wits about you—overcooked fish is terrible—but you will.

While the antipasto is being enjoyed, the second course—pasta with either blue crab or lobster sauce—is in its final stages. You have, obviously, made the sauce beforehand and are only heating water and cooking the pasta. You will need some help clearing the table. (We always had very good luck in asking our children to participate.) Then serve small portions of the pasta in warm soup bowls. You have undoubtedly noticed how I stress only small servings. As you work your way through seven courses there is a remarkable amount of food, and you want people to enjoy the last courses as much as they do the antipasto.

Fish course number six is usually a baked fish combination such as cod or red snapper slices with black olives and broccoli di rape. It, too, has been assembled ahead of time. However, you will have to allow time to blanch and sauté the rape before incorporating it into the final dish. (This should be done ahead of time.) As it finishes in the oven, fish number seven, a pan of sliced squid or cuttlefish in light tomato sauce with peas, is on top of the stove simply staying warm. In a break with tradition, these final courses are served on the same plate. In Italy each course would be served on a separate plate. Again, only small portions.

At our house we sit in the kitchen around a large round table that seats twelve. There are five in our family, so we never invite more than seven people because we feel we should all eat together. We dress as if we are going to the best restaurant in the country. It was always like that; even when I was a child we wore our best at the table. We drink lightly before dinner in order to savor the food and enjoy the excellent wines served with dinner. The wines served when I was a boy were ones my father had made, the best of them having been reserved for Christmas Eve. I, too, serve the best wines I make. Last year I served Cabernet, Merlot 1980, and a Chenin Blanc 1984.

My wife spends a great deal of time decorating the table and the house in general. The place mats we use, scenes from the Nativity, were painted by our children when they were young. Some of the plates are ones I painted years ago and gave to my wife. Many of the serving pieces were painted by the children fifteen years or so ago. I write the menu on the back of some abstract religious lithographs I made a number of years ago and place these menus in front of each guest, who takes the menu home. We eat slowly and relish the occasion so that it lasts as long as possible.

Christmas desserts are made by my wife. Pecan pie is one of our favorites, and her almond biscotti are wonderful, too. Espresso

Edward Giobbi

follows dessert, and then grappa and brandy. My wife always makes the bread, too.

After dinner we retire to the living room and gather around the fireplace to share a tradition that has existed since we have been married, one my wife is responsible for, one which our children adore. First my wife lights the candles and lowers the lights. Ellie then brings out a Bible that is read every Christmas Eve. Every year a guest is asked to read to the group a paragraph from St. Luke 2:1–20. The guests who have been asked to read have been Catholics, Protestants, Jews, and agnostics. Their names and the dates of their readings have been written in our Bible. Then we listen to a record of *A Child's Christmas in Wales*, written and narrated by Dylan Thomas. His beautiful, resonant voice, full of humor and emotion, is always an overwhelming experience. We sip our grappa and brandy in blissful contentment. Many are the times I have thought to myself, What a wonderful birthday!

For the Antipasto

Vongole Ripiene
(Baked Stuffed Littleneck Clams)

16 littleneck clams (or mussels)
½ cup breadcrumbs
½ teaspoon dried oregano
1 tablespoon minced Italian parsley
2 tablespoons freshly grated Parmigiano or Pecorino cheese
3 tablespoons good-quality olive oil
4 tablespoons dry white wine or vermouth
Salt and freshly ground black pepper to taste, or hot pepper flakes to taste
SERVES 8 AS PART OF THE ANTIPASTO

Inspect the clams and discard any clam that is not completely closed or does not close when dropped into cold water. Open the clams, loosen each one from its shell, and reserve its liquid. Discard the top shells. Place clams on the half shell on a baking sheet.

Combine the breadcrumbs, oregano, parsley, cheese, olive oil, 2 tablespoons of the wine, and salt and pepper to taste, and sprinkle a generous amount of this stuffing over the top of each clam. Strain the reserved clam juice and sprinkle it over the stuffing. Pour the remaining 2 tablespoons of wine into the bottom of the baking sheet.

Preheat the broiler for about 5 minutes. Then broil the clams under high heat until the breadcrumbs begin to brown. Pour the liquid in the baking sheet over the clams and serve immediately.

Grilled Long Island Scallops

1½ pounds Long Island or sea scallops
Olive oil
Fresh lemon juice
Freshly ground black pepper
SERVES 8 AS PART OF THE ANTIPASTO

Prepare a grill so that the coals are hot.

Arrange the scallops in a basket grill and grill them close to the heat until they just begin to brown. Turn and cook on the other side until they just begin to brown. Sprinkle with olive oil, lemon juice, and fresh pepper and serve at once.

Fried Whitebait with Lemon Wedges

1½ pounds fresh whitebait, 2 inches or under (if over 2 inches,
 fish should be gutted)
Corn or vegetable oil for frying
Flour
Salt
Lemon wedges
SERVES 8 AS PART OF THE ANTIPASTO

Carefully wash and pick over the whitebait. Wash again very well in cold water and drain.

227

Pour about 1 inch of the oil (I use corn oil) into a heavy skillet. When the oil is hot, flick a bit of flour into it. If the oil boils violently, it is hot enough to use. Dust the whitebait with flour and fry them, a batch at a time, for about 2 to 3 minutes, depending upon their size. Remove with a slotted spoon to paper towels to drain, sprinkle with salt, and serve while still warm with the lemon wedges.

Scampi e Carciofi alla San Benedetese
(Shrimp and Artichoke Hearts San Benedetto Style)

1 pound medium-size raw shrimp in the shells
1 (15-ounce) can or 2 jars artichoke hearts
Juice of 1 lemon
2 tablespoons extra virgin olive oil
2 teaspoons fine-chopped fresh mint, or 1 teaspoon dried
2 teaspoons fine-chopped Italian parsley
Salt and hot pepper flakes or freshly ground pepper to taste
SERVES 8 AS PART OF THE ANTIPASTO

Cook the shrimp in boiling water for 3 to 5 minutes, or until pink and just firm to the touch. Drain at once; when cool, shell and devein them. Slice the shrimp into pieces about ¼ inch thick and set aside.

Drain the artichoke hearts and chop into pieces no coarser than rough-cut breadcrumbs. Combine the shrimp and artichokes with the remaining ingredients and mix well. Serve at room temperature.

Linguini con Granchi
(Linguine with Crab Sauce)

You will note that the crabs used in this recipe are for flavor only. They are not served as part of the Christmas Eve dinner. There is a charming reason for this. Crabs are messy to eat and should really be eaten only with one's hands. On Christmas Eve everyone is dressed to the hilt. In truth, they are not right for the occasion, but are wonderful reserved for another time.

3 cups ripe tomatoes, peeled, seeded, and chopped
⅓ cup extra virgin olive oil
1 large red or green bell pepper, chopped fine
3 tablespoons chopped Italian parsley, plus additional for garnish
2 large garlic cloves, chopped fine
1 teaspoon dried oregano
1 tablespoon dried basil
Salt and freshly ground black pepper or hot pepper flakes to taste
1 pound dried linguine, preferably imported Italian
8 live blue crabs
¼ cup brandy
SERVES 8 AS THE PASTA COURSE OF CHRISTMAS EVE DINNER

Push the tomatoes through a sieve. In a wide, shallow saucepan just large enough to hold the crabs without overlapping, combine all the ingredients except the linguine, the crabs, and the brandy.

Clean the crabs: Turn each crab over, lift bottom flap, and pull off the top shell with your hands or force a thick-bladed knife under the shell to pry it loose. Rinse the crabs. (If you prefer not to clean the crabs yourself, have your fishmonger do it, but use them immediately.) Place the crabs in the sauce, partially cover, and bring to a boil. Boil gently for about 1 hour. Remove the crabs from the sauce and reserve them for another meal.

Cook the linguine in rapidly boiling salted water for about 7 minutes. Drain the linguine—it will be definitely undercooked and this is as it should be—add it to the sauce, and pour in the brandy. Cook the mixture, tossing constantly, over high heat for about 2 minutes, until the sauce thickens and the pasta is cooked al dente. Serve immediately on heated plates and garnish each portion with chopped parsley.

229

Baked Cod and Broccoli di Rape

10 cups broccoli di rape, or 1 large bunch broccoli
8 tablespoons extra virgin olive oil
6 garlic cloves, chopped fine
4 slices cod, haddock, or bass, each about 1 inch thick
½ cup dry white wine
24 dried black olives
Salt and hot pepper flakes to taste
ALLOW ½ SLICE PER PERSON FOR CHRISTMAS EVE
DINNER

Trim the broccoli di rape by discarding its tough leaves and tough, thick stems. Peel the tender stems and reserve. Cut the tender leaves into bite-size pieces. Cook the rape in boiling water for 3 minutes and drain well (if you use broccoli, cook for 5 minutes). In a large, wide skillet sauté the rape in 4 tablespoons of hot olive oil with half the chopped garlic for 5 minutes, turning it often. The rape is now ready to be combined with the fish. (For Christmas Eve, this can be done ahead of time.)

Preheat the oven to 500 degrees for about 15 minutes.

Arrange the fish slices in a baking pan and add 4 tablespoons oil, the remaining garlic, the wine and olives. Arrange the rape around the fish slices and add salt and hot pepper flakes to taste. Bake the fish, uncovered, for approximately 20 minutes, basting it occasionally, until it separates easily from the bone when tested with a fork or the tip of a sharp knife. Serve the fish with the rape. Garnish with a drizzling of extra virgin olive oil if desired.

Sepe con Piselli
(Cuttlefish with Peas)

4 tablespoons fine-chopped onion
3 tablespoons olive oil
1 teaspoon minced garlic
3 medium cuttlefish, cleaned (see Note) and cut into 2-by-½-
*   inch pieces (squid can be used instead of cuttlefish—use*
*   bone squid)*

Salt and freshly ground black pepper or hot pepper flakes to taste

2 tablespoons chopped parsley

4 tablespoons dry white wine

½ cup chicken broth

1½ cups fresh peas, boiled in salted water for 3 minutes and drained

SERVES 8 AS PART OF CHRISTMAS EVE DINNER

In a wide skillet sauté the onions in the olive oil over high heat until translucent. Add the garlic, cuttlefish, salt and pepper to taste, and parsley and cook, uncovered, over moderate heat, stirring constantly. When the liquid in the skillet has cooked down, add the wine, lower the heat, and cook until the wine evaporates. Add the chicken broth and peas, cover, and simmer for about 30 minutes, adding more broth if necessary to keep the peas moist.

NOTE: To clean cuttlefish, split open the cuttlefish with a sharp knife and remove and discard insides. Wash well and remove and discard skin. Cut off tentacles just below the eyes and remove and discard beak. Cut tentacles into serving pieces. Cut flesh into strips about ¼ inch wide.

Edward Giobbi

Bryan Miller

CHRISTMAS ABROAD: FRANCE AND SPAIN

Every week Bryan Miller keeps the readers of THE NEW YORK TIMES *up to date on that city's restaurant scene. His own food education began when he took a year-long sabbatical from newspapers to travel in Europe and then work in the kitchen of a French restaurant. But before that he had been introduced, one holiday season, to Christmas abroad.*

IN MY FAMILY THE CHRISTMAS HOLIDAYS were always a time of startling abundance, beginning on Christmas Eve and lasting right through New Year's Day. The menus never varied much from year to year, which was, now that I reflect upon it, part of the reassuring warmth of the season: the traditional Catholic fish feast on Christmas Eve, the roast turkey and ham the next day, with creamed onions, sweet potatoes, Grandmother's dense and chewy raisin bread, pickled beets, mounds of herb stuffing, and enough desserts to satisfy my elementary school for a week. Until I went to college, I simply assumed everybody had more or less the same culinary rituals. It was not until I spent my first Christmas and New Year's Eve abroad, in 1980, that my eyes were opened to the diverse delights of the holidays in other cultures.

Memories of my first Christmas in France are all the more special, of course, because everything was so deliciously exotic. I had been studying in Spain during the fall and went to France for the holiday break to visit my wife-to-be, Anne, in her hometown of Beziers, on the Mediterranean coast not far from the

233

Spanish border. Her family lived in a rambling 700-year-old manse surrounded by vineyards as far as you could see. A century ago it was a bustling spot where fifteen bedrooms and outbuildings were filled at harvest time with relatives and grape pickers. Most of the vineyards had since been sold and only a handful of the family still lived there year round. The Christmas dinner this year was to be held at Anne's cousin's home in Agde, a beach community nearby. The family always dined late on Christmas Eve, beginning about ten o'clock and continuing until well after midnight.

Before heading over we assembled in the living room of the big house to have an apéritif with Anne's father and another set of cousins. A stone hearth the size of some Manhattan studio apartments was festooned with seasonal greenery. Anne's father poured us *pastis*, my first exposure to the anise-flavored liqueur that is so popular in southern France and is usually cut with about five parts water. The experience was, to put it politely, unsettling. *Pastis*'s tart, vaguely medicinal flavor reminded me of licorice, which I had never liked. I wanted to pour the milky liqueur down the sink or give it to the dog, but being a first-time guest and wanting to make a good impression on my future in-laws, I decided to grin and bear it.

Along with the *pastis* we nibbled on chewy disks of *saucisson*, a dry garlic sausage produced locally, and French bread. Anne's father also passed around a crock containing a pâté-like substance, but it was unlike any pâté I had tasted before—very rich and highly seasoned, with a lingering aftertaste of garlic. It was called *rillettes*: shredded pork and duck preserved in jars under a layer of their own fat. *Rillettes* can also be made with rabbit, goose, and assorted game.

We drove to Agde about nine o'clock and met the rest of the family: Anne's cousins and aunt and her husband, their two rambunctious young boys, and her grandmother. At the time I spoke not a word of French, but the spirit of that evening needed no translation.

The first order of events was more *pastis*, which I now accepted politely and nursed for an hour as the boys tore open their gifts. Next we moved on to Champagne, along with bulbous Mediterranean oysters that had the most sublime briny flavor I had ever experienced. Unlike so many oysters I taste in restaurants in the United States, which are rinsed in the kitchen to remove grit— and, at the same time, much of the brine—these were as pure as a Mediterranean dawn, a shellfish epiphany. We also passed around plates of caviar with toast and slabs of velvety goose liver. I think it was the first time I ever tasted foie gras, and its ineffably luxurious texture combined with that unique lingering flavor made me an instant convert. I don't know if it was my imagination, but I believe my French comprehension improved with a few Champagnes.

Dinner was simple but so lovingly prepared and presented that it surpassed most multicourse feasts I have had since in restaurants around the world. We began with sparkling fresh sea scallops sautéed with cream and Cognac. It was the first time I had seen scallops served with their coral, the large orange sac attached to the white muscle. In the United States this sac is usually cut off and discarded for cosmetic reasons. I was a bit wary of this vaguely heart-shaped appendage, so I slowly munched on bread and watched what the others did. They devoured the sac with élan, so I joined in. It was remarkably good, as tender as fresh foie gras and with a wonderful hint of shellfish flavor.

For the next course we were served the traditional French Christmas lamb, blush-rose slices with garlic and mixed herbs. The French always eat their lamb extra rare. I can still smell the crust of rosemary, salt, and pepper. With the lamb we had fresh string beans and a salad of fragile lamb's lettuce tossed in strong olive oil and a dash of vinegar. We drank a dry, light-bodied red wine from a local cooperative that Anne's uncle stored in a twenty-gallon jug in the kitchen. It would win no highbrow wine competitions, but that night it seemed exquisite.

After I had consumed as much lamb as I thought a polite first-time guest should, we moved on to the cheese course with a bottle of Château Léoville-Las Cases, one of the great Bordeaux châteaux. The perfect match to this elegant wine was a rough-textured, striated hunk of Roquefort cheese. Not just any Roquefort for this occasion, though—this aged ewe's-milk beauty came directly from the famous cave in the town of Roquefort-sur-Soul-zon, about two hundred miles away. One of Anne's cousins worked there and brought it with her.

Finally came dessert, along with a bottle of a local sweet wine, Muscat de Frontignan, made from the muscat grape. Its thick, almost syrupy body takes some getting used to and is best sampled with something sweet to eat. In this case it was a charlotte of apples, a confection of ladyfingers set in a fluted mold filled with apples and ringed with raspberry sauce. It was so good I nearly scraped the decorative pattern off the china.

"*Joyeux Noël!*" we toasted with the last drops of Muscat, and I waddled off to bed with visions of charlottes dancing in my head.

The later part of the holiday was spent in Spain. On New Year's Eve I was on my way back to Salamanca and decided to make a detour en route to Valencia, where, I presumed, it would at least be sunny and warm. On the train I struck up a conversation with a lawyer from Barcelona named Jordi, who was on his way to a friend's house for the weekend.

"We have no families either, so why don't you join us?" he asked. I was a bit taken back at such an offer from a stranger, but decided that I had nothing to lose.

The friend in Valencia, Julio, was a poet and literary agent who lived in a cavernous turn-of-the-century apartment in a fashionable part of town. His *criada*, or maid, prepared a traditional Spanish New Year's Eve meal for us, which, in typical Spanish fashion, began about 10:30 that night. It was served on an antique table as large as a queen-sized bed and set with magnificent crystal, china, and monogrammed silver.

After a few glasses of Champagne and assorted olives, the meal began with a pale golden white wine from La Rioja, Spain's equivalent of Bordeaux, and a delicious onion and puréed-almond soup. This soup, as much a Christmas standard in that country as turkey is in the United States, tasted something like French onion soup, but with a nice hint of toastiness from the almonds. I remember how that steaming broth sent warmth to my toes in this typically underheated Spanish apartment.

Then came *angulas*, perhaps the most coveted delicacy in

Spain. *Angulas* are toothpick-sized white eels from rivers in the southwest. They spawn in the Sargasso Sea near Bermuda and then swim an incredible three thousand miles to Spain, where, after all that work, most get trapped in fine-mesh fishing nets. A traditional holiday treat, they are served in an earthenware crock with sizzling olive oil and shards of fresh garlic. You eat them like spaghetti, soaking up the garlic oil with bread.

I think Julio and Jordi were looking forward to a good laugh, figuring I would recoil at the idea of eating tiny eels, head and all. But I had eaten the eels before in the bars of Salamanca and had grown to enjoy their crunchy texture and oceanic flavor. So I devoured them eagerly, heeding the *angula* eater's credo: "Don't look them in the eyes."

The entrée was roast pork with red cabbage and apples. Pork is the most widely consumed meat in Spain and it is prepared dozens of ways—in *chorizo* sausages, in pies, in certain paellas, in soups, braised with various fruits, and, of course, as the famous roast suckling pig. On a tradition-bound day like Christmas it seemed appropriate. This pork was indeed special, or perhaps the circumstances added luster to it. But to this day I compare all pork dishes to it. With the meat course we had a ruby-colored red wine from La Rioja, bold and full-flavored.

The Spanish generally do not consume elaborate desserts, even on holidays. We finished our wine, then moved back to Champagne while nibbling on fresh figs, grapes, apples, and oranges. As the clock approached midnight, Jordi jumped up and came back into the room with an array of silly party hats, masks, and horns. We began tooting and howling like a gaggle of seven-year-olds at a birthday party. The maid appeared minutes before the magic moment and presented each of us with one dozen grapes, an old Spanish tradition. At precisely twelve seconds to midnight we all began popping grapes one by one into our mouths as the clock ticked toward the new year. Believe me, this is not so easy when the grapes have seeds. If you manage to consume all the grapes by midnight, good fortune will come your way in the new year. That year I could look forward to eight-twelfths of a good year, four parts having bounced onto the floor.

I missed my own family back in the United States that night,

Bryan Miller

237

but my worst fear—that of sitting desultorily in a Spanish café, alone, eating broiled fish with a half-bottle of wine—was avoided. At a festive table, I shared the generosity of strangers in a strange land. If that is not the holiday spirit, I don't know what is.

Christmas Leg of Lamb

1 6- to 7-pound leg of lamb
6 cloves garlic, slivered
1 tablespoon vegetable oil
1 tablespoon dried rosemary, crushed
1 medium onion, cut in half crosswise
Salt and freshly ground pepper to taste
6 TO 8 SERVINGS

Preheat the oven to 400 degrees.

Prepare the lamb for roasting by cutting away the hipbone and all the excess fat. Remove the cellophane-like fell.

With a paring knife make small incisions in the meat and insert the garlic slivers. Rub the lamb with oil and rosemary and place it in a heavy roasting pan, fat side down, along with the onion and the hipbone (with most of its fat removed). Sprinkle the meat with salt and pepper.

Roast the lamb on the floor of the oven (or the lowest rack, if in an electric oven), basting every 15 to 20 minutes. Turn fat side up after ½ hour. After 1 hour total cooking time, remove all liquid from the pan and pour ¾ cup water into the pan.

Continue roasting for 15 minutes. The internal temperature should reach at least 130 degrees for rare.

Remove from the oven and place the bone under the roast to serve as a rack in the pan, then let the lamb rest for 20 minutes as dripping juices enrich the gravy. Carve and serve with pan gravy.

Apple Charlotte

Bryan Miller

½ cup white raisins
¼ cup Cognac
7 to 8 thin slices white bread, or 1 package ladyfingers
½ cup (1 stick) butter
2½ pounds apples, peeled, cored, and sliced
½ cup sugar
1 tablespoon grated lemon rind
Apricot glaze (½ cup apricot preserves boiled with 2 tablespoons
    sugar)
Raspberry Sauce (see below)
SERVES 10

Soak the raisins in the Cognac for several hours.

Preheat the oven to 400 degrees.

Trim the crusts from the bread. Using about 2 tablespoons of butter, spread the slices on one side and toast only that side under the broiler.

Grease a 5-cup charlotte mold with 2 tablespoons of butter and line the wall with the ladyfingers or toasted bread, reserving one slice for the top. If using bread, press the untoasted sides firmly against the wall of the mold so they follow the contour. Place some of the bread (or ladyfingers), untoasted side down, on the bottom of the mold. (The untoasted sides will brown when the charlotte is baked.)

Melt 4 tablespoons of butter in a large skillet and sauté the apples with the sugar and lemon rind for about 10 minutes, or until tender. The idea is to remove much of the moisture in the apples. Turn the apples frequently.

Add the raisins and the Cognac and keep cooking until the liquid has evaporated so the apple slices will brown lightly. Spoon the apples into the mold. Cover the top with a slice of bread, toasted side down. Seal the charlotte closed by pressing the tops of the slices lining the wall inward so they fold over the slice capping the charlotte.

Place the mold in a shallow pan in which there is enough water to rise about 1½ inches up the side. Bring to a boil on top of the stove, then bake, uncovered, in the oven for 45 minutes.

Unmold by placing a platter on top of the charlotte and turning the charlotte upside down. Brush completely with apricot glaze. Serve hot or warm with Raspberry Sauce poured around each serving.

Raspberry Sauce

1 pint fresh raspberries, or one 10-ounce package frozen
Juice of half a lemon
¼ to ½ cup sugar
2 tablespoons framboise or Grand Marnier
ABOUT 1⅓ CUPS

If fresh raspberries are used, rinse and drain them. Put the fresh or frozen raspberries in the container of a food processor and add the lemon juice. Add ½ cup sugar for fresh berries; if frozen, add ¼ cup sugar. Blend thoroughly.

Add the framboise or Grand Marnier and blend.

Rillettes of Pork and Duck

Rillettes are easy to make. If well covered in the refrigerator they should keep for a week or more, ready to be served with cocktails. Here is a basic recipe that can be modified with other herbs and spices to suit individual tastes.

1½ pounds lean shoulder of pork cut into 2-inch cubes
1 pound duck meat, with skin and fat, cut into bite-size pieces
1 medium onion, peeled and studded with 3 cloves
1 large clove garlic, peeled
1½ cups dry white wine
Salt and freshly ground pepper to taste
⅛ teaspoon grated fresh nutmeg

Place the pork and duck in a saucepan, cover with water, and cook over medium heat for about 10 minutes.

Add the onion and garlic to the saucepan and cover tightly. Cook for 30 minutes, and then add the wine, salt and pepper.

Simmer for 3 hours, covered.

Discard the onion, remove the duck and pork with a slotted spoon, and let cool. When just cool enough to handle, place the duck meat and fat along with the pork in a bowl. Using a wooden spoon or wire whisk, work the meats and fat together. Add nutmeg and more salt and pepper if needed. The more the mixture is beaten, the whiter it becomes.

Taste for seasonings, and then spoon the *rillettes* into a terrine. Cover tightly and refrigerate. Serve cool with French bread and perhaps some Dijon mustard.

Helen Witty

"BREAKFAST FIRST"

Author most recently of FANCY PANTRY *and* MRS. WITTY'S MONSTER COOKIES, *Helen Witty is known for a kitchen that blossoms with abundant gifts of lovely food. These are gifts that fit everyone and, despite the Witty tradition of "breakfast first," should be opened before Christmas.*

WAYS OF KEEPING CHRISTMAS seem to drift down through the generations of a family, so it's likely that the holiday customs I grew up with had been established on one coast or the other long before my mother, from the East, and my father, from the West, met in the Puget Sound country, married, moved to Southern California, and began to bring up their own family. There, where snow and sleds and genuine holly were only a rumor, one family custom that came from somewhere was firmly maintained: The celebrations of Christmas Day began *after* breakfast, not before.

So well was our tribe imprinted with this custom, which some might think tantalizing to the point of cruelty, that it has been kept up in the families of all my siblings. This may be entirely out of respect for tradition, but I suspect "breakfast first" also survives because we've discovered that it helps preserve the frazzled nerves of parents obliged to spend Christmas Eve, until the small hours, deploying the presents and, even worse, assembling most of them.

By the time all my parents' big family had come along, any change in the pattern would have seemed very odd; Christmas just couldn't begin (as it seemed to, in some families) at midnight the night before or in an unruly raid on the presents at earliest morning light or indeed at any point at all before everyone was up, dressed, and comfortably fed.

It was hard for the children to be patient, even though our

custom included a token present waiting on the foot of each bed. But just as Christmas weather was always clear and sunny (that was back before smog) and the thermometer was expectably in the 80s, just as there were more palm trees than evergreens in the landscape, Christmas began after breakfast; that was the way it was.

So we took our places around the big dining-room table, excruciatingly close to the tree and the presents and the well-stuffed stockings visible beyond the dining-room door, and tucked into something more interesting to eat than the oatmeal, orange juice, and toast of every day. Dad liked to cook when he could, and he especially liked to fix breakfast, so he often turned out one of his Sunday specials on Christmas morning.

As a boy growing up on an island in Puget Sound, Dad had learned family-style cooking in a paradise of wild provender—salmon, shellfish, venison, wonderful berries—and had later sharpened his skills (for survival, he said) during youthful steam-boating and gold-seeking adventures in Alaska and the Yukon. (He never discovered a lot of gold, but I treasure a brooch set with a Ruby Creek nugget that he did find in those days and later presented to my mother.)

Although Dad's cookery was Western American, with Mid-west roots, he made chowders and some other dishes in ways I now recognize as pure New England, but how those ways traveled from one coast to the other I do not know. For breakfast he'd serve up sourdough pancakes with hot caramelized syrup he made himself, preferring it to store-bought maple syrup. His bacon was hand-cut and thick, and his even thicker slices of ham were sizzled in an iron skillet. He'd make "cream" gravy with the drippings, and often he'd bake big panfuls of yellow corn bread or the chil-dren's favorite—big, bumpy drop biscuits that were split, buttered, and heaped with boysenberry or youngberry or loganberry jam, or loquat or guava jelly, or the other preserves my mother made from the fruits of backyard trees. Dad also relished creamed cod-fish for breakfast (the salt fish came in little wooden boxes with sliding covers), or codfish cakes (New England again) if leftover mashed potatoes were on hand. His fried eggs were no-nonsense, turned and cooked decisively until firm. He'd scramble a bowlful of beaten eggs into great creamy curds, or scramble the eggs with poached and diced calves' brains for a most delicate dish.

More elegant breakfasts have been eaten since, but Dad's Christmas and Sunday cookery had an innocent zest I still remember.

Breakfast over, Christmas began. One child, or several in turn, played Santa and handed out the presents heaped under the tree glistening with hand-blown glass ornaments (commonplace then, priceless today) and swagged with ropes of cranberries and popcorn, garlands of spiky silver tinsel, and showers of metal-foil "icicles" that curdled intriguingly into wads if they fell to the floor. Banked on the piano and on a chair or two were all the dolls of Christmases past, even the raggedy ones. Our stockings hung above the fireplace; the bulge in the toe of each was an orange or a tangerine (tradition again, though neither fruit was exactly a rarity in that country of citrus groves). Among the small toys and candies and notebooks and pencils and puzzles in the stockings, the round lumps were walnuts.

There was always a box of ribbon candy we could raid at will—it was terrifyingly sweet then as now, but didn't it taste fruitier then? . . . There was a jar or two of soft-centered, satiny hard candies shaped like peanuts or raspberries or chunks of taffy . . . A platter of butter-cookie stars with candied cherries or sparkling sugar on top . . . Thick candy canes . . . Catnip for the cat, which was once intoxicated into climbing the Christmas tree . . . One year, there was an English wonder, a fruitcake topped with an inch of almond paste, made by the expatriate mother of a family friend. . . .

That was the Christmas I remember: a Sunday-special breakfast, then the presents, the toys and dolls, a day spent riding bikes or scooters or wagons in the sunny outdoors, with candies and nuts and cookies between meals quite remarkably allowed. Later, there'd be roast turkey for dinner, and chunky cranberry sauce, and mince pie—never mind the near-tropical reading on the thermometer.

As in my childhood home, Christmas morning at our house still starts with a not-for-everyday breakfast. As the "something

245

special," a yeast-raised stollen fragrant with lemon peel and spice, stuffed with dried fruits and almonds and snowy with powdered sugar, has become a tradition, but some other breads I've devised for the great day have also been well received.

And this is where family custom intersects with gift-giving. Because breakfast is the one holiday meal for which most store-bought gift foods—the ubiquitous assortments of cheeses and chocolates and charcuterie, fruitcakes and sweetmeats—aren't suitable, I'm likely to think of something for a pleasant yule breakfast when I'm contemplating gifts of food for friends. (Truth to tell, I also like to have a reason to make more than enough stollen, or hazelnut-cheese bread, or currant loaves, not the least because baking these good "keepers" can be fitted in well ahead of the holiday rush.)

A day or two before Christmas Day, then, the loaves are wrapped, often with an appropriate jar of preserves from the pantry shelf. Wild beach plum jelly, if we've had a good plum year here on the east end of Long Island, is a delectable companion for a "Christmas-card" currant loaf. Lemon curd, purple plum jam, or any really tart red jelly is most harmonious with cranberry-nut bubble bread. (The hazelnut-cheese bread needs nothing more than butter, though it's surprisingly toothsome with a fruit spread.)

As one package can look much like another, it's a good idea to attach a card or note alerting the recipient that the contents are to be enjoyed promptly, for breakfast or brunch or at will, and also telling how to warm the bread, if warming is appropriate, and how to store leftovers.

Not to be forgotten, of course, are the Christmas wishes for a merry breakfast, and for what comes after.

Hazelnut Cheddar Bread

Helen Witty

Devised for friends (and ourselves) who are best pleased by a zesty, nonsweet yuletide eye-opener, Hazelnut Cheddar Bread is meant to be toasted lightly and spread with the best butter. The flavors burgeon for a day or two after baking, so if you're making it for yourself, this isn't a bread to serve hot from the oven.

1½ cups milk
4 tablespoons (½ stick) unsalted butter
1 teaspoon salt
Pinch of sugar
1 envelope (1 scant tablespoon) active dry yeast
1 egg, beaten
About 5 cups all-purpose flour
2 cups (6 ounces) fine-grated extra-sharp natural cheddar cheese
1 cup coarse-chopped toasted and skinned hazelnuts (filberts)
Melted butter for pans and tops
MAKES 2 LARGE LOAVES

Heat milk with butter and salt until butter melts; cool until tepid, 100 to 110 degrees.

Combine the pinch of sugar with ¼ cup lukewarm water in a mixing bowl (or the large bowl of an electric mixer) and stir in the yeast; leave until foamy, about 10 minutes.

Add the tepid milk mixture to the yeast mixture; beat in the egg, then 2 cups of flour, one cup at a time, to make a smooth batter.

Stir 2 cups of the remaining flour together with the cheese, reserving the rest. Beat the floured cheese and the hazelnuts into the batter until well mixed, then beat hard (or knead by hand in the bowl) for 2 minutes, or beat at medium mixer speed for 1 minute.

Turn the dough out onto a floured surface and knead until dough is smooth and elastic but still somewhat soft, adding more of the flour as needed. (If mixing by machine, change to the dough hook and knead the dough at low speed for 2 minutes, then at medium speed for 2 minutes.) Form the dough into a ball.

Butter a large bowl, turn the dough around in it until coated, cover, and let rise until doubled, about 1¼ hours. Punch the dough down, turn it over, and let it double again, about 45 minutes.

Turn dough out onto a floured surface, flatten it to expel air, and cut in two. Form each half into a fat cylinder and place it in a buttered 8- to 10-cup bundt or kugelhopf mold, pinching the ends together. (Or use two standard loaf pans.) Cover and let rise until doubled, about 45 minutes.

Before rising is complete, preheat the oven to 400 degrees.

Brush the tops of the loaves with melted butter. Bake the bread in the center of the oven for 10 minutes. Lower the heat to 350 degrees; bake 30 to 40 minutes longer, until the tops are golden-brown and the loaves have shrunk slightly from the pan sides.

Turn the loaves onto a rack, cover with a towel, and cool. Wrap in foil or plastic and store 24 hours or longer before slicing.

NOTE: This bread keeps for several days at room or refrigerator temperature, or freezes for up to 6 months. Thaw completely before unwrapping.

One Dough, Two Christmas Breads

Use this fragrant sweet dough for two edible "Christmas cards"—glossy brown currant loaves sporting baked-on greetings in the style of Mexican carnival bread—or for two festively glazed cranberry-and-walnut bubble or "monkey" breads. First, the basic dough.

Sweet Dough for Christmas Breads

⅔ cup milk
⅔ cup sugar
1⅓ teaspoons salt
6 tablespoons unsalted butter, cut into slices
Pinch of sugar
4 teaspoons (about 1⅓ envelopes) active dry yeast
4 eggs, lightly beaten

2 packed teaspoons grated or fine-chopped lemon zest
About 6 cups all-purpose flour
MAKES 2 GENEROUS LOAVES

Heat milk to simmering. Stir in ⅔ cup sugar, salt, and butter; stir until dissolved; cool to tepid (100 to 110 degrees).

Combine ¼ cup lukewarm water and the pinch of sugar in a mixing bowl and stir in the yeast; leave until foamy, about 10 minutes.

Combine tepid milk mixture with yeast mixture; add eggs and lemon zest; beat to mix. Beat in most of the flour, a cupful at a time, reserving about 1 cup; beat well, by hand or machine.

Turn dough out onto a kneading surface spread with half the remaining flour and repeatedly scrape, turn, and cut the soft dough, using a dough scraper or a wide spatula, until the flour is incorporated. Sprinkling with more flour as needed, knead the dough until it is smooth and elastic; form into a ball. (A mixer with a dough hook may be used for these steps; knead about 4 minutes.)

Butter a large bowl, turn the dough around in it until coated, cover, and let the dough rise until doubled, 2 hours or more, depending on room temperature.

Christmas-Greeting Currant Loaves

Sweet Dough for Christmas Breads (see above), fully risen
1 cup currants

GLAZE
1 egg yolk beaten with 2 tablespoons milk, or use about 2
  tablespoons cream

PIPING PASTE FOR DECORATING LOAVES
4 tablespoons soft butter blended with 4 tablespoons flour and
  1½ teaspoons water, placed in pastry bag or decorating
  syringe fitted with plain writing tip
MAKES 2 LOAVES

Turn out the risen dough onto a lightly floured surface and knead in the currants.

Cut the dough in half; form each piece into a smooth ball higher than it is wide. Place each ball in a buttered 9- or 10-inch pie plate. Cover with a towel and let rise until doubled, about 45 minutes.

Before the final rising is complete, preheat oven to 350 degrees.

Brush the risen loaves with glaze. With the piping paste in a pastry bag or decorating syringe, write Christmas greetings on the tops of the loaves—MERRY XMAS or NOËL fits well—or make decorations (such as holly-leaf outlines or a simple wreath). Reserve unused piping paste for possible repairs during baking.

Bake loaves in the center of the preheated oven for 15 minutes, then check the decorations. If there are any small breaks, patch them with remaining paste. Bake the bread 15 to 20 minutes longer, until loaves are firm and hollow-sounding when tapped; they will be glossy-brown around the pale decorations.

Cool the loaves on racks. Wrap airtight and store or freeze.

NOTE: These loaves keep up to 4 days at room or refrigerator temperature, or freeze for up to 2 months. Thaw before unwrapping.

Cranberry-Walnut Bubble Rings

Sweet Dough for Christmas Breads (see above), fully risen
2 cups coarse-chopped cranberries
12 tablespoons (1½ sticks) butter
1½ cups light brown sugar, or ¾ cup each light brown and white sugar
1½ cups coarse-chopped walnuts
MAKES 2 LOAVES

While the dough is rising, combine the cranberries, butter, and sugar in a saucepan and cook them over low heat, stirring, until the sugar and butter melt and the cranberries soften slightly, 3 to 5 minutes. Cool. Stir in the nuts.

Turn the risen dough out onto a lightly floured surface and flatten to remove air. Cut the dough in two. Form each half into 1-inch balls. Spoon a generous layer of cranberry-nut sauce into each of two well-buttered 10-cup bundt or one-piece tube pans. Arrange a layer of dough balls ½ inch apart in each pan; scatter some of the cranberry and nut mixture over the layer; repeat layers, dividing ingredients equally, until dough and sauce have been used. Cover pans with towels and let rise until dough has doubled, about 1 hour.

Before rising is complete, preheat oven to 350 degrees.

Bake loaves in the center of the oven for 35 to 40 minutes, or until the tops are moderately brown and the sides have shrunk slightly from the pans.

Cool loaves in pans for a few minutes, then turn onto racks and cool completely. Wrap in foil or plastic and store.

N O T E : These will keep for several days if refrigerated; they may be frozen for up to 2 months. Thaw before unwrapping.

Helen Witty

251

Jehane Benoit

THE TRADITIONAL CHRISTMAS FEAST IN QUEBEC

This is one of the last pieces Jehane Benoit wrote before her death in late 1987. The best-known writer and speaker on food in Canada, Mme Benoit was leaving for a lecture tour when she called to say her article was in the mail. "It is the authentic Quebec Christmas," she said in her rich voice, beautifully touched with French overtones. She recalled the formality of the Christmas dinner set off by the cold weather and the excitement of Midnight Mass.

I AM HAPPY TO SAY that in the countryside of Quebec traditional Christmas celebrations have changed very little over the years, and even in the cities there are still many traditional festivities. For me Christmas traditions began with my own Christmas at my grandparents' home and at my parents', when as many as forty of us sat around the table.

The pleasurable anticipation of Christmas dinner is still very much with me, and I prepare for it the way we did when I was a child. The excitement then began to build up at least a month before Christmas, when the best secret recipes, handed down from mother to daughter, were taken out. Twenty years ago, in the country, the main course was a saddle of lamb or a haunch of venison marinated in red wine before roasting. This was served on a bed of puréed chestnuts. As a saddle of lamb is difficult to come by, I now sometimes roast a turkey, which, maintaining

253

tradition, is served on a bed of puréed chestnuts (they may be served apart).

Nobody seemed to worry much about vegetables, which are not a part of the northern winter. The favorite was usually cauliflower topped with a fresh herb butter, as both were a luxury at Christmas, this very cold time of year. When frozen vegetables became available, we added turnips cooked with peas. No Christmas dinner would have been complete without a plum pudding brought flaming into the dining room on a large silver platter.

Adults and children were all seated together at our long table, which was covered with the finest, largest, purest white damask. Cut glass and old silver were a must, shining to perfection. The Noel of long ago is something that I will never forget, and the festive meal with my children and grandchildren seated around the table is now a part of my tradition.

Noel Galantine

An important traditional dish or first course at our Christmas dinners, which everyone loved, was the Noel galantine. It is, in fact, a recipe passed on to us by the Naspakis Indians, who were here long before we arrived. They made it with venison instead of pork. Some people who have access to venison still make it that way.

4-pound loin roast of pork or a 4-to-5-pound boned shoulder of
    pork
2 pounds pig's feet
Good-sized piece of pork rind (optional)
2 large onions, minced
1 tablespoon coarse salt
¼ teaspoon ground cloves
1 teaspoon savory
1 cup boiling water
½ cup strong tea

Use a large cast-iron pan, or an enameled cast-iron Dutch oven. First place the pork loin or shoulder in the pan, fat side up, then place the pig's feet, each cut in three pieces, around the meat. If you have a pork rind, place it on top of the meat. Combine the minced onion and seasonings and distribute over all. Roast at 325 degrees for 2½ hours, without covering, basting, or stirring.

Then pour a cup of boiling water over the meat. Cover but do not stir, and cook another hour. By this time, the meat will be very well cooked.

Remove the meat from the juice. When it is cool enough to handle, remove the bones and cut the meat into coarse shreds with two forks. Cut the rind and the pig's feet into very small pieces. Place the meat in a mold of your choice.

Set the roasting pan over direct heat. Add ½ cup strong black tea to the juices in the pan (my grandmother and mother always used green tea). Scrape the bottom of the pan to remove all crunchy pieces. Pour the liquid through a fine strainer over the meat. Let it cool. Cover and refrigerate. When ready to serve, remove the meat from the mold and arrange on a platter with pickled onions, beets, and small gherkins. Serve very cold—and with lots of homemade bread.

Tourtière Tartlets

These tartlets were served as an appetizer either at the table or in the "salon" with small red linen napkins.

Jehane Benoit

PASTRY

2 cups all-purpose flour
1 teaspoon salt
½ teaspoon baking soda
Pinch of turmeric
¼ teaspoon savory
½ cup lard
⅓ cup ice water
⅓ cup (5⅓ tablespoons) butter

Stir the flour, salt, baking soda, turmeric, and savory together in a bowl. Cut in the lard with a pastry blender or two knives until the particles are about the size of peas. Add ice water by the tablespoon, stirring with a fork or the tips of your fingers, until just enough has been added so that you can pat the dough lightly into a ball. (Since flour varies, you may not need all the water.) Handle the dough as little as possible at this stage. Roll out the pastry, dot with the butter, and roll up toward you like a jelly roll, and roll out again in a flat sheet. Roll up and roll out again 2 or 3 times. Chill.

FILLING

1 pound ground pork
2 medium potatoes, peeled and grated
1 small onion, chopped
1 garlic clove, minced
1 teaspoon salt
½ teaspoon savory
¼ teaspoon ground cloves
1 egg beaten with 2 tablespoons water

Place all the ingredients except the egg in a saucepan. Bring to a boil, stirring to break the meat into small pieces. Cover and simmer for 30 minutes. Remove from heat and cool.

Roll out the chilled pastry to ⅛ inch thickness. Cut into small circles and use to line small tartlet molds or individual pie plates. Fill each pastry shell generously with the meat mixture. Cover with another circle of pastry and pinch the edges together. Brush the top with the egg glaze. Bake at 400 degrees until golden brown. Serve the tartlets hot.

The centerpiece of our dinner was most often a roast saddle of lamb. There were many Scottish people living in Quebec, and that is probably the source of this dish there. A magnificent roast standing proudly on the Christmas table was "hospitality sitting with gladness."

Nowadays serving a saddle of lamb (one piece containing both loins) is quite a luxury and it is not always possible to find one; if your butcher carries this cut, it usually has to be ordered in advance. The curry flavoring, which is definitely not French Qué-bec, was brought to us by a Scottish friend, and one custom associated with the saddle of lamb followed by my grandparents was also brought to Quebec by Scottish settlers. The roast was placed on the table in front of my grandfather, accompanied by some hot whiskey or brandy, which he poured on top and lit. While the saddle was flaming, everyone kissed his or her dinner partner and wished him or her the very best, with my grandfather offering best wishes to all.

Saddle of Lamb

¼ *cup vegetable or olive oil*
1 *teaspoon dry mustard*
1 *teaspoon salt*
½ *teaspoon freshly ground black pepper*
½ *teaspoon rosemary*
½ *teaspoon dried basil*
1 *saddle of lamb, 8 to 12 pounds*
2 *cups Lamb Stock (see below)*
2 *tablespoons butter, at room temperature*
1 *teaspoon curry powder*
2 *tablespoons all-purpose flour*

Stir together the oil, dry mustard, salt, pepper, rosemary, and basil. Place the saddle of lamb in a roasting pan and spread mixture on top. Roast at 400 degrees, allowing 10 to 15 minutes per pound.

When done and a deep, golden brown, with a lovely fragrance, remove the meat to a warm serving platter, cover with wax paper, and set aside in a warm place while you make the gravy. (The saddle comes to its point of perfection after a rest of 20 minutes.)

Pour off fat from roasting pan, add the Lamb Stock to the drippings over moderate heat, and stir all the crusty bits from the sides and bottom of the pan into the stock. Make a ball of the butter, curry powder, and flour. Add to the boiling stock in the roasting pan and stir quickly over low heat until creamy and smooth. Simmer 5 minutes and adjust seasoning.

Lamb Stock

Ask your butcher to give you the saddle trimmings. Discard as much fat as possible and place the bones and scraps of meat in a kettle. Add 4 cups water, a stick of celery, a small onion halved, 1 bay leaf, and salt and pepper to taste. Cover and simmer for 3 hours, then strain. The stock should be prepared in advance. Refrigerate it, remove hardened fat, and pour the cold stock over the drippings in roasting pan.

Vegetables, as I've said, were not central to our Christmas cooking; nevertheless, there were some traditional favorites. The combination of turnips and peas is a somewhat surprising one, but it was well loved, and no Christmas dinner was complete without it.

Mashed Turnip Petits Pois

1 large yellow turnip (rutabaga)
1 teaspoon sugar
3 to 4 tablespoons butter
½ teaspoon freshly ground black pepper
Juice of 1 lemon
2 cups frozen tiny green peas, cooked
Salt to taste

Don't peel the turnip until you're ready to cook it. Remove a thick layer of the peel, enough to eliminate the color line that is clearly seen between the turnip and the rind—this is where the bitterness is. Slice the turnip and scald with just enough boiling water to generously cover it. Then add the sugar.

Boil rapidly, uncovered, for 20 minutes. (Prolonged cooking darkens the color of the turnip and gives it a strong flavor.) Drain and mash; then add the butter, pepper, and lemon juice. Beat well and fold in the cooked green peas, making sure they have been well drained. Salt to taste and serve.

Golden Fan Potatoes

These potatoes were served on a large silver platter, surrounded by little colored paper fans with special good wishes personal to each guest.

> 12 medium potatoes, peeled
> Tray of ice cubes
> Paprika
> ¼ cup (½ stick) butter

Cut down through the top of each potato, making thin slices but keeping it together by not slicing right to the bottom. Leave about ¼ inch below. Place the potatoes in a bowl of cold water, cover with ice cubes, and let stand 1 hour. Drain and dry in absorbent cloth. Roll in paprika until they're well coated and blushing pink.

Melt the butter in a large frying pan and cook the potatoes, uncovered, over low heat. Turn them often, until tender and golden brown, about 35 to 40 minutes. (The cut side of the potatoes will open up like a fan.)

Plum Pudding

No Christmas meal could be traditional without the flaming plum pudding. For years and years, my daughter and I served the pudding immediately as it first emerged from the steamer because we found it was light textured and delicious, although lighter in color and a shade less rich than the usual mellowed version. However, if you belong to the old school and prefer to make your pudding ahead of time, this one keeps well for six months and can be frozen for as long as a year.

Either way, it would not seem possible to bring a pudding to the table without setting it on a silver platter together with all that is needed to flame it, and that is done by the master, as they used to say, or the man of the house.

PUDDING
2 cups currants
1 cup seeded muscat raisins
1 cup seedless golden raisins
1 cup fine-chopped mixed candied citrus peel
¾ cup brandy
1 cup unblanched almonds, sliced lengthwise
1 cup grated carrots
¼ cup unsifted all-purpose flour
1 tablespoon ground allspice
2⅓ cups fine-chopped chopped beef suet
6 cups fine, soft breadcrumbs (no crust)
8 large eggs, separated
1¼ cups brown sugar, well packed

MOLDS
4 tablespoons soft butter
½ cup brown sugar, well packed
10 to 12 glacéed red cherries
Cinnamon
10 to 12 thin strips candied citron

Combine currants, raisins, and mixed peels in a large bowl. Add brandy and toss ingredients lightly. Cover bowl and let mixture stand overnight.

Prepare pudding molds the following day before combining remaining ingredients. To do this, spread 2 tablespoons soft butter over the bottom and sides of each of two 7- or 8-cup crockery molds or bowls. Evenly pat ¼ cup well-packed brown sugar over butter in each mold; decorate the bottom of each one with 5 or 6 glacéed cherries. Lightly sprinkle cinnamon over the sugar, then arrange 5 or 6 strips of citron, in a vertical position, around the sides of each mold. (To keep them in position, press citron strips against the sides of the molds.) Refrigerate molds until you are ready to use them.

Add almonds, carrots, flour, and allspice to the brandied fruit mixture, tossing lightly but thoroughly. Stir in suet and bread-crumbs and lightly toss again.

Beat egg whites at high speed in an electric mixer until they are stiff but not dry, then reduce to medium speed and add the yolks, one at a time. As soon as the yolks are blended into the whites, gradually add 1¼ cups well-packed brown sugar. Stop beating as soon as the sugar and eggs are blended.

Fold the egg mixture into the fruit mixture; a rubber spatula is good for this. Turn the batter into the prepared molds, dividing it equally between the two. Place a large square of heavy-duty aluminum foil over each mold; press down on the sides of the foil, fitting it tightly around each mold. Secure the foil in place with string. Place each mold in a separate steamer. (To create a steamer, see the instructions for Steamed Persimmon Pudding on page 143.) Steam puddings for 3 hours, adding more boiling water to steamers as required. Remove the molds from the steamers and let stand on wire cake racks, without removing the aluminum foil, until the puddings are cold. It is customary to store puddings in a cool, dry place for at least 3 weeks before using. This gives them a chance to ripen. Each one makes 8 to 10 servings.

TO PREPARE A PUDDING FOR SERVING
Steam the pudding for 30 to 40 minutes, then unmold it onto a heated platter with sides. Spoon ½ cup flaming brandy over the pudding (see below) and serve with hard sauce or with Caramel Sauce (see below).

HOW TO FLAME A PUDDING
There are many ways to flame a pudding. My favorite is easy and reliable, and it can be done right at the table.

Set up a small silver tray with cubes of sugar, a little plate with a good-sized piece of butter, and a long-handled jug of hot rum or brandy. (Less expensive "young" alcohol flames better than fine old types.) Place the pudding on a silver or flameproof glass platter. Put a good-sized pat of butter on top of the pudding, stick into it 6 to 8 cubes of sugar, then pour the hot brandy or rum over it. Light it and, without delay, start basting by pouring the rum or brandy back on top of the pudding. Keep pressing the sugar gently with the back of the spoon and continue to baste until the flames die out naturally. The more you baste, the more it will flame.

It is important to have the hot pudding on a hot plate, because the hotter the platter, the longer the alcohol will keep warm—and the longer the flame will last.

My Grandmother's Caramel Sauce for Plum Pudding

Contrary to the English tradition of serving the plum pudding with hard sauce, the French Québecois flame it and serve it with caramel sauce.

3 tablespoons all-purpose flour
½ cup brown sugar, well packed
Pinch of salt
2 to 3 tablespoons butter
1 teaspoon vanilla extract
¼ teaspoon almond extract

Place in a saucepan the flour, brown sugar, and salt. Mix well and add 1 cup of cold water. Cook over medium heat, stirring all the time, until the sugar is melted; then continue cooking until smooth and creamy. Remove from heat, add the butter and vanilla and almond extracts. Serve hot. (The sauce will keep refrigerated for 10 to 12 days.)

Our Family Christmas Eggnog

Jehane Benoit

Grand Marnier may come as a surprise, but we always had it only during the month of December, to be used on Christmas and New Year's. Once you try it, you will never use a different recipe. In my youth, this was served to the children in small liqueur glasses, so we could join in with the elders in offering our good wishes.

> *6 egg yolks; retain whites*
> *1 cup maple syrup or granulated sugar*
> *1 cup rum*
> *1 cup Grand Marnier*
> *Grated rind of 1 orange*
> *½ cup brandy*
> *1 vanilla bean*
> *6 cups milk*
> *3 cups heavy cream*
> *6 egg whites, beaten stiff*
> *Freshly grated nutmeg*
> SERVES 20

Beat the egg yolks and the maple syrup or sugar with an electric beater until very creamy and light. Keep beating as you add the rum, Grand Marnier, grated orange rind, and brandy. Cover and chill 2 hours. Meantime, add the vanilla bean to the milk and let stand.

When 2 hours are up, remove the vanilla bean from the milk and slowly add the milk (while stirring) to the egg-yolk mixture. Whip the cream until it stands in soft peaks and gently fold in until it is well blended. Then fold in the beaten egg whites. At this point, the eggnog can be covered and will stay perfect for 12 to 24 hours. Sprinkle a bit of freshly grated nutmeg over each serving.

Pour any leftover eggnog into a container, cover, and freeze. Serve it as a frozen dessert, or thaw out and serve as a drink.

Robert Farrar Capon

THE GROANING

BOARD

In his SUPPER OF THE LAMB *Father Robert Farrar Capon wrote of his reverence for the taste and feel of food and the pleasure he takes in them. Here he mixes the ingredients of a full-scale family Christmas in exciting and exhausting detail.*

CHRISTMAS AFTERNOON IS FOREVER. In my household in the early 1960s, that was no pious sentiment. My wife and I, parents of six children, did not deliberately conspire to turn Christmas Day into an endless trial by wrapping paper, but somehow, holiday after holiday, we did just that. As the years passed, we took the simple Christmas-present routine of my childhood and complicated it to the point of insanity. As a boy, I had received all my presents either on Christmas morning under the tree or at the dinner table with my relatives. But as a young parish priest and a budding paterfamilias in the 1950s, I, like almost everyone else raising a family in those days, went out of my way to look for "traditions" with which to embellish (perhaps "load down" is a better phrase) our life. By 1962, the cement of our acquired customs had set pretty much like this:

Borrowing from the German background of my "aunt" Lotte (of whom more later), I had instituted the practice of giving presents on Christmas Eve as well as on Christmas Day. But since I had young children who were not supposed to be up for the festivities after Midnight Mass, I had ordained that there would be one round of presents given at suppertime on December 24. Predictably, these toddlers paid no attention to what anyone expected, so during the elaborate buffet after church, while the

265

second round of gifts was being given, they were also present, tearing up and down the staircase.

Then at 2:00 or 3:00 A.M. there followed the endless job of setting out the Santa Claus presents for Christmas morning. This meant, of course, getting out half the tools in the basement and trying to put together two-story dollhouses and pedal-driven fire trucks with the nonhelp of assembly instructions written by first-year students of English in Hong Kong. It also meant keeping six children at bay upstairs, not only during the time of putting tab "A" into slot "B," but also afterward, while my wife and I tried to get a few hours' rest.

In the morning, after the Santa Claus presents, there was a small additional round of token family gifts. Then the day began in earnest. Grandparents arrived at eleven o'clock in the morning. More small gifts. Then there was dinner at 1:00 or so, no mean affair. We had a standing rib roast of beef, wild rice, Yorkshire pudding, roast potatoes, mashed potatoes, as many vegetables as we had had at Thanksgiving, and enough good Burgundy to float a yacht.

My memory at this point becomes hazy. The two grand-mothers, I believe, decided that the formal giving of grandparental gifts should be deferred until after dessert—which, in turn, should be deferred until after the dinner dishes were done. Thus re-prieved, I withdrew quietly to my study, stretched out on the couch, and slept the sleep of the well-oiled just.

The next thing I remember was being slid off the couch and onto the floor by three of my children, and then dragged the length of the house by my two sons. Deposited unceremoniously in the middle of the family-room floor and slowly buried under a mountain of empty boxes, gift wrap, and bows—all the while muttering as best I could how nice these socks or that Sunday dress would look on their several recipients.

At 5:00 P.M., my own father decided, as he always did, that it was time for cold roast beef sandwiches and more wine (there were giants in the earth in those days). So up I got, carved again, laid out a spread, and settled down in my chair for a Christmas cigar just in time to hear the doorbell ring, announcing the arrival of a brace of aunts with, of course, yet another round of presents.

I remember nothing else, other than waking up late the next morning and mumbling to myself in tombstone Latin: *Hic jacet Robertus; obiit surfetii traditionum.* "Here lies Robert; he died of a surfeit of traditions."

Still, by the next Christmas I would surely be ready as ever to plunge into the ordeal again—in particular, the midnight buffet on Christmas Eve. This was not a tradition I had picked up from my own family; rather, it came to me from across the street, where my best friend, Arthur Beer, lived. His mother, Lotte, my "aunt" by friendship, was a first-rate cook who, whenever she decided to indulge in a fit of German cookery, insisted that I call her Tante Löttchen.

Even when Arthur was not around, I hung out in Tante Löttchen's kitchen, especially before Christmas, when the Germanic mood was upon her in earnest. My own family background was predominantly British (two grandfathers), with one Swedish and one Scottish grandmother tossed in. Christmas at our house, therefore, had a good deal of English reserve about it. But Christmas across the street was something else.

There, the entire festivity took place on Christmas Eve. Better yet, the whole performance—drinks, presents, and food—was in full swing from the moment you came through the door. There was no waiting; you simply walked in after Christmas Eve church services and dug in. Later on, as a priest, I developed a theological rationale for Tante Löttchen's style of celebration. I decided that my own family's restrained festivities gave the wrong impression. What was the point of rejoicing in church over the birth of the Redeemer if all you did afterward was go home and sleep it off? Tante, I concluded, had a much better idea: once the ecclesiastical party was over, you went straight into the domestic one.

Her house on Christmas Eve was the diametric opposite of my funereally quiet home. First, there were platoons of people: all her German relatives, plus a host of neighbors and friends. Second, the welcome was warm, even hot. Literally, because Tante Löttchen kept her house at 83 degrees; but it was also figuratively warm. Both my Uncle Otto (Tante's husband) and his brother Emil always seemed to have started their Christmas libations somewhere around noon on December 24; by the time of the party

267

they were energetically pressing drinks on anyone over four feet tall.

But third, there was the buffet itself, all laid out on the table, desserts included, from the start. There was Kartoffelsalat and Böhnensalat; there were breads—Westphalian pumpernickel and Vollkornbrot, Roggenbrot and Bauernbrot; there was Apfelkuchen with pitchers of heavy cream for the restrained and bowls of Schlagsahne for the serious eaters. But above all, there were Wursts. To this day, I can still see them, arranged on her table like the sections of an orchestra—a kind of philharmonic of pork. Liverwursts on the left: Kassler Leberwurst, Zwiebel Leberwurst, Gänseleberwurst, Kalbsleberwurst, and Braunschweiger; hot Wursts on the right: Niersteiner Mettwurst, Thüringer Mettwurst, Bauernwurst, Bratwurst, Weisswurst, and Knackwurst—(all accompanied by bowls of sauerkraut with caraway seeds and by red cabbage with apples. And then there were the cold cuts—the woodwinds, brass, and percussion of the performance. Let me simply list them as they sat there, sliced or whole: Jaegerwurst, Gelbwurst, Speckwurst, Ham Bologna, Ring Bologna, Bauernschinken, Westfälisher Schinken, Schwarzwälder Rauchfleisch, Landjaeger, Touristenwurst, Blutwurst—all of that, plus herrings, rollmops, cold ham, and roast beef (with sliced turkey for the timid), along with endless supplies of cheese, butter, mayonnaise, and the king of mustards, Düsseldorfer Löwensenf.

Since no one except ancient aunts drank wine at parties in those days, beer, whiskey, and (I do not lie) cream soda were the beverages of the evening—and it was by the working of the first two that the scheduling of the party's only *de rigueur* event was determined. All the adults exchanged presents as they came into the house, opening them as they greeted each other and leaving gift wrappings everywhere. But when Uncle Emil had progressed from two sheets to the wind to three, it was time for him to put on his Santa Claus suit and give out small favors to the children. The performance, from his constantly slipping pillow stuffing to his alarmingly secular line of patter, was something that even the smallest child's belief in St. Nick could hardly survive. Later on, I developed a theological justification for that, too. God did not save the world by uplift. He came down to our level and was born in the back of a barn; I decided, therefore, that we do ill when we gussy up the earthiness of our salvation with too many coats of propriety. I do not think that Jesus, the friend of publicans and sinners, would have found Uncle Emil anything but delightful. Both were the salt of the earth.

So when I came to establish my own style of celebrating Christmas, it was Tante Löttchen's party that was my paradigm. Every other year, I regaled my family and friends with a German Christmas Eve. What did we do in the off years? Well, I mentioned that my paternal grandmother was Swedish. Accordingly, the party in those other years was an authentic Swedish smörgåsbord.

My grandmother Amanda Anderson came to this country in the early 1890s as a young widow with one daughter. She worked here as a household cook and met my grandfather, a butler, at the French Cooks' Ball in New York City. So I came by my love of cooking in a direct line. My Swedish traditions, however, reached me by a kind of cushion shot. Amanda did not do very much Swedish cookery, having been trained and employed in places that looked more to France for culinary inspiration. Her sister in Boston, though—my great-aunt Anna—wore her Swedishness like a badge; it was from her hands that I first experienced Scandinavian Christmas fare, although not a lot of it. I remember clearly only *wörtlimpa* (orange-anise rye bread), herring in various guises, and *lutfisk*, the lye-soaked Swedish version of dried codfish, which I absolutely despised.

This meager beginning was launched into high orbit in 1950 when Amanda's daughter, my Aunt Edith, gave me a copy of *Good Food from Sweden* by Inga Norberg, the book that to this day remains my bible of Swedish cookery, and I promptly cooked my way through it. I baked *limpa* and *saffransbröd*, I did everything the book suggested with salt herring. I cooked pot roast with anchovies, basted my roast lamb with a cup of sugared and creamed coffee, served *lutfisk* and boiled potatoes to my family on Christmas Eve (my children hated it even more that I had—the meal was, besides strange-tasting, of a whiteness uniform enough to cause snow-blindness). I also kept *knäckebröd* (Swedish hardtack) on hand at all times. I mention this last item because I was able to do with it something my grandmother had always forbidden.

Knäckebröd has deep holes on the top side and only minor irregularities on the bottom. Amanda, being frugal, never allowed you to butter the side with the holes, lest you get the idea that butter was to be spread about with abandon. In my own house, therefore, I invariably buttered the top.

My grandmother tasted my Swedish extravagances only once or twice, but she had mellowed a bit with age and made agreeable Swedish noises as she sampled my handiwork. She never got to attend the Christmas Eve smörgåsbord in alternate years, but I am sure she would have approved. And so I give you our family smörgåsbord and bring this piece to a rest. After all the work of producing such a spread over so many years, what remains is a deep tug at the heart. I don't really remember the labor. I remember the sights and sounds of my own family: eight of us around the Christmas Eve supper table at 6:00 P.M. eating finnan haddie or smoked haddock or smoked codfish in cheddar-cheese sauce and singing carols in four parts. I remember Midnight Mass with the whole parish out and the church redolent of incense and Scotch-scented breath. I remember the party after Mass with our friends and their children, and our children's friends, and their children's friends. And last but not least, I remember the great Christmas dinner and the endless afternoon. Over the decades, we have not always done the best we could by each other, but by George, we did Christmas with both hands. It was no small thing, and I thank everyone for the company these long, short years.

Some Recipes for the Smörgåsbord

Robert Farrar
Capon

Herring is practically the backbone of the Swedish buffet, but in order to do justice to it, you will need to make your own from scratch. Salt Holland Herring, packed in 5-pound plastic barrels, is available in many markets and in cheese or specialty stores. Buy a barrel marked "mixed" (meaning males and females) so you will have roe for the Mock Oyster Pudding.

Pickled Herring Three Ways

HERRING IN WINE SAUCE
3 to 4 salt herring
½ cup white wine
½ cup vinegar
¼ cup sugar, or to taste
2 tablespoons pickling spice
1 tablespoon white peppercorns
1 small onion, sliced

Soak whole salt herring for 12 hours in several changes of cold water. Remove herring from water and bone and skin them, producing 6 or 8 fillets.

Combine remaining ingredients and bring to the boil. Remove from heat and cool completely.

Put the fillets in a suitable shallow dish, strain the pickling liquid over them, and marinate overnight in the refrigerator. Cut the herring into bite-size pieces before serving.

HERRING IN DILL SAUCE
½ cup white wine
½ cup vinegar
⅓ cup sugar, or to taste
3 tablespoons dried dill weed, or to taste
6 or 8 salt herring fillets, prepared as in step 1 above

Bring first 4 ingredients to boil. Remove from heat and cool completely.

271

Put herring fillets in a suitable dish, pour unstrained pickling liquid over them, and marinate overnight in refrigerator. Cut into bite-size pieces before serving.

HERRING IN SOUR CREAM

6 or 8 salt herring fillets, prepared and pickled as in first recipe above
1 cup sour cream
⅓ cup strained pickling liquid (from first recipe above)
2 or more medium onions, sliced thin

Cut herring fillets into bite-size pieces, mix with sour cream, pickling liquid, and onion. Refrigerate for at least several hours before serving.

Herring Salad

6 or 8 herring fillets pickled in dill sauce, diced
¼ cup vinegar
½ teaspoon white pepper
1 to 2 tablespoons sugar
1 cup cooked beef, veal, lamb, or pork, diced
1 cup cooked beets, diced
1 cup cooked potatoes, diced
2 sweet gherkins, diced
2 peeled, cored apples, diced
1 cup unsweetened, lightly salted whipped cream or 1 cup mayonnaise delicately colored with beet juice
2 or 3 hard-boiled eggs, sliced
6 or more cherry tomatoes, halved
Parsley for garnish

Mix first 9 ingredients thoroughly and pack into a 6-cup fish-shaped mold (or other suitable mold) that has been rinsed with cold water. Refrigerate.

Unmold the salad onto a platter, cover completely with whipped cream or mayonnaise, and decorate with sliced eggs, tomatoes, and parsley.

Herring Savory

2 salt herring
⅓ cup dry breadcrumbs
3 tablespoons butter
½ cup cream
1 tablespoon chopped chives

Soak whole salt herring for 12 hours in several changes of cold water. Remove from water and bone and skin them, producing 4 fillets.

Preheat oven to 400 degrees.

Coat fillets thoroughly with breadcrumbs. Butter a small gratin dish with 1 tablespoon butter, lay on the fillets, and dot with the remaining butter. Pour cream over and bake 5 to 10 minutes. Sprinkle with chopped chives before serving.

Mock Oyster Pudding

3 pairs salt herring roe
⅔ cup dry breadcrumbs
2 cups half-and-half
6 tablespoons melted butter
5 eggs, beaten
1 teaspoon sugar
⅛ teaspoon nutmeg
4 tablespoons butter
½ cup fine, fresh breadcrumbs

Rinse the roe well and soak in cold water for 3 hours. Drain and chop fine.

Preheat the oven to 350 degrees.

Mix the chopped roe with ⅔ cup dry breadcrumbs, the half-and-half, the melted butter, and the eggs. Season with sugar and nutmeg.

Grease a baking dish with 4 tablespoons butter and press ½ cup fresh breadcrumbs into the butter. Pour in the roe mixture and bake for 30 to 40 minutes, or until the center is nicely puffed.

Robert Farrar
Capon

273

Recipes Using Swedish Anchovies

Swedish anchovies (*ansjövis sprats*) are preserved in a sweet, spicy sauce. They are available in cheese shops and specialty stores, and they provide the characteristic "Swedishness" of the following dishes. NOTE WELL: Italian or other Mediterranean anchovies are *not* a substitute for the Swedish sprats; there is no substitute.

Anchovy Eye

6 to 8 Swedish anchovy fillets, chopped fine
1 raw egg yolk
1 medium onion, chopped fine

Arrange the chopped anchovies in a circular mound in the center of a small plate and make a well in the middle.

Carefully slip the egg yolk into the well.

Arrange chopped onion around the outside of the anchovies so that the onions have the shape of the white of an eye. First guest to tackle this dish has the privilege of mixing the ingredients together.

Janssons Frestelse
(Jansson's Temptation—Swedish Scalloped Potatoes)

6 tablespoons butter
10 potatoes, peeled and sliced
10 Swedish anchovy fillets, cut into small pieces, reserving liquid
2 onions, chopped fine
3 tablespoons all-purpose flour
Salt to taste
White pepper to taste
1½ cups cream

Preheat the oven to 375 degrees.

Grease a casserole with 2 tablespoons butter. Place a third of the potatoes in the bottom of the casserole. Add half the anchovies, onions, and flour, plus 2 tablespoons butter, and salt and pepper to taste. Top with a layer of potatoes. Add the remaining anchovies, onions, flour, butter, and seasonings. Cover with the remaining potatoes.

Pour on cream to which has been added the anchovy liquid (about 1 teaspoon or less). Add salt and pepper to taste.

Bake, covered, for 1 hour.

Uncover and continue to bake until brown on top, about 20 minutes.

Gentleman's Relish
(Old Man's Hash)

3 large onions, chopped
3 tablespoons butter
12 Swedish anchovy fillets, chopped fine
6 hard-cooked eggs, chopped
1 teaspoon anchovy liquid
¼ cup heavy cream, or more, to taste

Sauté onion in butter until transparent.

Add chopped anchovies, remove from heat, and add remaining ingredients. Mix well and serve warm.

Other Items for the Smörgåsbord

Rabiff
(Swedish Steak Tartare)

1 pound top-quality lean beef, chopped fine (see Note)
4 tablespoons capers, chopped
Salt to taste
1 raw egg yolk
2 medium-size cold boiled potatoes, cut into small dice
2 medium-size cooked beets, cut into small dice
4 tablespoons red onion, chopped

Mix the first 3 ingredients together and arrange in a flat mound in the center of a serving plate.

Score a pleasing pattern on the mound with the back of a knife blade. Make a well in the middle and slip the egg yolk into the well.

Garnish the edge of the plate attractively with the remaining 3 ingredients. Serve with *knäckbröd* and butter.

NOTE: To ensure freshness, quality, and integrity, this dish is best made from raw beef purchased from a reliable butcher and ground at home.

Kalvsylta
(Jellied Veal)

2 pounds neck of veal
1 veal knuckle
Salt to taste
½ teaspoon white pepper
2 tablespoons vinegar, or to taste
1 teaspoon powdered plain gelatin, softened in 1 tablespoon cold
*   water (use more gelatin if you want very firm results)*

Combine the meats in a kettle and add water to cover. Season with salt and simmer for 2 to 3 hours, or until very tender.

Take out the meat, cool, remove bones and sinews, and cut

it into small pieces. Meanwhile, let the stock boil hard to reduce slightly.

Strain the stock, add the meat, pepper, and vinegar, correct seasonings, and add the softened gelatin.

Cool 10 minutes, pour into a suitable mold such as a loaf pan, and refrigerate overnight.

Unmold and cut into slices. Arrange on a platter and garnish with pickled beets (see below).

Bruna Bönor
(Brown Beans)

2 cups Swedish brown or red kidney beans (canned red kidney beans can be used to avoid preliminary cooking)
Salt to taste
¼ cup golden syrup, or to taste (dark Karo syrup can be substituted)
¼ cup vinegar, or to taste

Rinse dry beans, if used, and place in a pot with 5 cups water and salt to taste. Simmer until tender, 1 to 2 hours. Add more water if beans begin to boil dry.

When beans are cooked, add syrup and vinegar, adjust seasonings, and serve hot. The dish can be prepared the day before.

Pickled Beets

⅔ cup vinegar
½ cup beet liquid reserved from cans
1 cup sugar, or to taste
Salt to taste
2 tablespoons pickling spice
2 (16 ounce) cans whole beets
2 medium onions, sliced into rings

Bring the first 5 ingredients to the boil.

Slice beets thin and put into a bowl; strain the hot pickling liquid over them. Cool; refrigerate overnight.

Add onion rings an hour before serving.

Christmas Breads and Cakes

Vörtlimpa
(Swedish Holiday Rye Bread)

3 cups dark beer or stout
2 teaspoons salt
¼ cup (½ stick) butter
1 cup molasses
3 packages active dry yeast
Peel of 4 whole oranges (white pulp removed), chopped fine
2 tablespoons fennel seeds, well pounded in a mortar (or 2 teaspoons ground fennel)
6 cups rye flour
3 cups white bread flour
Cornmeal
MAKES 6 OVAL LOAVES

Heat the first 3 ingredients in a large pot till the butter melts. Remove from the heat, stir in the molasses, and cool to luke-warm—or to body temperature when tested on the wrist. Sprinkle the yeast, orange peel, and fennel over the mixture and blend well.

Add one-third of each kind of flour and beat until smooth. Add another one-third of each kind of flour and mix vigorously.

Add the remainder of the flours (using more white flour if extra flour is needed), mix, turn out onto a floured board, and knead for 10 to 15 minutes, or until smooth and elastic.

Put the dough into a buttered bowl, cover with a damp towel, and let rise until doubled in bulk (about 2 hours).

Turn the dough out onto a floured board and divide it into 6 pieces. Shape into longish loaves and place them, seam side down, on baking sheets lightly dusted with cornmeal.

Let rise, covered lightly with wax paper, for about 2 hours, prick the tops with a buttered skewer, and bake at 300 to 325 degrees for 40 to 50 minutes, or until the loaves sound hollow when tapped. After 20 minutes of baking, and again at the end, brush the loaves with water to which a little molasses has been added. When they are cool, wrap them in plastic bags to keep the crust soft.

Stollen

2 cups milk
2 teaspoons salt
½ teaspoon nutmeg
1 cup (2 sticks) butter
1¼ cups granulated sugar
2 eggs, beaten
2 packages active dry yeast
6 to 7 cups bread flour
1 cup raisins
½ cup chopped blanched almonds
½ cup chopped citron
Grated rind of 4 lemons, or to taste
Confectioner's sugar
MAKES 1 LOAF

Heat the first 5 ingredients in a large pot until the butter melts and the sugar is dissolved. Cool to lukewarm (baby's-bottle temperature).

Add the eggs, sprinkle the yeast over the mixture, and blend well. Add 3 cups flour and beat until smooth. Blend in all the remaining ingredients, using enough flour to make a soft dough. Turn the mixture out onto a floured board and knead 10 to 15 minutes, or until the dough is satiny and elastic.

Put the dough into a buttered bowl, cover with a damp towel, and let rise in a warm place (85 degrees) for about 2 hours, or until doubled in bulk.

Turn the dough out onto a floured board and divide it into 3 pieces: one piece being one-half of the whole, the second one-third, and the last one-sixth. Take the largest piece, cut it into 4 equal pieces, and squeeze each one into a thin, 2-foot-long rope. Make a braid of the 4 ropes, and place the braid on a lightly

279

buttered baking sheet. (If braiding four strands stumps you, cut the piece into three sections and make a braid of three.)

Divide the next largest piece into 3 equal pieces, squeeze them into ropes, and make a braid of three. Place it on top of the four-braid (it should be narrower and shorter; flatten the four-braid down the middle to make room for it).

Squeeze the last piece into a long rope. Make a twist of two out of it and set it on top of the others. Firm all together and let rise, covered lightly with wax paper, for about 2 hours. Bake at 300 to 325 degrees for 1½ hours, or until the loaf sounds hollow when tapped. (Lower the temperature if the bread begins to brown excessively.)

When done, place on a rack and sprinkle immediately and liberally with confectioner's sugar. (The finished loaf is supposed to represent the Infant in swaddling clothes, but since it also looks like a white, braided model of the *Merrimac*, you can take your pick of symbols.)

White Fruitcake

2 cups (4 sticks) butter, at room temperature
2 cups sugar
6 eggs
4 cups all-purpose flour
2 teaspoons baking powder
2 teaspoons salt
1 tablespoon vanilla extract
¼ cup Cognac
2½ cups (a 15½-ounce box) seedless raisins
2 cups (a 10-ounce box) dried currants
½ cup chopped candied orange peel
½ cup chopped candied lemon peel
½ cup chopped candied citron peel
Confectioner's Sugar Icing (see page 58)
MAKES 1 LARGE FRUITCAKE
OR 6 SMALL LOAF CAKES

Preheat the oven to 325 degrees.

Cream together the butter and sugar. Beat in the eggs, one at a time, until incorporated. Stir the flour, baking powder, and salt together and fold into the mixture. Add vanilla, Cognac, and all the fruits and mix well.

Pour into a well-buttered tube pan or into small loaf pans and bake 1½ to 2 hours (a shorter time for small loaves), or until a cake tester inserted in the center comes out clean.

Allow to cool somewhat and remove from pan. Glaze while still warm with Confectioner's Sugar Icing, to which a little grated lemon rind has been added.

Mazarin Cake

PASTRY SHORTPASTE
1⅔ cups all-purpose flour
1 teaspoon baking powder
⅓ cup sugar
½ cup (1 stick) butter, at room temperature
1 egg

THE FILLING
2 cups grated blanched almonds
2 cups sugar
1 cup (2 sticks) butter, at room temperature
4 eggs
2 teaspoons almond extract
4 tablespoons raspberry jam
MAKES 1 CAKE

To prepare shortpaste: Sift the flour and baking powder into a bowl and work in the remaining 3 ingredients in the order given until you have a smooth paste. Set aside.

To prepare filling: Work the first 3 ingredients together by hand, then beat in the eggs with a wooden spoon. Beat in almond extract.

Preheat the oven to 325 degrees.

Divide the shortpaste in half and, using fingers, press it into two 9-inch tart pans, lining them completely.

Spread 2 tablespoons raspberry jam over the bottom of the pastry in each pan and divide the filling evenly between them.

Bake for 1 hour, or until the centers are well puffed. Cool and serve in small wedges.

Irena Chalmers

LINKS IN

THE CHAIN OF

MEMORY

It has been more than twenty-five years since Irena Chalmers left Great Britain and became a publisher and author of cookbooks in the United States. But her holiday thoughts always drift to her childhood home and a cloud of steamy English cooking.

IT'S A LOT LIKE GETTING MARRIED. There has to be a beautiful, solemn bride in a long white dress and everyone gasping as she comes down the aisle. And all of us, craning to catch a glimpse of her as though we had never seen her before. And then a heart-stopping moment when for a terrible second we all fear that he really *has* forgotten the ring. And then, of course, the best man finds it in his other pocket and the tension make the relief all the sweeter. And in moments they are safely across the high wire and the vows are all completed and the organ is crashing out the Wedding March and the couple is dancing down the aisle and all the guests break out from the orderly rows to greet the bride and groom, and each other, and the party is ready to begin. . . .

It's like that with Christmas dinner. Once you've embarked on it you've got to go the whole way: do it up properly with the plumpest turkey that ever there was and the sage and onion dressing and the chipolata sausages and the lumpy mashed potatoes and the gravy and the Brussels sprouts and the gooseberry sauce. And then, when there is not an inch of room left, the lights

283

are turned out and in comes Father carrying the plum pudding borne on the silver platter as though it were the head of John the Baptist, and he looking as proud as if he had made it himself, though he had nothing to do with it; and Mother warning him nervously, as she does every year that I can ever remember, to be careful or the flames from the brandy will burn his hands and set him on fire too, and us saying hooray. And then Mother serving the pudding onto the very best plates that were inherited from her great-grandmother, so precious that this is the only time they are used each year, and the plates being passed around and us all helping ourselves to hard sauce and then us all singing out "Happy Christmas!" But we hardly eat any of the pudding because we've already had more helpings of turkey than anyone would have thought humanly possible. And that is because Mother relates the hours she spent in the kitchen and the amount of food we eat through some Einsteinian theory of the more we eat the more we love her.

So the table is cleared and heaped again with Stilton and walnuts and fresh fruit and the black bun and shortbread from our relatives in Scotland and the glacéed apricots from our relatives in Australia and the dates from Algeria, in their familiar box with the funny little fork that breaks the moment anyone tries to use it for prying out the first date from its tightly packed row, and the Turkish delight so thickly covered in sugar that when you try to bite into a piece it showers you in a storm of white powder and when you try to brush it off yourself it smears even worse. And, of course, some port. We always have port right after Christmas dinner and just before the Queen. The Queen's speech always comes on the radio at 3:00. "My loyal subjects," she begins, and we all sigh with full bellies and thankful hearts, and we stagger from the table still heaped with dishes and flop into armchairs around the fire with Yes please, I think I will have just another small—very small, thank you—glass of port. "My husband and I," the Queen intones, and there are more mentions of her loyal subjects and the Commonwealth and this and that . . . and was that the beginnings of a snore I heard? And then the message (it's always the same message) is over, and the dishes are not yet washed and won't be until someone hits on the idea of having a turkey sandwich. Very late that night, after we have all gone to bed, I creep downstairs again to have just one spoonful of cold plum pudding. It is by far at its best then, when it is black-solid, rich as rich can be, and descends with a thud into the tummy. Blessed sweet sleep follows and another Christmas has come and gone. The cold plum pudding is always the epilogue, for only with that last morsel can we know that we have survived another year with all the rituals intact and are prepared to leap into the New Year.

It is the rituals that count more than anything. It is the predictability that we cherish—the fact that we have our own particular traditional way of doing things. As I look back on the Christmas dinners of my childhood, I realize, somewhat to my surprise, now that I've lived in the United States for more than twenty-five years and my own children are grown, that we too have adopted many of the same rhythms and that we nourish them year after year.

It is surely that way with the tree. To begin with, we can hardly ever settle on a time when we are going to get the tree, and stick to it. Someone always has to go somewhere else at the last minute, and one person is left thinking the unthinkable: Let's not have a tree this year.

But we always *do* have a tree and we almost always buy it at the last minute. Often only straggly trees are left by that time, but we console ourselves by saying that we can turn the sparse branches toward the wall and no one will ever know.

This year it will be just the same.

We don't have what you might describe as a theme tree, the kind that designers and celebrities have. We never have a tree that is all white, for instance—two hundred white doves and dainty bows of white velvet ribbon, that sort of thing. Instead, we have a motley assortment of what could loosely be described as "objects"—things that we have acquired over the years.

And as we unwrap each ornament from its nesting of tissue paper, we exclaim over it and remember when we got it and who was there and how pretty—or awful—it is and we hang it on a branch no matter what it looks like, because each ornament "belongs," simply because it is ours.

Irena Chalmers

285

Irena Chalmers

We play old records while we are decorating. It is all part of the ritual. Every year we play the same music, nothing uplifting like the *Messiah*, but more along the lines of (maybe you remember it) "All I Want for Christmas Is My Two Front Teeth."

Finally, when everything is finished and the tree is twinkling with fairy lights and surrounded by far too many packages—because we always fear that we have not bought enough presents for each other—we step back and declare that this is absolutely the best tree we have ever had. And it always is.

It's the same with the dinner. Basically we hold hands with the generations past but forge our own unique links in the chain of memories.

My own earliest memories of Christmas dinner recall England during the war, when in order to help our country in some way that was never entirely clear to me, we were all supposed to raise chickens. We were the only family in our neighborhood that heeded this particular call to patriotism. Our chickens were always getting out and running into other people's gardens, and it used to be my job to try to corner them, cow them into submission, and carry them home, quivering in my arms. They needn't have been afraid—we never ate any of them. One in particular became a family pet. Her name was Lucy and she was very tame. I used to wheel her around in my doll's pram. She would lie there quite quietly, her head resting on the dolly pillow and one beady eye watching me. I covered her with a soft blanket to keep her feathers warm.

We had fifteen chickens.

You will be wondering why on earth I am talking about chickens here, but they feature large in my memories of Christmas dinner because they had to be fed, and every few days my mother would boil up a huge bucket of potatoes for them and sometimes the potatoes smelled so good my sister and I would steal one and eat it before the chickens ever got to them. On normal days, days when there wasn't a Christmas dinner cooking, the chickens' potatoes didn't loom so large, but on Christmas Day the steam from the potatoes was a major contributor to the dense fog that filled the kitchen.

My mother, a woman of tradition if ever there was one,

followed custom hallowed by English cooks from time immemorial. Having put the pail of potatoes on to cook, she then started everything else as close to all at once as possible. No sooner was the turkey put in the oven to roast than the Brussels sprouts were set to cooking and so were the chipolatas. Chipolatas, in case these are foreign to you, are little pork sausages—the backbone of the British Empire, some say. They are very small, hardly bigger than an index finger. Five minutes is about as much time as it takes to cook them. My mother cooked them for about an hour, just to be on the safe side, then she left them to "keep warm" on top of the stove, where they continued to cook, marginally, for about another five hours until the turkey was done.

What with the steam from the chickens' potatoes and our potatoes, and the sprouts and the gently boiling plum pudding, you could hardly see across the room. The windows were totally fogged up, so to see if the sun was still weakly shining you had to use your sleeve to wipe away the condensation. It all added to the atmosphere and the anticipation. That entry into the warm, steam-laden kitchen was a big part of time-honored custom.

I think about all this now that I am doing the cooking instead of my mother. Long gone are the war and the chickens, and we don't hear the Queen's speech in New York. We remember our Scottish heritage, not with black bun but with the long tartan scarves that run the length of our old wooden table. The fireplace, too, is garlanded with tartan and holly, and everywhere there are red candles, tall and thin, fat and round, to flicker their light and echo the flames from the burning logs. We eat almost exactly the same things, but the emphasis on some things is ever so slightly different. We still have turkey, though the composition of the stuffing has changed. The chipolatas have been replaced with oysters and the gooseberry sauce has become cranberry, but the Brussels sprouts are still there and the mashed potatoes are still as lumpy as ever they were. And to crown this license for supremely wonderful overindulgence there is always the plum pudding.

Tradition says that plum pudding is the symbol of Christmas. The round pudding represents the good and abundant earth. The holly berries stand for the blood of Christ. The flames of brandy are the flames of hell that are rapidly burned away as goodness triumphs over all. If plum pudding can mean all that—then let's raise our forks in celebration of life renewed.

Stir-up Sunday is the Sunday before Advent Sunday when the Church of England collect begins, "Stir up, we beseech Thee, O Lord, the wills of Thy faithful people: that they, plenteously bringing forth the fruit of good works . . ." Irreverent choirboys parodied this with:

> *Stir up, we beseech Thee,*
> *The pudding in the pot.*
> *And when we do get home tonight*
> *We'll eat it up all hot.*

The prayer is a reminder to stir up real as well as spiritual goodies, and this is traditionally the day on which the family gathers together to make the plum pudding. They have been doing this since the beginning of time, or if not the beginning, way back yonder in time. Not everyone understands it. In 1658 the Chevalier d'Arvieux described the plum pudding as "a detestable compound of scraped biscuits of flour, suet, currants, salt and pepper made into a paste, wrapped in a cloth, and boiled in a pot of broth." Well, what did he know? He was a foreigner. Besides, whether you like it or not is wholly irrelevant. It is something you have to have. It is a kind of gastronomic patriotism, though it began humbly enough.

It started as a kind of porridge, a soft gruel or soup, at first made with plums but later with raisins and currants and spices, especially ginger. These were stirred into a broth made from beef or mutton and thickened with brown bread crumbs. It didn't evolve into the admirable pudding as we know it today until well into the late 1600s. It needed time to transform itself into the real thing, a noble pudding that would culminate the dinner with a flaming climax.

Henry VIII understood these matters. At his Tudor court at Christmas, peacocks were roasted and sewn back into their plumage; each beak was gilded with gold leaf and within the beak was stuffed a ball of cotton, first soaked in spirits, that was set alight—an early attention-getting device. There were others. There was always the boar's head, symbolizing Frey, the Norse god of fertility, with its apple and oranges to remind the guests of the promise of the reward of the fruits of the labors and the return of the sun. Now, this was a time when if you were invited for dinner you could also be confident of being served a noble feast of venison and grouse, pheasant and partridge, wild duck and goose. There would be roast swans and larks and capons and mince pies, which before the Reformation were baked into an oblong shape to symbolize a manger, and often there would be the tiny figure of the baby Jesus on top of the pie. There would be minstrels and music and a lot of noisy entertainment and roaring fires and wassail by the bowl—some contrast, you might note, to what we have become accustomed to today: a factory-fabricated, microwave-ready, prebasted, tasteless turkey, central air conditioning, and our little nuclear family sitting around an electrically illuminated dead tree watching the VCR and drinking a wine cooler! But through it all the plum pudding has kept its place in our affections—everywhere.

Some families still make their own plum pudding, remembering to stir it clockwise, as the earth moves on its axis, for this will bring good luck and another wish may be granted as the pudding is stirred. And more luck will come to the person who finds in the pudding a coin, a ring, or a charm. The notion is that a coin will bring a year of wealth, obviously a ring will be a wedding, and a silver thimble means a happy life, but one of a spinster.

Queen Victoria was the one who introduced the idea of adding trinkets to the pudding, and here is a charming story told in the December 1956 issue of *Country Life*: As Stir-up Sunday in 1887 drew near it was suggested that, this being the year of the Queen's Golden Jubilee, the old recipe books might be discarded for once. It was thought the ladies should make a Jubilee Christmas pudding in accordance with the instructions below, and many of them did so. "Fifty sweet almonds, number equal to years of Her Majesty's reign; five ounces of bread crumbs, number of Her Majesty's daughters; four ounces of flour, number of Her Majesty's sons; three ounces of cocoanut, cut into thirty-two pieces, number of

Her Majesty's grandchildren; two ounces of sugar, number of Her Majesty's great-grandchildren; five ounces of suet chopped into as many pieces as Her Majesty has subjects in every town; five eggs well beaten up, representing England, Scotland, Wales, Ireland and our Colonies. Mix these well together with half a pint (4,980 drops) of milk representing the ages in months of Her Majesty and her children. Boil two hours and sixteen minutes, or twice sixty-eight minutes, the age of Her Majesty in Jubilee Year."

The present Queen and her husband, Prince Philip, Duke of Edinburgh, still distribute 1,400 puddings to people who are associated with the royal household at Buckingham Palace, and other homes.

The Queen's Christmas Pudding, borne blue and blazing with brandy by the Queen's Page to the dining table at Windsor Castle, will be made as usual from a seventeenth-century recipe first used in the days of King George I. Here is the recipe as it has been preserved ever since in an old book in the library at Windsor:

Christmas Pudding for Royal Family

1¼ lb. suet
1 lb. demerara sugar
1 lb. raisins
1 lb. sultanas
4 oz. citron peel
1 teaspoonful mixed spice
1½ teaspoonful nutmeg
1 lb. breadcrumbs
1½ lb. sifted flour
1 lb. eggs (weighed in their shells)
1 wineglassful brandy
1½ pints milk

Prepare all ingredients, well whip the eggs, add to milk, and thoroughly mix. Let stand for 12 hours in a cool place, add brandy and put into well-greased basins and boil 8 hours or longer. Sufficient for twenty to twenty-eight people.

Julee Rosso

OLD-FASHIONED CHRISTMAS IN MICHIGAN

Julee Rosso's childhood Christmases were the stuff holiday dreams are made of— snow, sleigh bells, a large gathering of family and friends, and hours of loving preparation. All of this was background for the success of the Silver Palate, started with Sheila Lukins, one of the biggest little stores in the United States.

I HAVE NEVER GROWN UP, and I don't think I want to, at least not as far as Christmas is concerned. But then I don't think that most of us ever do. My childhood memories of the mystery and of the anticipation that surrounded the most magical days of the year are as vivid as if they were yesterday and not over thirty years ago.

Of course, for the past eleven years, since the creation of the Silver Palate, Christmas has begun in April and worked itself into a frenzy as summer turns to fall. As the season approaches, we cheer one another with Secret Santas, and try somehow to find moments to gather gifts for friends and family. But, finally, as Christmas arrives and work subsides, it is memories of one's past that condense and become unutterably delicious. I think of the Christmases of my childhood in Michigan, and clearly I treasure them. They were, after all, the times when my every wish was anticipated, fulfilled, and surpassed.

We knew my mom had Christmas on her mind earlier, because various closets and the cedar chest had been announced as "off limits," but Christmas actually began in our house two Saturdays before December 25. That was the day my little brother Rick and I went out to buy Mom's and Dad's presents. I was the adviser as to what we should buy them, but Rick had invariably saved all the money. After that annual shopping expedition, we'd arrive home to find my dad testing string after string of outdoor Christmas lights and my mom elbow deep in flour and sugar, baking up a storm for our annual open house—pinwheels, butterballs, whiskey cake, date nut pudding, macaroons, toffee bars, lemon squares, fruitcake, Christmas cookies, candy cane baskets, and taffy. It was always much more of an adventure to help Dad— or Shrank, as I always called him—so we joined him outdoors testing lights, knowing that with our every trip through the kitchen we could still test Mom's efforts as well.

We lived in Kalamazoo on Pinehurst Boulevard, so named because of the thirty- and forty-foot pine trees down the center of the street. At Christmas we focused on our own twenty-five-foot front-yard blue spruce tree that was to be trimmed with lights. As neighbors wandered over to help (or drive us crazy by "borrowing" lights from the tree), they were all aware of the Rosso family challenge: the best helper placed the star on top. It was Rick who usually won, particularly since I was frequently sidetracked in the kitchen testing and tasting. Eventually there was that special moment in the late-afternoon twilight when the lights of the tree were turned on. That was really the beginning of the Christmas season for us.

The next afternoon we always spent in front of a fire addressing Christmas cards, drinking hot chocolate, and making a giant wreath to hang over the fireplace. Mom and I started with coat hangers wound together in a thirty-six-inch-diameter base, adding pine branches, magnolia leaves, pinecones, walnuts, pecans, acorns, chestnuts, juniper branches, eucalyptus, sprigs of holly, tartan ribbon bows, and a few antique ornaments. Sometimes we would leave it natural and other years we would spray the entire thing antique gold.

During the following week, school life largely kept me away from home, along with lots of Christmas parties, rehearsals, caroling at the hospital and home for the aged, ice-skating parties, tobogganing at Echo Valley, Girl Scouts gathering food for the needy, and the gym club's Secret Santas. Not that it was quiet at home, where there was a constant aroma of baking and candy making, present wrapping and Christmas card writing. In the midst of all this, one evening was set aside to put up our Christmas tree. Some years we went to our farm outside of Kalamazoo to chop it down; other years we would visit the local volunteer firemen's tree sale to help the underprivileged.

Of course, I always wanted the tallest tree possible, and getting it selected and set up straight was a nightmare. But once it was draped in tiny white lights and sugary fruit ornaments, paper chains, cranberry and popcorn strings, ribbons, tinsel, and snow, it was worth the hassle. We placed a manger under the tree, mounded the mantel with boughs of holly, hung our homemade wreath, put red candles in the silver hurricane candlesticks, retrieved Mom's damson plum brandy from the cellar (grownups drank brandy, kids got ice cream with brandied plums on top, Dad got both), lit a fire, and almost as if on cue, our cocker spaniel Tiny would topple the tree. We'd all jump to attention for fear Dad would kill Tiny, but the tree would be righted and we'd wander off to bed knowing that Christmas was just around the corner.

The Sunday before Christmas was traditionally candlelight service at church, followed by our open house. The day was spent decorating the house and bringing tray after silver tray of the holly-decorated sweets that Mom had been baking for weeks. Dad put Tom and Jerrys in the punchbowl for the adults as Rick, the eggnog expert, made his specialty for the kids and I supervised the hot chocolate, plum brandy, and mulled cider.

Candlelight service was at five o'clock, and whether I was singing in the choir or sitting in one of the pews, this was when the awesome wonder of the historical Christmas seemed so very real to me. Our church was a great Gothic cathedral that towered above us. As we entered, there were mountains of white poinsettias and garlands wrapping huge pillars. Candelabra were placed at the end of every aisle, and the altar was covered with more white poinsettias, masses of candles, and clusters of stately twenty-foot pines decorated with herbs and flowers and sea-blue lights. As the Christmas Story was read and the carols were sung,

Julee Rosso

293

yet more candles were lighted, until the church radiated a loving glow and warmth that crept inside us to warm the cockles of your heart, as my grandfather would say.

Then it was home to light the fires and greet our own guests. This was the one day of the year when almost everyone we knew in Kalamazoo was in our house at once. It made my world seem ever so right, and it lasted way into the night as we caroled everyone home.

Around noon on Christmas Eve day our family piled into the car—dog, presents, and us—and headed to see our two sets of grandparents, zillions of aunts, uncles, and cousins, and lots of old friends on the other side of the state. It was a three- to four-hour trip in those days on old two-lane highways, and we sang our way with my dad leading—"Over the River and through the Woods," "Jingle Bells," and "White Christmas" over and over and over again. We arrived first at my mom's parents', where we would base ourselves. Grandma had cookies waiting and a piece of mince pie for Dad (Shrank loved his pie). My great-uncle and my "aunt grandma" would be there, and as we had coffee and cookies, Grandma "just this time" let me dunk my chocolate-chip cookies in her coffee, even though they broke and made a terrible mess. It was the best!

Then we dressed quickly and drove another hour to my grandfather and grandmother Rosso's farm. As we arrived, Grandma Rosso was always just finishing the last pie (I think she secretly wanted to show her daughters-in-law that she never measured anything). Rick and I would head out to the barns to join our cousins, teasing Billy the bull along the way. Farmhands were busy hooking up the Clydesdales, Molly and Maude, to the big sleigh, and our job was to fill it with plenty of hay and lots of blankets. When we were ready, the grownups would join us for a sleigh ride, crisscrossing the land until the brilliant moon was high overhead or our teeth were chattering too much to sing carols anymore.

Then it was back to my grandparents' house for Christmas Eve dinner. My dad always carved the turkey. He loved the ritual, bringing out the long, bone-handled carving knife and sharpening it on a long, thin steel with a matching handle, carving with precision and confidence, as we all watched with awe. When my dad finished, his father presented a drumstick to the youngest grandchild. Then Shrank always placed the turkey on the buffet table with a big "Ho, ho, ho, Merry Christmas!" and it was time for dinner to begin.

We gathered in the huge cabbage-rose living room that had twenty-foot trees in each of its corners. This was my grandmother's favorite treat for all of us. In one corner her Harvest Tree was covered with fruit, tartan ribbons, tiny baskets, straw figures, miniature gourds, nuts, and strings of cranberry and popcorn. In another corner the Spice Tree had gingerbread men, pomanders, nosegays of rosemary, nutmeg, and cinnamon sticks, and candy canes. The Peace Tree was a vision of white with wild juniper, white doves, dried sea lavender, angels, baby's breath, and a dusting of snow. Finally, there was a silvery green Herb Tree laden with sprays of rose hips, lavender, sage, lamb's ears, thyme, rosemary, and light-green and white ribbons sprinkled with silver glitter.

At each of the fifteen tables for four there were bouquets of pink tea roses from Grandma's greenhouses surrounded by votive candles. I remember how dining by the candlelight added to the sense of mystery and expectation we felt.

Dinner finished, the tables were cleared in a flurry, and the lights went on. Bowls of nuts and chocolates were put out, Mom's plum brandy was served, and—wondrously—sleigh bells would ring and in would come Santa with a twinkle in his eye and the biggest bag of presents I'd ever seen. With so many of us, it took forever to deliver all the presents and unwrap them, but around midnight we'd trundle off into the snow for our drive back to my other grandma and grandpa's house.

I remember it was always very crisp and clear, with the snow squeaking underfoot. If we dozed on the way home, it was only for a moment, because somewhere out there in a sky with stars tumbling to the ground, if we looked very hard, we could see where Santa was trailing across the sky.

When we arrived home we set out cookies and milk for Santa and a carrot for Rudolph, read the Christmas Story one more time, kissed everyone good night, said our prayers, and tried to fall

Julee Rosso

asleep watching the Star of Bethlehem out of the window but really wondering where Santa was in his journey. It all made for the most wonderful dreams.

Christmas morning we were up with the dawn, and Rick and I would creep down the stairs to see if Santa had been there. The rule was: No presents could be opened until everyone was up, and getting our ancient great-aunt and uncle cracking was no easy task. But once we had seen the piles of presents, there was no stopping us. I must say there is something to being the only grandchildren in a household of six adults. It was overwhelming!

Finally we were finished with presents, and dragging new toys with us, we trooped to the breakfast table. It was always the same: broiled grapefruit made from the citrus shipments that Great-aunt Helen always sent from Sebring, Florida; bismarcks—puffy pancakes sprinkled with blueberries, lemon juice, and powdered sugar (a recipe from the hotel in Indiana where my grandparents spent their honeymoon); sausage made at the Rosso farm; Angie's coffeecake (made by a neighbor in Kalamazoo); and hot chocolate.

After breakfast Grandpa took us sledding at the country club with friends from early elementary school. My favorite years were when we had sliding saucers, because all alone you could fly over the moguls and icy patches. After two or three hours, when we were frozen to the bone, we would give up and go back home, stopping along the way to deliver presents to special families my grandpa liked to help out. We went to the same houses every year, and those seven families became very much a part of our extended family and our Christmas tradition.

Mom and Grandma had worked all morning long cooking, and when we walked back into the house, all the flavors of their labors hit us. Our feast's menu varied little from year to year, and for a child that was part of knowing there were certain things you could count on:

Sherried Lobster Bisque
Scalloped Oysters
Roast Goose with Apple and Pecan Stuffing
Broccoli Florets with Hollandaise Sauce

Julienne Green Beans with Pearl Onions
Yams with Mango Chutney
Waldorf Salad
Pickled Peaches
Watermelon Pickles
Cranberry Orange Relish
Date Nut Pudding with Whipped Cream
Mince Pie with Whiskey Sauce

Julee Rosso

After the table was cleared and the wishbone set out to dry, Rick, Grandpa, and I always went to watch Sonja Henie skate in the Christmas show at Olympic Stadium. I was sure that if I just wished hard enough, I too would grow up to be a beautiful and graceful figure skater. Meanwhile, at home a lot of our old friends had gathered. The grownups played cards, and we played with our toys until one by one we all wandered off to a comfy cushion or couch to slip into sleep and dream of tomorrows.

Those years are long gone, and since that time there have been many Christmases in faraway places—some just like those you dream of having as a child. We've found ourselves in Paris, New York, Vienna, Rome, Monte Carlo, and the Caribbean at Christmas time, and while it is ever so nice to visit other countries at Christmas, I'd give almost anything for one of those Christmases in Michigan, just once more.

Bismarcks

A light and wonderful way to begin a Sunday any time of the year.

½ cup (1 stick) unsalted butter
½ cup milk
½ cup all-purpose flour
2 eggs
Fresh lemon juice to taste
Confectioner's sugar for dusting
SERVES 2

Put butter in a heavy frying pan or a shallow casserole. Place in an oven set at 475 degrees.

Meanwhile, mix milk, flour, and eggs lightly to make a batter.

When the butter has melted, pour the batter into the heated pan and bake for 12 minutes. Remove from the oven and place the bismarck on a plate.

Pour a little of the melted butter on the pancake and squeeze on a little lemon juice to taste. Roll it up like a loose jelly roll and sprinkle with confectioner's sugar.

VARIATIONS
- Sprinkle with brown sugar.
- Forget the sugar and use a fruit or maple-flavored syrup.
- Spread with a favorite fruit preserve or fresh berries.
- Lightly sprinkle with Grand Marnier.
- Fill with chestnut cream.
- Top with cooked link sausages after 4 minutes' baking time.

Angie's Coffeecake

1 package active dry yeast
1 cup lukewarm milk
3 tablespoons granulated sugar
4 cups all-purpose flour

1 teaspoon salt
1¼ cups solid vegetable shortening
2 whole eggs
1 egg, separated
2 cups (4 sticks) unsalted butter, at room temperature
2 cups brown sugar, packed
2 cups coarse-chopped shelled pecans
3 cups chopped dates
3 teaspoons cinnamon
2½ cups confectioner's sugar
2 tablespoons warm honey
½ cup fresh lemon juice (2 or 3 lemons)
3 COFFEECAKES, EACH 9 × 13 INCHES

Dissolve the yeast in the lukewarm milk in a small bowl. Stir in the granulated sugar and let stand for 10 minutes.

Sift the flour and salt together. Cut in the vegetable shortening until the mixture resembles rolled oats. Stir in the milk and yeast mixture. Beat the whole eggs and the egg yolk together and stir gently but thoroughly into the dough. Cover with a towel and set aside to rise until tripled, about 3 hours.

Grease three jelly-roll pans, 9 by 13 inches. Turn the dough out onto a floured surface and divide into thirds. Roll out one piece of dough into a thin rectangle about three times the size of a jelly-roll pan. Slide a pan under the center third of the dough.

Set aside a third of the softened butter. Divide the remaining butter into thirds and spread half of one portion over the center portion of the dough in the pan. Sprinkle ⅓ cup of the brown sugar, ⅓ cup of the chopped pecans, and ½ cup of the chopped dates evenly over the buttered center section of the dough. Sprinkle with ½ teaspoon of the cinnamon. Fold one side of the dough over the center section. Again spread with softened butter and sprinkle with the same amounts of brown sugar, pecans, and dates. Fold the final third of the dough over the center section, cover, and set aside for 2½ to 3 hours. Repeat with remaining dough and ingredients.

Preheat the oven to 400 degrees.

Mix together the reserved butter, 1 cup of the confectioner's sugar, the reserved egg white, and the warmed honey. Cut 3 deep decorative slits in the risen coffeecakes, being careful not to cut through the bottom layer. Spread the honey mixture evenly over the tops of the cakes.

Set the two cakes on the middle rack of the oven and bake for 25 to 30 minutes, or until puffed, brown, and firm. Remove and cool slightly. When the first two cakes are finished, the third can be baked, or it can be frozen for another time.

Mix together the remaining confectioner's sugar and the lemon juice and drizzle over the warm coffeecakes. To serve, cut into narrow strips and serve warm.

The coffeecake can be wrapped in foil and frozen. Defrost and rewarm slightly before serving.

Date-Nut Pudding

½ cup (1 stick) unsalted butter
1 cup sugar
2 eggs, beaten
1 cup milk
1½ tablespoons all-purpose flour
1½ teaspoons baking powder
1 cup coarse-chopped pitted dates
1 cup coarse-chopped shelled walnuts
1 cup heavy cream, chilled
8 PORTIONS

Preheat oven to 325 degrees. Grease well a 9-by-13-by-2-inch glass or ceramic baking dish.

Cream the butter, gradually adding the sugar and beating until light.

Add the eggs, milk, flour, and baking powder; mix well. Fold in dates and walnuts.

Turn into the prepared baking dish and place on the middle rack of the oven. Bake for 50 to 60 minutes, or until set.

Serve slightly warm or at room temperature with spoonfuls of the cream, whipped to soft peaks, on the side.

Taffy

2 cups sugar
½ cup light corn syrup
¼ teaspoon cream of tartar
1 teaspoon vanilla
MAKES 2 DOZEN PIECES

Combine in a large saucepan the sugar, corn syrup, and cream of tartar with ½ cup water and stir over low heat until the sugar dissolves.

Bring to a boil, cook for 2 minutes covered, then remove the cover and continue cooking without stirring until a little of the syrup forms a hard ball when dropped into cold water (265 degrees on a candy thermometer). Remove from heat and stir in the vanilla.

Pour the mixture onto a greased platter. When it is cool enough to handle, lift the ends and pull with buttered hands until the taffy is snow white and almost hard.

Twist into ropes and cut with scissors into 1-inch pieces.

Whiskey Cake

1 two-layer white or yellow cake (select your very favorite)
2½ cups coarse-chopped pecans
3½ cups grated dried coconut
¾ pound candied cherries
12 egg yolks
1¾ cups sugar
½ teaspoon salt
¾ cup (1½ sticks) butter
¾ cup rye or bourbon

Prepare cake and let cool for 2 hours. Split each layer in half.

Meanwhile, combine the pecans, coconut, and candied cherries in a bowl. Set aside.

Place the egg yolks in a double boiler over simmering water. Beat slightly with a whisk. Add the sugar, salt, and butter. Cook until the sugar is dissolved, the butter melted, and the mixture is slightly thickened, stirring constantly. Do not let the mixture overcook or the egg yolks will become scrambled.

Remove from the heat and add the rye or bourbon. Beat vigorously for 1 minute with a wire whisk.

Pour the mixture over the pecans, coconut, and cherries and mix well.

Place one of the split cake layers in the center of a platter and spread generously with the frosting mixture. Top with the remaining layers, spreading the mixture generously over each layer.

Refrigerate until frosting is set. Decorate the cake platter with holly.

Whiskey Sauce

½ cup (1 stick) butter, at room temperature
1 cup sugar
1 cup hot cream
4 large egg yolks, beaten
Pinch of salt
2 tablespoons whiskey
MAKES 4 CUPS

Cream together butter and sugar until light and fluffy.

Heat the cream in a medium saucepan until hot but not boiling. Remove from the heat and stir in the butter-sugar mixture, the beaten egg yolks, and the salt. Beat until well blended.

Return the saucepan to the stove and cook over low heat, stirring constantly, until the mixture is thick.

Stir in the whiskey. Pour into a sauceboat and serve hot with mince pie. This sauce is also great on gingerbread, chocolate cake, baked apples, and apple pies.

Eggnog

6 eggs
¾ cup granulated sugar
1½ cups brandy

½ cup rum
4 cups heavy cream
4 cups milk
½ cup confectioner's sugar
Nutmeg
MAKES 26 PORTIONS

Separate egg whites from yolks. Beat yolks until very light.

Add sugar and continue beating until well blended. Slowly add brandy and rum.

Mix in 3 cups of the cream and all the milk.

In a separate bowl, using clean beaters, beat the egg whites until stiff but not dry. Fold into the eggnog before serving.

Whip the remaining cup of cream and add the confectioner's sugar. Top each glass of eggnog with the sweetened whipped cream and sprinkle with nutmeg.

Scalloped Oysters

1 pint oysters
1½ cups cracker crumbs
½ cup (1 stick) unsalted butter, melted
2 teaspoons lemon juice
Salt and freshly ground pepper to taste
¾ cup heavy cream
⅓ cup oyster juice
1 tablespoon sherry
Dash Worcestershire sauce
SERVES 4

Drain the oysters, reserving the juice. Preheat the oven to 350 degrees.

Combine the crumbs, butter, lemon juice, salt, and pepper. Sprinkle one-third of the crumbs over the bottom of a 3-cup buttered gratin dish. Cover with half the drained oysters.

Sprinkle another third of the crumbs over the oysters. Make another layer over the crumbs with the remaining oysters.

303

Whisk together the heavy cream, oyster juice, sherry, and Worcestershire sauce. Pour over the oysters.

Top the casserole with the remaining one-third of crumbs. Bake for 40 minutes.

Classic Turkey Stuffing

1 cup raisins
1½ cups Grand Marnier
1 cup (2 sticks) unsalted butter
2 cups chopped celery
1 large yellow onion, chopped
1 pound spicy breakfast sausage or Italian hot sausage, casing removed
1 pound herb stuffing mix
1 cup coarse-chopped pecans
4 Granny Smith apples, peeled, cored, and cut into 1-inch chunks
2 cups chicken stock
2 teaspoons dried thyme or 4 teaspoons fresh sage
Salt and freshly ground pepper to taste
ENOUGH FOR AN 18-TO-20-POUND TURKEY

Place the raisins in a small saucepan and cover with 1 cup of Grand Marnier. Bring to a boil, then remove from heat and set aside.

In a large skillet, melt 1 stick of butter. Add the celery and onion and sauté over medium heat for 10 minutes. Transfer to a large mixing bowl.

In the same skillet, cook the sausage, crumbling with a fork, until brown all over. Remove from heat and combine with the celery-onion mixture.

Add the stuffing mix to the vegetables and sausage. Stir in the raisins, liquid included. Add pecans and apples and combine thoroughly.

Melt the remaining stick of butter with the chicken stock in a saucepan. Pour over the stuffing along with the remaining ½ cup of Grand Marnier. Stir well; the stuffing should be moist all over. Season with thyme or sage, salt, and pepper.

Index

Index

Index

Index

3 1 1

Index

312

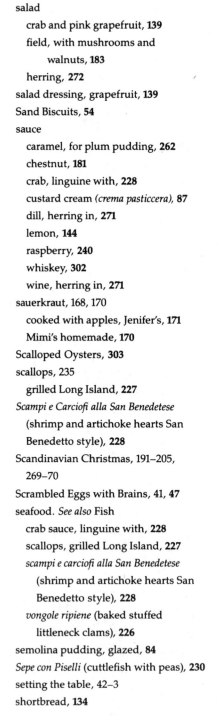

Index

314

Index